THEATER
IN THE
AMERICAS

A Series from
Southern
Illinois
University
Press
ROBERT A.
SCHANKE
Series Editor

Ghost Light

Ghost Light

An Introductory Handbook
for Dramaturgy

Michael Mark Chemers

Southern Illinois University Press
Carbondale and Edwardsville

Library of Congress Cataloging-in-Publication Data
Chemers, Michael M.
 Ghost light : an introductory handbook for dramaturgy
/ Michael Mark Chemers.
     p. cm. — (Theater in the Americas)
Includes bibliographical references and index.
ISBN-13: 978-0-8093-2952-6 (alk. paper)
ISBN-10: 0-8093-2952-2 (alk. paper)
1. Theater—Production and direction. 2. Drama—
Technique. I. Title.
PN2053.C428 2010
792.02′3—dc22
2009022486

"The Ballad of Jed Clampett" written by Paul Henning.
Copyright © 1962 Carolintone Music Company, Inc.
Copyright renewed. International copyright secured.
Used by permission. All rights reserved.

To Brian Johnston
Dramaturg, historian, critic, scholar, mentor, friend

Contents

Preface

Ghost Light is an introductory handbook for the art and science of dramaturgy specifically as it is practiced in the American theater. Written with the undergraduate student in mind, this handbook is a useful tool not only for students of dramatic literature in general and those who wish to become professional dramaturgs but also for directors, designers, actors, and anyone else who wishes to improve his or her ability to do dramaturgy and to work *with* dramaturgs. This book presents an approach to dramaturgy that maximizes a dramaturg's utility in the production of theatrical art as well as his or her leadership in the ongoing development of dramaturgy as a critical slice of the American theatrical pie. It is grounded in the writings of dramaturgs of the distant past and informed by current debates among American dramaturgs, directors, and playwrights about the nature and purpose of dramaturgy in our theater.

By writing this book, I hope to advance the discipline of dramaturgy in the United States by encouraging students to explore the field and follow their passions. I have felt the call to dramaturgy because the skills I need to succeed in the other fields in which I work (theater history, critical theory, playwriting, teaching, and the study of dramatic literature) have direct applications here to the creation of a work of living art. Dramaturgy keeps me involved in the electric excitement of theatrical creation. I am fortunate to have been involved as a dramaturg in productions in which my input was deeply valued, in which I had significant positive effect on a production, and in which I could create important bridges between administrators and artists, among the artists themselves, between the production and the script, and between the company and the audience. With some companies, I have been intimately involved in the selection of entire seasons of shows; with others, I have been asked to read and comment on a few script submissions. I have adapted classical and foreign-language texts for contemporary productions. I have had working relationships with playwrights, directors and artistic directors that were good, bad, and ugly (or at least indifferent). I have also worked with dramaturgs as a playwright myself, and I have worked as part of a dramaturgical team on international, multilanguage productions. Most American dramaturgs have similarly variegated work histories; what unites us is our love of theatrical discovery and the shared secret that dramaturgy, though difficult if it's done well, is immeasurably rewarding and tremendously fun.

Because dramaturgy is such a multifaceted discipline, not everyone who reads this book will find its conclusions consistent with his or her own practice or experience, nor can this book substitute for the critical training that an emerging dramaturg gets in the rehearsal hall and by working with more senior dramaturgs. The book is not meant to define once-and-for-all what dramaturgs can or should do. It is only meant to be an introduction to the discipline and to provide the basic intellectual and artistic equipment necessary for the new dramaturg to define through practice what constitutes his or her unique dramaturgy. Dramaturgy is truly a world of limitless possibilities, and it is a great joy and privilege to share it.

Ghost Light has three sections: philosophy, analysis, and practice. The first section gives the practitioner a solid background in the history and utility of the discipline by describing dramaturgy's extensive history and arguing why it is as indispensable as costume design or box office as American theater struggles to increase its relevance, depth, and breadth. . The second section works the most important skill set of the dramaturg, reading and writing, and describes a variety of techniques for skillful interpretation, diagnosis, and deep critical engagement with scripts and provides techniques for writing fluidly and meaningfully about them. Although the title of chapter 4, "The Twelve-Step Program," alludes to the twelve-step model of recovery employed by addiction recovery groups like Alcoholics Anonymous, it is not meant to be taken literally or explored *too* extensively. The model of analysis in this book does share with the twelve-step model of recovery certain key aspects; it is holistic, emphasizes personal humility and responsibility, is process-oriented, and provides tools that should guide the reader for the remainder of his or her life. The third section discusses how a dramaturg presents him or herself to the director as a fellow artist and collaborator, works with cast, crew, and audience to enrich the theatrical experience, and works in the development of new plays, devised theater, documentary theater, and adaptation.

At the end of most chapters are three exercises ready-made for course assignments. All of these exercises, adapted from actual tasks that professional dramaturgs are often asked to do and so hone specific practical skills, are broken down into three categories:

- *Go deep!* These exercises are designed as intensive and self-contained tasks to immerse the student in the theory and/or practice of the material of the chapter.
- *Go wide!* These exercises are designed to help the student integrate the chapter's material into a larger, contemporary social context. This category demonstrates how the knowledge presented in the chapter affects, and is affected by, circumstances of everyday life in the twenty-first-century United States and across the globe.
- *Go long!* These exercises help the student historicize the material (that is, to put it into the context of a long conversation among theater practitioners, historians, and critics in changing social conditions through time) and/or to compile the various aspects of a professional project into a synthetic whole.

At the end of the book is a collection of appendixes giving guidance on how to build a dramaturgical casebook and presenting lists of up-to-date and useful resources available around the world.

This book is by no means the first attempt to pragmatically define dramaturgy: on the contrary, there is a dedicated (if small) canon of books on dramaturgy written in the past few years. The flagship among them is *Dramaturgy in American Theatre: A Source Book*, edited by Susan Jonas, Geoffrey S. Proehl, and Michael Lupu (1997), an indispensable collection of essays by prominent dramaturgs, playwrights, and directors. *Words at Play: Creative Writing and Dramaturgy* by Felicia Hardison Londré (2005) is a useful text focusing mainly on dramaturgy as a form of and a technique for improving creative writing. Mary Luckhurst's *Dramaturgy: A Revolution in Theatre* (2006) provides a comprehensive history of dramaturgy and its discontents, and for more advanced students of dramaturgy, Cathy Turner and Synne K. Behrndt's *Dramaturgy and Performance* (2008) is a must-have resource. There are numerous scholarly articles and essays on various aspects of the discipline as well, and dramaturgy research groups meet regularly at various conventions around the world. The best online source for keeping up with the art form is the Literary Managers and Dramaturgs of the Americas Web site, http://www.lmda.org. More resources are listed in the appendixes of this book. A serious student, starting with *Ghost Light*, will explore all of these sources to get a full appreciation for the many approaches that the cutting-edge practitioners of dramaturgy are taking.

Also, *Ghost Light* touches only lightly on the dramaturgy that attends the plays of William Shakespeare. Rather than attempt to grapple with this important topic in a diluted way, with perhaps only a single chapter, I instead direct the reader to Andrew James Hartley's book *The Shakespearean Dramaturg:*

A Theoretical and Practical Guide (2005). Since Shakespeare is probably the single author who will provide the most regular work to dramaturgs in the United States, it behooves the student dramaturg to focus strongly on the current techniques and debates employed by dramaturgs to solve the production problems of Shakespeare.

Knowledgeable readers will notice that the book's historical content tends to gravitate towards the German Enlightenment, perhaps at the expense of other significant dramaturgical thinkers in other periods and places. The choices in the history are meant to provide a muscular, cross-disciplinary approach as a productive paradigm for the advancement of dramaturgy in the United States, without intentionally excluding any particular period or place. The ghost-light concept of dramaturgy puts the dramaturg at the very center of aesthetic, political, and philosophical discourses of theater making, where the dramaturg can make the most significant contributions not only to single productions but to fostering theater in his or her community, but it is only the first step in the development of a student's skills and knowledge. I have striven to be widely inclusive, but for this introductory text, I wish to present a model for dramaturgy that is enthusiastic, powerful, politically engaged, humanist, and dialectical, and the German Enlightenment presents this model forcefully. This is not to say that other dramaturgies do not, and the serious student of dramaturgy must make any and all authors of dramatic theory and dramaturgy and the productions they engendered a high priority. The dramatic critics and philosophers of France and England, particularly, have a rich history that is only briefly examined here. To cast a wider net here, as I would very much love to do, would begin to engage arguments about dramaturgical methods that (although productive and essential to more advanced training) would complicate this book's simple mission and interfere with its utility as an introduction. Throughout the book, I have given citations and suggestions for further reading for any students who wish to pursue particular threads of this vast and fascinating discipline.

Acknowledgments

No undertaking of this kind is executed in isolation. My views on dramaturgy have developed in conversation with artists and scholars over many years of working in the theater. I am indebted to the scholar-dramaturgs Carlyn Aquiline, J. A. Ball, Mark Bly, Ken Cerniglia (special thanks for his editorial eye), Sergio Costola, Michele di Pietro, Heather Helinsky, Kimberly Jannarone, Ben Nadler, and Irina Rudakova; to directors Mark Bell, Anne Bogart, Steve Cosson, Kathy Fletcher, Jed Allen Harris, Sasha Ilyev, Mladen Kiselov, Rajendrah Ramoon Maharaj, Vladimir Mirodan, S. Michael Thompson, and Marianne Weems and who were all willing to share their insights with me; to playwrights Steven Dietz, Dennis Reardon, and Milan Stitt; to my teachers Sarah Bryant-Bertail, Roger Herzel, Odai Johnson, David Krasner, Joseph Roach, Ron Wainscott, Albert Wertheim, and Barry Witham; and to the theater scholars, dramaturgy researchers, and practitioners at the American Society for Theatre Research (ASTR), the Association for Theatre in Higher Education (ATHE), and the Literary Managers and Dramaturgs of the Americas (LMDA). To Oliver Gerlund and Tom Shafer, thanks for giving me my first dramaturgical jobs. I owe a debt to Robert A. Schanke, Kristine Priddy, and my readers at Southern Illinois University Press for conscientiously shepherding this project to completion. Thanks to my research assistants, Brianna Allen, Alan Katz, and Rose Sengenberger. To them and to all the rest of my students, who have forced me to refine my thoughts on this topic and whose innovations and energy are constant sources of inspiration, my sincerest gratitude. For overall support in a strange career, thanks, Mom and Ed, Dad and Barb, and Rafia and Mohammed Basha.

Special thanks are due to Elizabeth Bradley, Dick Block, and rest of the faculty of the Carnegie Mellon University School of Drama, whose advice and support have been profoundly generous and necessary. Immense gratitude is owed to my Carnegie Mellon colleagues Wendy Arons, David Holcomb, Brian Johnston, Anne Mundell, Tina Shackleford, and Kristina Straub, who were so generous with their advice in the process of writing this text. Thanks also to the Wimmer Family Foundation and the Eberly Center for Teaching Excellence for providing a fellowship that supported the development of this book.

A moment of acknowledgment is required for the Ghost Light Collective, the fine working group of faculty, student, and professional dramaturgs who have helped to build the Production Dramaturgy Program at Carnegie Mellon University's School of Drama. All of them contributed in some significant way to the assembly of knowledge this book contains, even if by only listening: Brianna Allen, Carlyn Aquiline, Corinna Archer, Wendy Arons, Anthea Carns, Kendra Chapman, Michael Christie, Elias Diamond, Clare Graziano, Kate Goldstein, Timothy Israel, Lavina Jadhwani, Brian Johnston, Alan Katz, Mary-Margaret Kunze, Kendra Lee, Molly McCurdy, Alexander Miller, Nick Mudd, Stefano Muneroni, Nicole Ogurek, Lauren Parks, Rose Sengenberger, Dana Shaw, Greg Van Horn, Ismail Smith Wade-El, Amy Young, and Breanna Zwart.

To Martin Christoffel, without whom I never would have become a dramaturg in the first place, thank you.

Most important, to my wife, Farhana, and son, Zain, thank you.

ONE

Philosophy

What the #$%@ Is a Dramaturg?

> Dramaturge. And what does that mean? Having the word is very useful; it's
> pregnant with associations and I'm obliged to whoever coined it. But—!
> —John Brunner, *The Dramaturges of Yan*

> AUDIENCE MEMBER: What did you, as dramaturg, actually *do* for this produc-
> tion? What appeared on stage that is a result of what you did?
> MARK BLY: I can't point to anything specifically, but if you took a knife to that
> play, it would bleed me.
> —Overheard by the author, 23 August 2007, Arena Stage talkback

Mark Bly, former chair of the Dramaturgy and Playwriting Program at Yale
University and currently senior dramaturg at Houston's Alley Theatre, comes
as close as anyone ever has to explaining the function of the dramaturg[1] in
modern theater practice. *Dramaturgy* is a term that refers to both the *aesthetic
architecture* of a piece of dramatic literature (its structure, themes, goals, and
conventions) and the *practical philosophy* of theater practice employed to create
a full performance. Together, dramaturgy is the very blood coursing through
the veins of any theatrical production.

In practice, dramaturgy refers to the accumulated techniques that all theatrical artists employ to do three things:

1. Determine what the aesthetic architecture of a piece of dramatic literature
   actually is (analysis)
2. Discover everything needed to transform that inert script into a living
   piece of theater (research)
3. Apply that knowledge in a way that makes sense to a living audience at
   this time in this place (practical application)

Of course, no play gets produced without these three elements; directors, designers, actors, and production teams all do these for every show. There is no theatrical production without dramaturgy. None. Zero. Zip. Nada. The question is merely how it gets done, and by whom.

Asking Questions

The question that forms the title of this chapter is one that dramaturgs get asked all the time. I asked it myself for the first time in 1990, when director Oliver Gerlund invited me to act as dramaturg for a production of Czech playwright Václav Havel's political comedy *Largo Desolato*. Thanks to Gerlund's willingness to incorporate me into the process, I had a really terrific time, and it opened a whole new door for me in the theater—one that unites my passions for script analysis, historical research, theoretical exploration, dramatic literature, and the magic of live theater. Now, two decades later, I find I have done a lot of it, but I still get asked this question almost every day, and almost every day I also ask it of myself.

In John Brunner's 1972 pulp science-fiction fairy tale *The Dramaturges of Yan*, quoted above, the fate of an entire planet rides on the answer, but for most of us, the question begins a discussion of the centrality and necessity of dramaturgy to the creation of every kind of theatrical production.

Now, of course, there is no production without lighting design, either. Even a production held outside in daylight needs a practical theory about how the natural light will be employed—someone has to be thinking about that. And although one may be able to mount an installation without any visible humans, generally in theater we like to see actors on stage as well. And then, of course, one needs a costume designer. Even if it's only T-shirts and jeans, such a "non-design" has an effect on the audience, and someone needs to be thinking about that, too. The space in which the actors will perform requires someone who knows how to think about scenic design. And a sound designer would also be nice. And a fight master, a choreographer, a technical director, a stage manager, and a production team are all probably going to be required and some front-of-house staff as well, and someone to lead the whole project with a directorial vision, and perhaps someone could write a beautiful, moving script.

Do we need *any* of these people to do theater? British director Peter Brook famously wrote that all theater strictly needs is an empty space, and someone walking across it could be engaging in an act of theater. But such ascetic performances are rare; most performances require considerably more. Bly, in his 1996 essay "Bristling with Multiple Possibilities," ponders the existence of a dramaturg:

We should remember, perhaps with a prescient grin, that the dramaturg's function in the theater now is in an embryonic stage not unlike the role of the director nearly two centuries ago, when actors and playwrights wondered why this strange creature should be allowed to exist within their magic circle.[2]

A few centuries ago, Bly reminds us, directors were unknown, although what we think of as the director's *function* was executed by nonspecialists (senior actors, the writer, the producer, and the like). But for the past two hundred or so years, we have had directors, and now it's hard to imagine working without one. Since the Renaissance, innovations in technology, design, architecture, staging, and playwriting have all increasingly required *specialists* in these subdivisions of the dramatic arts, who need specialized training, and who understand exactly what their roles will be when they sign their contracts. Some people think of dramaturgs as a "luxury," but if that's the case, then so are designers and directors. We don't strictly *need* any of these people, apart from the single actor who walks across the empty space, but the more well-trained specialists on the team, the better the work is likely to be and the greater the possibility that the art form will continue to evolve and increase in relevance and power.

So what is a dramaturg? A *dramaturg* is a member of the artistic team of a production who is a specialist in the transformation of a dramatic script into a meaningful living performance. This is somewhat different from the role of a director, who provides the leadership and vision necessary to the function of the company, although directors and dramaturgs look at plays and theater practice similarly. It is also different from the function of the theatrical critic; a dramaturg is a theater practitioner and an artist while a critic is a journalist, although again critics and dramaturgs look at plays from a similar perspective and often seek out the same kind of training. But critics engage the product at the site of public contact, the end of the process, while dramaturgs help to build the theatrical product from conception. I think it is helpful to look at the dramaturg as a source of what the Ancient Greek philosopher (and dramaturg) Aristotle called *phronesis*.

Phronesis is one of two "intellectual virtues" that Aristotle discusses in his moral handbook *Nicomachean Ethics*. The other virtue is *sophia*, or "scientific wisdom," knowledge derived from the rational contemplation of first principles. Phronesis is "practical wisdom," which includes everything one must know in order to live a good and harmonious life. Phronesis is employed to advance the greater good for oneself and one's society in general. It seeks truth and knowledge but specifically for the creation of happiness and harmony for humanity. In the world of the theater, dramaturgs are the "phroneticists," keepers both of the knowledge of theater practice of the past and of the wisdom necessary to apply that knowledge to create the theater of the future.

Since the late 1990s, the artistic necessity of dramaturgy has become far better understood in America than it was previously, largely thanks to the courage and skill of the younger generation of dramaturgs. The more dramaturgs work with some of the nation's top directors, designers, actors, and producers, the less commonly they have to answer the question "What is a dramaturg?" and the more often they find themselves engaged in serious discussions of history, theory, practice, and aesthetic philosophy. Recently, the Artistic Director of the Minneapolis Repertory Theatre, Joe Hanreddy, told a group of students, that "the dramaturg is the guy you go to when you're in trouble. I want that guy close."[3] Furthermore, according to a survey conducted by Dr. Jay Malarcher for the American Society of Theatre Research (ASTR) in 2005, some 35 percent of theater programs in the United States offer at least introductory dramaturgy courses, and that number is increasing as American professional theater continues to become smarter, more topical, and more curious about what is going on beyond the borders of the United States; dramaturgs, with their analytic acumen and international perspective, are becoming more critical to the process, and there is a growing need for plays to be translated into (and from) English and adapted for audiences around the world. Undeniably, there are increasing opportunities for dramaturgs at home and abroad.

So, the times they are a-changin'; where dramaturgy was once barely understood in this country, it is increasingly becoming a necessary component of work as theater artists. That you're reading a book like this one is a sign of that change. A lot of ignorance is out there about what dramaturgs do, but as dramaturgs continue to generate phronesis and break down some barriers, we are swiftly moving toward an era of American theater when working without a dramaturg will become as inconceivable as working without a director.

What Kind of Person Becomes a Dramaturg?

All over America tonight, millions of children will lie in their beds and dream of becoming an actor; some fewer will dream of designing a smash show; some fewer will dream of being a visionary director. Very few will dream of becoming a dramaturg. This is not because dramaturgy is not a powerful, rewarding, and immensely fun way to live an artistic life but simply because very few people even know that such a position exists until they start working in professional or college theaters. Now that dramaturgy has come into its own as an art form that is in many ways discrete from (yet connected to) all others in the theater, it attracts people from a wide variety of backgrounds—I know dramaturgs who began their careers as designers, actors, stage managers, directors, playwrights, political scientists, social activists, philosophers, historians, cultural anthropologists, and even one statistician; all were, at some point, seduced by the boundless artistic possibilities dramaturgy has to offer. Each background brings its own unique perspectives and priorities, and each is deeply valuable to the progress of the discipline. What do they have in common?

- They think deeply about dramatic texts and their production.
- They are experts in aesthetic philosophy and theater history.
- They are strong and versatile writers.
- They are committed and visionary artists who love being in rehearsal and collaborating with other artists.
- They are not scared of libraries.
- They are devoted to the principle that theater should be socially as well as artistically relevant.
- They are deeply driven by the "ah-ha!" of discovery.
- They are intrepid, frontline operators, willing to go boldly where no one has gone before.
- They are versatile and adaptable, ready to wear a variety of hats in a variety of contexts.

If this list describes your own hopes and dreams, dramaturgy might be for you, too. What's more, people with dramaturgical training do a lot more than production dramaturgy, although that is the main focus of this book. Dramaturgs often shift emphasis in their careers to become excellent screenwriters and playwrights, directors, artistic directors, critics, literary managers, story editors for television and film, teachers and professors, and theater theorists and historians. For many of the professionals I know, production dramaturgy is just one facet of what they do, and they do it because they love it.

Forking Paths and Ghost Lights

Jorge Luis Borges's short story "The Garden of Forking Paths" [4] describes the desperate flight of Dr. Yu Tsun, a former literature professor turned German double-agent during World War II, who has been discovered by British authorities. He is fleeing for his life with important strategic information, and, fearing arrest, he forms a desperate plan to communicate to his chief. For this, he requires a man of a certain name. As it happens, the only man with that name in the region is a British sinologist. Journeying there, Dr. Tsun muses on his ancestor, Ts'ui Pên, a governor who gave up his power and wealth to write a great novel and to build a labyrinth in which anyone would become lost. The ancestor was murdered, having completed only a fragmented series of chapters of his novel, *The Garden of Forking Paths*, and none of the labyrinth. When Dr. Tsun finds his quarry, Dr. Stephen Albert, he discovers that the sinologist's life work has been in recreating and unlocking the secrets of Ts'ui Pên's work. He argues that the novel is not only complete but in fact *is* the labyrinth; its fragmented nature is actually an extremely erudite and complex riddle about the nature of time. In regular novels, a character sees two futures open before him; he chooses one, and the possibilities of the other collapse. But in Ts'ui Pên's narrative "garden," there are many branching paths, loops, crossovers, intersections, bridges, hidden passages, throughways, and opportunities to double back on or to skip to another route. In this novel, the reader can choose *all* possibilities, and the same instance can even be repeated under different circumstances. The dead can live again, and two persons who meet as enemies might have the same meeting as friends. Since its writing in 1941, Borges's compelling garden has been used as a metaphor to describe radical reconceptions of topics as diverse as quantum mechanics, metaphysics, history, and genetic evolution.

Borges's garden is also a compelling metaphor for dramaturgy. In his 1996 essay, Bly provides a liberating perspective on the art and craft of the dramaturg. If every practitioner of theater arts does dramaturgy, is a dramaturg not redundant? Perhaps, but Bly insists that in a garden of forking paths like the theater, such redundancy is a cause for celebration. It enables theater artists to remain supremely flexible, ready to bend back over themselves for a different solution or to find some alternate path, and to mutate as they go:

> On individual projects, the dramaturg can be the artist who functions in a multifaceted manner helping the director and other artists to develop and shape the sociological, textual, directing, acting, and design values. . . . Alternately, a dramaturg may appear to overlap with other artists in their duties, especially in interpreting the play and shaping the production, so that an apparent redundancy may be manifested. But it is a redundancy that often leads to increased creativity. . . . Redundancy, in both cases, can be a creative fount in service of a larger artistic impulse underlying the production's development.[5]

When we are granted the freedom to pursue our own curiosities wherever they take us, to wander down unexplored and overlapping paths, and to define our work ourselves as dramaturgs, then we develop the skills necessary to enrich and empower the process of theater making at all of its multifarious and polymorphous levels. Bly actually advocates *not* defining dramaturgy any further than necessary:

> I believe such attempts to codify the behavior of dramaturgs and to circumscribe the sphere of their influence have been not only counter-

productive and limiting, but also harmful to our collective evolution as artists. . . . [W]hen pressed for a definition of what it is that I do as a dramaturg, both in a rehearsal hall and in the theater at large, I generally answer 'I question.'[6]

Bly's understanding of the dramaturg as the one who doubts is a very powerful idea. It presents the dramaturg as a unique kind of scientist, critically engaged not only with the minutiae of the artistic production at every stage of its evolution but also with questioning the very role and function of theater in society. Like scientists, dramaturgs ask questions at every step and test their answers. Like scientists, dramaturgs often have to look back in time for answers. Like scientists, dramaturgs often have to backtrack and repeat and experiment with different pathways and look for hidden connections and causes. And like scientists, dramaturgs often have to move in unexplored, sometimes dangerous territories.

All of which brings us to the defining metaphor of this book: the concept of the dramaturg as a ghost light.

A *ghost light* is in reality nothing more than a lighting instrument left illuminated in the middle of the stage when no one is working in the theater. Use of ghost lights dates at least as far back as the sixteenth century—there is an obvious need for such an instrument anywhere theaters are constructed with roofs. There are a lot of urban legends about the origins of ghost lights: my personal favorite is that they were originally left onstage to propitiate (or abjure) the ghosts that were known to congregate in theaters where the metaphysical barriers between this world and the next are notoriously thin. Legends aside, the ghost light is a simple safety feature to respond to the fact that the interior of a dark theater is an extremely dangerous place. So indispensable are ghost lights that it is now almost impossible to find a theater anywhere in the world without one.

But the legends about the ghost light are entirely understandable. There is something almost mystically compelling about this figure, nowadays just a bare bulb on a pole in the middle of a cavernous darkness, the only sign of life in a place that seems even more eerily empty by the lack of players and audiences, loud and colorful, that are somehow all the more present for their absence. The ghost light's lonesome existence is dedicated to protecting us, just in case we wish to venture into the dangerous space. The ghost light is a beacon in a world of darkness, where a single step (say, off the stage into the pit or off a catwalk) could be the last mistake one ever makes. It is this sense of the ghost light's function that compelled the respected American theater critic Frank Rich to choose it as the dominant image of his 2001 memoir, because he saw the theater itself as a beacon in the darkness of his tumultuous early life.[7] Like Rich, I find myself drawn to ghost lights both figurative and actual. An empty theater is a space of ghosts (that is to say, of the echoes of the past), but it is also like Ts'ui Pên's garden a place of infinite possibilities, a place where, literally, dreams become real. Ghost lights remind me of dramaturgs at their best—venturing, usually alone, into dark places for the benefit of others, to illuminate potential hazards, prevent missteps, and navigate across that most perilous of all terrains, the living stage.

But what does all this ectoplasmic metaphor actually mean for the boots-on-the-ground dramaturg? If the dramaturg is the one who questions to become the light in the darkness, what do we actually *do?* Well, in many parts of the world dramaturgs are considered essential to the process. In Latin America and many parts of Europe, *dramaturgistos* are often listed on programs right below artistic directors and *above* directors. There were times in recent history when failing to listen to a dramaturg (or listening to the *wrong* dramaturg) could get the company shut down or even get you arrested, exiled, tortured, or executed. Dramaturgs have become critical to all aspects of theatrical production, and in America, many dramaturgs have been working hard to foster what is sometimes called German model dramaturgy." Chicago dramaturg Sarah Gubbins (who worked extensively with dramaturgs in Berlin, Germany) describes this model:

> The German model is more formal than the American one. It's always an institutional position that requires extensive knowledge of philosophy, languages, social policy and literature. The structure in a German theatre is that of co-artistic heads—the artistic director, who deals with the practicalities of implementing an artistic vision; and the dramaturg, who is responsible for soliciting new scripts and placing a work in a socio-political context. . . . The dramaturg is considered a diplomat in constant dialogue with the artists and the community at large.[8]

If we are really committed to the idea that dramaturgy is such an integral part of the theater-making process that it requires a highly trained specialist, then it makes a lot of sense to consider this German model as we forge a new sense of our work as American dramaturgs. This model encourages dramaturgs to be experts in the application of critical philosophy and aesthetics to dramatic production, to be able to comparatively analyze texts in multiple languages and from multiple historical periods, and to be able to develop strategies for putting even ancient scripts into contexts that make them relevant and immediate for modern audiences. These are special skills, and they require a special kind of person with a special kind of training, *starting* with:

- Historical knowledge both broad and deep, spanning multiple cultures and periods and the ability to do historical research, especially in the area of theater production, in any period or milieu
- Comprehension of world history of theatrical practice and theory
- Mastery of the fundamentals of theatrical practice from directing to playwriting to set building to show calling to lighting design to run crew to costume fitting to marketing to season selection
- Facility with the many roles that theater can play in society
- Fluent and precise writing ability at many levels for different audiences
- Top-notch research skills and the power to present findings in useful ways to many different audiences
- Meaningful collaboration with other theater makers from every aspect of the process

At the end of the training process, the dramaturg becomes a total theater specialist, an artist whose passion for the theater is matched only by practical knowledge of the form, vitally integrated into the production process. In this model, dramaturgs are *practical aesthetic philosophers* whose collaboration in the process of theater making is as essential as that of the director. Defining dramaturgy in this way, as an indispensable specialization and source of phronesis in American theater, is the aim of this book.

Historicizing Dramaturgy

> When you come into the theater, you have to be willing to say, "We're all here to undergo a communion, to find out what the hell is going on in this world." If you're not willing to say that, what you get is entertainment instead of art, and poor entertainment at that.
>
> —David Mamet, *Three Uses of a Knife*

> The drama is not dead but liveth, and contains the germs of better things. It lies with criticism to foster these germs, and, in the very effort, to develop its own possibilities.
>
> —William Archer, *About the Theatre*

It is always a good idea to *historicize* (that is, put into a historical context) any concept when it is first encountered. Historicizing reminds you that concepts and terms change, sometimes fairly drastically, over time and distance, and sometimes two authors or thinkers who might appear to be dealing with the same issue have wildly divergent ideas. Conversely, sometimes two people who use different terminology might be talking about exactly the same thing. Remember always that history, like the theater itself, is really a garden of forking paths; sometimes, while you are doggedly pursuing some elusive idea through this maze you run into yourself coming back the other way.

Origins

Historicizing a concept like dramaturgy is unsurprisingly not easy. If you go back to the original ancient Greek source of the word *dramaturgy*, δραματουργία (dramatourgia), you get *drama* plus *urgia*, literally "making drama," and the term referred generally to playwrights and producers. The ancients did not, to the best of our knowledge, employ a dedicated dramaturg the way we think of the role today. But luckily for us, quite a few individuals throughout history have spent a lot of time theorizing and writing in a dedicated philosophical (as well as artistic) manner about the role that theater plays in society and in the individual human psyche. These writers go beyond playwriting and even beyond theater criticism to achieve the position of what we now think of as a dramaturg, a *practical aesthetic philosopher* who thinks about theater in a theorized but very pragmatic way for the end goal of improving the theater's phronesis on the community that generates it. The purpose of this chapter is to introduce some of these protodramaturgs in a global context to trace a few discourses of deep thought on the subject of drama back to the very origins of theatrical art.

Theatrical institutions, in their diverse and polymorphous manifestations, appear and disappear in many places throughout the world, playing vastly different social roles in each period. They generate controversies. The historical record is murky and full of intrigues. Very different traditions of sophisticated, literary dramatic writing and performance can be said to have definite recorded "origins" not only in fifth-century BCE Athens but also in nineteenth-century BCE Egypt, eighth-century BCE China, second-century BCE India, tenth-century Europe, and fifteenth-century Japan, among other times and places. Each of these traditions provides writings and other historical traces that give great insight into the roles that theater played for those artists. It behooves emerging dramaturgs to look at as many different approaches to theater practice as possible, so that dramaturgy may be not only the custodian of sophisticated aesthetics from many traditions but also may advocate for more rarely heard voices in our own societies and around the world.

We have plenty of evidence to suggest that we can do both, often at the same time, but even better is the discovery that in the process of interrogating these old ideas, we discover rich new veins of intellectual and aesthetic history to mine, and that's what being a dramaturg is all about. For instance, in the tenth century during a time when it seemed that Athenian-style drama was completely dead in Europe and when the society was dominated by what we are told was an ultraconservative, paranoid theocracy that both denigrated women and suppressed performance, Hrosvitha of Gandersheim emerges: a woman dramaturg and Roman-style playwright whose writings not only revolutionize the role of theater in her society but also seem to provide subtle and deeply sophisticated criticisms of theocracy and patriarchy. She's been sitting there in the historical record for a thousand years and was quite celebrated back in the fourteenth century for a while, but lately she was ignored because she didn't fit into the "correct" idea of the evolution of drama in the Dark Ages. To old-school historians, she was an aberration. To a dramaturg, discovering Hrosvitha is like finding a twenty-four-carat diamond in a sewer.

Challenging old-guard traditional ideas about culture and society and theater's role therein opens us up to multiple possibilities. It makes us dynamic thinkers and writers and gives us new gardens of forking paths to explore and new dark terrain for us to ghost light.

Dramaturgy in History

Dramaturgy's roots are as ancient and polymorphous as those of the theater itself. We may deduce the dramaturgies that drove the creation of some plays by examining the plays themselves with historical research or theoretical interpretations, but documents of self-conscious dramaturgical inquiries, like casebooks, esoteric aesthetic texts, or dramatic criticism are rare. But some such texts survive, and a quick survey of a few of the most influential writers reveals some astonishing facts. These protodramaturgs were men and women of great passion as well as devastating intellect, and they directed both their passion and their intellect to maximizing the potential of theater to affect audiences and improve society. They include not only cultural philosophers and theater critics but also doctors, scientists, humanists, soldiers, aristocrats, religious leaders, spies, and adventurers. Some of them risked their safety, their freedom, even their very lives for their ideas about art and culture. Despite their age, the writings of these inspirational figures continue to shape how we think about and practice theater to this very day. As emerging dramaturgs, it is useful (and invigorating) to see our work as part of an ongoing discussion with these figures and others not yet born.

I have assembled such a survey here. Many thousands of documents of dramaturgy and theater criticism survive in the historical record, but I have chosen these specific writers for this chapter either because their writings emerge at critical moments in theater history or because their writings are deeply influential to the dramaturgies of later periods. Listing these dramaturgs in this fashion provides a framework for tracing certain long discourses of aesthetic criticism as they are influenced by events and changes in philosophy, technology, and aesthetics. This is not meant to be an end-all-be-all of historical dramaturgy but rather the beginning of a lifelong study of critical contexts that helps the student dramaturg understand his or her own work as part of one (or actually several) very ancient philosophical traditions that have profoundly influenced the development of dramatic art.

Ikhernofret (ca. 1820 BCE)

Possibly the earliest dramaturgical casebook on record is the Ikhernofret Stela, a stone tablet dated to around 1820 BCE, upon which an actor named Ikhernofret discusses his performance in a huge pageant, held in the Egyptian city of Abydos, of the kind we now call Osiris passion plays. Ikhernofret was an aristocrat and dynastic heir, and his day job was chief treasurer to the Pharaoh Senusret III. But by royal command (owing to his good looks, his high character, and his facility for speaking well, according to the stela), he played the role of Osiris's son in the procession. If you care to examine this stone (it can now be examined in the Agptisches Museum in Berlin) and if you can translate it, you will discover a detailed account of the pageant with a sort of running commentary that concerns the importance of the pageant to the people who witnessed it. It was lavish, subsidized by the pharaoh, and included dramatizations not only of mythological and religious stories but also of real political events such as the unification of Upper and Lower Egypt. The Greek historian Herodotus witnessed one of these spectacles many centuries later and described it in detail in his own work. The procession, conducted annually for thousands of years, seemed (apart from a colossal spectacle) to be a performance that helped the Egyptians to unite their terrestrial history with their cosmic one. Ikhernofret's painstaking (but tantalizingly short) account of this colossal festival provides a keen insight into the role that this kind of performance played in that culture: to provide, apparently, a glorious, celebratory context that explained political events in terms of spiritual ones, for the purpose of creating a unified society.[1]

Plato (424?–347 BCE)

A devoted student of Socrates and the progenitor of all academics (he founded the Academy), Plato is perhaps the most influential author in the Western canon. Luckily, a great deal of his writing survives, and much of it is concerned with analyzing the role drama plays in social life. Alas, he was not exactly a fan of the theater.

Plato's thoughts on the subject of dramatic poetry (and other arts) and its effects on the body politic are sometimes hard to decipher; if there is one unifying theme throughout, it has to do with Plato's concept that knowledge was not gleaned by observation and experience but transmitted from the gods by divine energy. All other kinds of knowledge are derived from acts of imitation (*mimesis*) of this higher kind of knowledge and are therefore inferior, as a digital scan of the Mona Lisa would be in comparison to the original hanging in the Louvre. Dramatic poets and actors compound the problem because they are imitating what is already just an imitation. Plato felt that when men, particularly the theater-loving Athenians, put their faith in this form of inferior knowledge, they are spiritually and politically deranged by it. In one of his early dialogues, *Ion*, Plato has his teacher Socrates confronting and shamelessly outwitting an actor of the heroic musical theater genre, also called a *reciter* or a *rhapsode*. At one point, Socrates tricks Ion into making a rather extravagant claim:

SOCRATES: What will a [reciter] know then, since he will not know everything?

ION: What is proper for a man to say—so at least I take it, or what for a woman, what for a slave or what for a free man, what for a subject or what for a ruler.

SOCRATES: Do you mean, what is proper to say for the ruler of a ship in a storm at sea? Will the reciter know that better than the pilot?

ION: Oh no, the pilot will know that better.

SOCRATES: And what the ruler of a sick man ought to say: Will the reciter know that better than the doctor?

ION: No, he won't know that either.

SOCRATES: But you say he knows what a slave ought to say?

ION: Yes.

SOCRATES: If, for example, the slave is an oxherd, and his cattle are wild and he wants to calm them, you say the reciter will know what he ought to say, and not the oxherd?

ION: Oh, dear, no.

SOCRATES: Then, what a woman ought to say about working wool, a woman whose business is to spin?

ION: No.

SOCRATES: Then he will know what a man ought to say if he is a general encouraging his troops?

ION: Yes, that is the sort of thing a reciter will know.

SOCRATES: Oh, the reciter's art is the general's art?

ION: I should know, at any rate, what the general ought to say . . .

SOCRATES: Then whoever is a good reciter is also really a good general?

ION: Certainly, my dear Socrates.

SOCRATES: Then whoever is really a good general is also a good reciter?

ION: No, I don't think that.

SOCRATES: But you do think that whoever is a good reciter is also a good general?

ION: By all means.

SOCRATES: Well, you are the best reciter in Hellas?

ION: Much the best, my dear Socrates.

SOCRATES: Then are you also the best general in Hellas?

ION: Yes, I assure you, Socrates; and I learnt it all from Homer.[2]

Ion's fatuous conclusion that being a good rhapsode makes him qualified to lead troops in battle is really a device designed to illustrate Plato's point; that Ion's knowledge as an actor is actually utterly useless, even less useful than the knowledge of slaves and women (Plato didn't think much of *them*, either), which Ion does not even claim to possess. Offering his poor befuddled friend a meretricious way out, Socrates gets Ion to admit that he feels divinely inspired when he performs, that he actually senses a spiritual connection with his audience that causes them to feel the same transcendent emotions regardless of what words are actually being sung. Socrates then presents poor Ion with an awful choice; either to admit that as an artist, he is engaged in a complex deception of his audience or to acknowledge that his ability to engage audiences is divinely inspired:

> SOCRATES: Choose, then, which you prefer us to believe you, a cheat or one divine.
> ION: A great difference there, Socrates! It is much finer to be considered divine!
> SOCRATES: Then that finer thing is yours, Ion, in our belief; you are divine, and not an artist, when you eulogize Homer.[3]

With this apparently lighthearted dialogue, Socrates has actually managed to get Ion to repudiate the entire theatrical enterprise. By choosing divine ecstasy over the careful disciplined craft of the artist, Ion has admitted that both the performance and appreciation of drama is a derangement of the senses—in effect, madness (albeit sacred). But for Socrates, theatrical art as a form of divine madness is preferable to theatrical art as a natural phenomenon and a human skill, for the natural world and all things that come from it are "bad."

In his later dialogue *The Republic*, Plato makes a special point of continuing this vilification of artists in general, and dramatic poets and actors in particular. In book 10, he goes so far as to say to his friend Glaukon: "Between ourselves—for I'm sure you will not betray me to the tragic poets and the other imitators—all such things are the ruin of the hearer's minds, unless they possess the antidote, knowledge of what such things really are." Tragedies really, according to Plato, are lies, deceit, trickery, and willing domination and derangement of the rational mind by the senses, a recipe for disaster in the perfect state he is hoping to achieve: "Hymns to the gods and praises of famous men are the only poetry that should be admitted into our State. For if you go beyond this and allow the honeyed muse to enter, either in epic or lyric verse, not law and the reason of mankind, which by common consent ever have been deemed best, but pleasure and pain will be the rulers of our state."[4]

But a dramaturgical eye will catch a very interesting contradiction here. Rejecting the old concept of "mere information" (*noesis*), which is static, for "true knowledge" (*dianoia*), Plato articulates one of the core values of the

Athenians: that true knowledge takes the form of a dialogue, in effect a contest between ideas that can result in the revelation of a third, even better idea. The Greeks called this *dialectics*. Because of Plato's commitment to this kind of knowledge, almost all of his writings are actual dialogues: little performable plays (and some, like *The Symposium*, actually have accounts of performances in them). Plato himself was a dramatic poet! In multiple occurrences in his dialogues, Plato does actually admit to loving drama and poetry . . . and hating himself for it.

The debate over what Plato actually meant to say about drama in these books has raged for millennia, but as dramaturgs, it is important to study Plato for several reasons. First, his philosophies will become the basis of antitheatrical arguments proffered over centuries (*The Republic* is directly quoted, for instance, by Saint Augustine in *The City of God* (426 CE) in support of banishing theater), and it's critical that we know the terms and conditions of those conflicts. Second, and perhaps more important, we need to study Plato because of his immense influence on his pupil who would become the first truly self-conscious dramaturg and the first champion of dramatic art in opposition to his master over the millennia: Aristotle.

Aristotle (384–322 BCE)

Although Plato was *arguably* the most influential writer in the Western philosophical canon, most people contend that it was his pupil Aristotle who had the greater impact. Aristotle was born into the aristocratic class of Macedon (his father, Nicomachus, was the king's personal doctor). At eighteen, he attended the Academy of Athens, where he studied under Plato for nearly twenty years until the elder man's death, in 347 BCE. He then traveled the known world to research botany and zoology and was hired by King Philip of Macedon to be tutor to his son, Alexander (later known as "the Great"). Aristotle then returned to Athens to found in 335 BCE his own school of higher education, the Lyceum, where he taught for a dozen years while writing erudite treatises on topics including logic, physics, metaphysics, optics, ethics, rhetoric, politics, biology, psychology, music, and theater.

Aristotle's philosophical works, particularly on the drama, have only increased in importance since his death. The Roman statesman and philosopher Cicero called these writings "a river of gold." Thought lost to Europe after the fall of Rome, Aristotle's dramaturgical text *Poetics* captivated Byzantine and Muslim philosophers like Ibn Rushd (Averroës). Even during the Dark Ages, elite Christian theologians debated the virtues of *Poetics*, which they had acquired in fragments from Arabic translations. Thanks largely to the influential theologian Thomas Aquinas, Aristotle experienced a tremendous resurgence in popularity in the West in the thirteenth century, and *Poetics* would become the single most influential dramaturgical text of the Renaissance. *Poetics* remains the touchstone for literary drama, the measure against which the great playwrights of history have compared their own writing and the standards of their societies, and shows no sign whatsoever of diminishing in importance.

Poetics can be called the Ur-dramaturgy. It is an attempt to define the nature of drama scientifically, according to "first principles" and observable data, classifying it into genres and discerning its components, commenting on its history and its role in the social matrix, and making evaluative judgments about the worth of individual pieces. There is not space to go into great detail on the contents of the book here; however, it is worthwhile to briefly encapsulate Aristotle's view of the theater, particularly in contrast to that of his teacher Plato. As opposed to a divine inspiration, Aristotle identified dramatic art as a *tekne*, a learnable human skill. He saw a tragedy as composed of six constituent elements, which he lists and explains in order of their importance to the ideal, as he saw it, performance experience: action (or plot), character, thought, diction (or lexical choices), rhythm (including sounds and music), and spectacle (visual elements). The greatest dramas, he said, had but a single action (plotline), which permitted the playwright to delve deeply into the total meaning of a single event. He wrote that the virtue of the tragic drama (as opposed to the "lesser" comedy and epic forms) is both social and psychological, in that it generates both *pity* (an emotional reaction derived from seeing in a horrible occurrence someone suffering more than they deserve to) and *fear* (an emotional reaction derived from the realization that the person in danger *might* somehow turn out to be oneself). When pity and fear are both cultivated to a high enough pitch, the observer will achieve *katharsis* (literally, "purgation"). A transcendent emotional experience, one of the profoundest possible for humans to feel, *katharsis* is a purification of the mind and spirit. But Aristotle's most influential contribution lies in his observation that the structure of a dramatic piece is itself the source of the audience's profound reaction: "Fear and pity may be aroused by spectacular means, but they may also result from the inner structure of the piece, which is the better way, and indicates a superior poet. For the plot ought to be so constructed that, even without the aid of the eye, he who hears the tale told will thrill with horror and melt to pity at what takes place."[5]

In part 4 of *Poetics*, Aristotle writes about the origins of dramatic poetry:

Poetry in general seems to have sprung from two causes, each of them lying deep in our nature. First, the instinct of imitation is implanted in man from childhood, one difference between him and the other animals being that he is the most imitative of living creatures; and through imitation he learns his earliest lessons; and no less universal is the pleasure felt in things imitated. We have evidence of this in the facts of experience. Objects which in themselves we view with pain, we delight to contemplate when reproduced with minute fidelity: such as the forms of the most ignoble animals and of dead bodies. The cause of this again is, that to learn gives the liveliest pleasure, not only to philosophers but to men in general. . . . Imitation, then, is one instinct of our nature. Next, there is the instinct for "harmony" and rhythm, meters being manifestly sections of rhythm. Persons, therefore, starting with this natural gift developed by degrees their special aptitudes, till their rude improvisations gave birth to Poetry.[6]

Although both Plato and Aristotle are deeply committed to the idea of dialectical knowledge, Aristotle here shows a significant divergence from Plato's teachings. Whereas Plato is pessimistic about general humanity's ability to determine its own path, Aristotle is full of hope. Whereas Plato fears the irrational aspects of humans (in himself as well as in humankind), Aristotle embraces them as part of the total human experience. Aristotle's dramaturgy is unflaggingly positive and affirmative of the human impulse to improve—for him, dramatic poetry and other arts are the highest achievements of human nature, setting us apart from other animals and bringing us closest to the gods. Plato devalues all things of the natural world, arts particularly: for Aristotle, the arts are a natural (and therefore "good") product of the very human psychological condition that *learning* gives us *pleasure*. Since we learn by imitation *(mimesis)*, what could be more natural, good, useful, and pleasurable than elevating *mimesis* into a high art? In so doing, Aristotle makes a very profound argument—that the drama is psychologically and sociologically therapeutic. This observation is one that many important psychologists (like Sigmund Freud) and sociologists (like Erving Goffman) explored in great detail and that became critically important to playwrights of the social-realist school, which has dominated mainstream playwriting in Europe and the United States for a century.

Quintus Horatius Flaccus (Horace) (65–8 BCE)

Born the son of a freed slave in a border town of the Roman Empire, Horace was educated in Rome and Athens, served in the military under Brutus in a civil uprising against Augustus (Brutus lost), and, after an amnesty was declared, worked his way out of poverty as a scribe in the administration of the victorious Augustus (he and the emperor eventually became close friends). While holding down that job, Horace secured his position as one of the greatest poets of the Western canon, ranked by Dante with Ovid and Virgil.

In 18 BCE, Horace penned a letter to his friends, the Piso family, which was later published; today we know it as the *Ars Poetica* (The Art of Poetry) (the term *poetry* was used by classical authors to mean both written poems and works of dramatic literature). *Ars Poetica* was perhaps second only to Aristotle's in terms of its effect on the dramaturgy of the Middle Ages and the Renaissance and is engaged very deeply by Gotthold Ephraim Lessing and others, including Alexander Pope and Horace Walpole. It is a friendly, humorous, ambling text (indeed, it is actually a poem itself, leading by example) that discusses many aspects of poetry and drama but most significantly to our study presents the idea of *decorum*.

Decorum is as central to Horatian dramaturgy as mimesis is to Aristotelian. For Horace, *decorum* is not only a guide for writing and performing but also for judging whether a cultural product is any good. Thinking about art, Horace also here coins the phrase *ut pictura poesis* (literally, "as painting, so poetry"), by which he meant that poetry should be treated with the same level of critical engagement as was at that time reserved for painting. Written arts, he argued, were to be acknowledged to be as complex and sophisticated (and deserving of complex and sophisticated criticism) as visual ones. Written arts, he writes, should furthermore be created with similarly deep, introspective, and, above all, artful care: "Latium would not be mightier in valor or feats of arms than in letters, if only her poets, one and all, did not scorn the long labor of the file. Do you, O Pisos, sprung from Numa, censure the poem that has not been pruned by time and many a cancellation—corrected ten times over and finished to the finger-nail."[7] This is critical, because for Horace, poetry is the protector of civilization itself, which as a veteran of a losing war he sees as desperately fragile, primed for destruction should its delicate balances be upset. A good poet, by exhibiting such balance, acts as a guide and a grand unifier of a just and moral society while a bad poet will be hounded and persecuted for upsetting the balance. *Decorum* has many constituent elements all interrelated, but they may be described in three broad categories:

- *Unity.* Horace argues that although poets should be granted license for flights of fancy, there are obvious limits, and these are determined, once again, by balance. Drama, he suggests ought to be unified in terms not only of action, with extraneous plotlines and filigrees trimmed away, but also of tone as well; one should not mix the wild and the tame, for instance. Styles employed by the poet should always be appropriate to the subject matter, and the poet should strive to be "charming."
- *Internal balance.* Horace is all for inventiveness as long as it falls within certain proscribed boundaries. Specifically, he is against slavish, robotic

replication of the Greeks, without heart or novelty, but he discourages the Pisos from diverging too far from acceptable custom. Horace is also deeply concerned that poets should strike careful balances between their responsibility to uplift and edify their audiences and their desire to provide titillating fare to sell their books and plays. He was seriously committed to the necessity of revision, of not trusting the first impulse; he favored artists who were not only blessed with natural skill but also dedicated to improving their craft through genuine critical engagement and study, eschewing flattery and other distractions.

- **Decency.** Horace encouraged artists to be true to life but to avoid at all costs lewdness, undue violence, indiscriminate sexual behavior, profanity, and indecency, because he contested that poetry was, since the dawn of time, the medium for the communication of proper thought and action. To a twenty-first-century American reader, this may seem unnecessarily prudish, but remember that Horace believed that poetry had tremendous power to affect the way people think and act, and to him the consequences of misusing that power were extremely grave.

Horace's popularity throughout the Middle Ages and the Renaissance was so extensive that he was often mentioned in the same breath as Aristotle, and his influence would eventually spark the development of an entire aesthetic movement.

Bharatamuni (fourth century BCE to second century CE)

Little is known about the Indian sage (*muni*) Bharata, except that he was of the Brahmin caste and authored a comprehensive guide to dramatic art and musical performance, known as the *Natyasastra* (literally, "the skill" [*sastra*] "of performance" [*natya*]). Written in Sanskrit, it is one of the most comprehensive dramaturgies ever created and provides insight into the nature of Indian performance art and its social role during one of its golden ages. The *Natyasastra* is a foundational text both for modern Indian performance aesthetics *and* for a populist branch of Hindu theology.

According to the book, which like Plato's work is presented as dialogue, Bharata tells a group of other sages that he received a divine message from the god Brahma (the world soul), who was concerned that despite the completed transmission of the four *Vedas* (holy texts that contain information about the nature of the universe and proper moral codes of behavior that humans must follow), only the men of the priestly Brahmin class could understand the *vedas*. Most humans still lived in barbarism and violence. What was needed, therefore, was a tool for communicating Vedic wisdom to non-Brahmin men (and to women of all castes).

Brahma therefore devised the *Natya Veda*, instructions for the creation of a performative medium through which wisdom could be transmitted to humans who lacked Brahmin training. Bharata piously assembled a theatrical troupe, which included angels of various kinds created especially for the purpose and Bharata's many sons, who rehearsed and performed a play about the victory of the celestials over their demonic enemies, the *asuras* and *davanas*. The gods were pleased and showered the actors with gifts. Unfortunately, the demons, who were also watching, felt maligned by the show and voiced their criticism by rushing the stage and with their dark magic attacking the defenseless actors. The god Indra thrashed the demons with a flagpole, and Brahma later brought in a celestial architect who built a special performance temple (a *natyavesman*) around Indra's flagpole that would be proof against demons (theaters in India are still built according to this plan). The gods themselves protected the actors personally. Brahma then assured the demons that their points of view and their own good acts would be given fair representation in future dramas.[8] The book goes on to describe in great detail all the various aspects of theater life, including the diet and physique of actors, dance, music, composition, architecture, design, direction, makeup, costume, and gesture.

Like *Poetics*, *Natyasastra* is a self-conscious, esoteric dramaturgical text that is responsible to its own self-contained aesthetic philosophy. It claims theatrical art to be divinely inspired, as did Plato, but like Aristotle, Bharata treats drama as a learnable and valuable human skill (*sastra*). Whereas Aristotle was concerned with *mimesis*, Bharata describes *Bhava-Rasa*, a similar process in which actors produce *bhavas* (imitations of emotions) that elicit *rasas* (sentiments in the audience). Each *rasa* constitutes a particular genre, or "flavor," of performance (rage, heroism, awe, disgust, eroticism, compassion, terror, and laughter); Bharata advised against mixing the *rasas*. While Greek theater employed mythological stories as source material for many plays, *natya* engaged *itihasa*, sacred spiritual histories. Where Aristotle seeks *katharsis*, Bharata seeks Vedic enlightenment for his audiences; as does Horace, Bharata argues that the drama is necessary to keep humanity out of barbarism and misery; performance

> teaches duty to those bent on doing their duty, love to those who are eager for its fulfillment and chastises those who are ill-bred or unruly, promotes self-restraint in those who are disciplined, gives courage to cowards, energy to heroic persons, enlightens men of poor intellect and gives wisdom to the learned. It gives diversion to kings and firmness of mind to persons afflicted with sorrow. It provides hints to acquire wealth to those who are after it and brings composure to persons who are agitated in mind.[9]

Natyasastra, then, is not merely a dramaturgy but a religious text, so critical to Indian spirituality that it is often referred to as the "fifth Veda," presenting an egalitarian inclusiveness where previously only the elite (and men) had access to *itihasa* and its sacred wisdom. And it is plain to see that actors all over the world still struggle constantly with "demons" of various kinds and with varying results.

Aelius Donatus (fourth century CE)

This much we know about Aelius Donatus: he was a teacher of rhetoric and a grammarian in Rome in the fourth century of the common era, and one of his pupils was Eusebius Heironymous, later known as Saint Jerome. He wrote a comprehensive textbook on the function of the various parts of speech that was extremely popular in the Middle Ages (so popular that educational treatises of all kinds were commonly referred to as "donets"). He also wrote a *Life of Virgil* (not to be confused with the *Interpretationes Vergilianae*, a commentary on the *Aeneid*, written by Tiberius Claudius Donatus later in the fourth century). But it is his treatise *On Comedy and Tragedy* that chiefly interests us as dramaturgs, in which he writes that "comedy employs a story involving the various peculiarities of public and private behavior, which teaches us what is practical in life and what on the contrary is to be avoided."[10]

The treatise is interesting from many perspectives, not least because it gives detailed descriptions of fourth-century performance practices, including genres, characterizations, costumes, scenic dressing, writing and musical composition, production practices, and performance. But it was in this treatise that Donatus presented his scheme for breaking down the action of a dramatic piece into four parts.

The first part of a drama is the *prologue*, which Donatus describes as merely a presentation of the play's "argument," that is, a quick summary of its action and themes. In Roman drama, this was presented by a single actor prior to the beginning of the plot. Once the action of the play begins, we move into the *protasis*, the introductory part of the play, wherein *exposition* occurs (that is, part of the argument is revealed but part is concealed to build tension). In the next part, the *epitasis* (or the "intensification"), the plot is "complicated" as the conflict is increased. In the final part, the *catastasis* (literally, the "settling"), events reach their final outcome; occurring within this part is the *catastrophe* (literally, the "down turn"), which is the event that resolves the play's action and completes the argument.

So influential was Donatus on the education of Middle Ages Europe that his conception of dramatic structure has become part of the basic assumptions we make. Playwrights, consciously or no, often build the acts of plays around this concept, and if a play does not progress more or less in this fashion, it feels very strange to the modern audience.

Hrosvitha of Gandersheim (930?–1002?)

Hrosvitha, also known as Roswitha, Hrotsvita, and Hrotsuit, was born Helena von Rossow to an aristocratic German family and became a Benedictine nun when very young. In the convent, famed for its classical library and learning in a culturally rich region, Hrosvitha (literally, "mighty voice") became one of the most accomplished women of the Middle Ages. She became a canoness (with a specific mission to minister to laypersons) and a widely respected author, whose works were proudly displayed by the Emperor Otto as part of what is now known as the Ottonian Renaissance. Hrosvitha herself divided her literary works into three categories: legends, Latin poems, and dramas.

Hrosvitha was both a playwright and a dramaturg who crafted esoteric commentaries about drama and its social function. She self-consciously emulated the dramatic structure of the Roman comedy playwright Terence to create six compelling plays about the lives of martyrs and saints. What was a Benedictine nun doing messing around with a pagan poet to whom Christian morality was utterly unknown? Hrosvitha herself, now wearing her dramaturgical hat (or in this case, cowl), explains her own motives in an introduction to her work:

> Lamenting the fact that many Christians, carried away by the beauty of the play, take delight in the comedies of Terence and thereby learn many impure things, she determines to copy closely his style, in order to adapt the same methods to the extolling of triumphant purity in saintly virgins, as he has used to depict the victory of vice. A blush often mounted to her cheeks when in obedience to the laws of her chosen form of poetical expressions she was compelled to portray the detestable madness of unholy love.[11]

Whether this canny canoness actually blushed or no, Hrosvitha's dramaturgy was specifically designed to "rehabilitate" theater into the service of Christian ministry. The utility, and permissibility, of such an enterprise had been debated for centuries; while the early Church fathers Tertullian and Saint Augustine preached in unequivocal terms that theater and Christianity were utterly incompatible, Saint Isidore of Seville (last of the Latin fathers) argued in the seventh century that theater, with its emphasis on dialectical knowledge, was but one form of pagan wisdom among many that could be employed in the service of Christian ministry. But although the theological debates are well documented,[12] we have little evidence of the presence of Athenian-style literary drama in this period (although we do have evidence of jongleurs, bards, skalds, jesters, fools, minstrels, mimes, *ioculatores*, performing monks, liturgical dramas, mystery and miracle plays, pageants, and mobile amateur and professional theatrical companies). Hrosvitha is the only known author of such "poetic drama" for hundreds of years on either side. Notes in the text (and the practical playability of her plays) suggest that her plays were staged, likely in her abbey or in Otto's court, possibly directed by her as well. It is pleasant to imagine (in the absence of hard evidence) Hrosvitha herself taking a role, using her mighty voice on stage and in rehearsal. After the Ottonian Renaissance, her works suffered critical neglect until they were rediscovered by a fourteenth-century humanist and became wildly popular again, to slip into obscurity yet once more in the Victorian era. Today, scholars and university dramatists are experiencing a renewed interest in Hrosvitha and her body of work.

Hrosvitha's plays bear out her dramaturgy minutely. In her famous *Paphnutius*, a holy hermit disguises himself as a rich merchant in order to get close to Thaïs, a successful and powerful prostitute. When he reveals himself to her, she instantly repents of her sinful life and accompanies him to willingly undergo horrifying deprivations in order to purify her soul. Such an intrigue of disguise was common, of course, in Terence, but Hrosvitha here appears to be using it as an example of how a minor falsehood (like the impersonations endemic to theatrical performance) can be employed in the service of a greater truth. However, while she is accomplishing this overt task, she is also providing some very surprising characterizations of women. Her female characters are righteous, profoundly virtuous, and immeasurably brave and pious and are often shown in positions of some power. They are in control of their own destinies, and they choose rightly. Some critics have argued that the portrayal of women in her plays indicates a streak of subversive protofeminism, a subtle critique of the Christian patriarchy. Whether this is the case or not, as a beacon in the darkness of the Dark Ages, Hrosvitha is one of the greatest of ghost lighters, shedding a powerful radiance on a period of drama that is otherwise quite obscure and still providing a model dramaturgy for adaptors.

Zeami Motokiyo (1363?—1443?)

During the early years of his reign, the Shogun Ashikaga Yoshimitsu brought to his court the greatest actor of the day, Kan'ami, and his son Zeami Motokiyo. Together, they established the ground rules for Sarugaku-Nōh, the performance style that would become the tradition of Nōh theater. Zeami would write a dramaturgy of the Nōh, titled *Fushi-Kaden*, or "the Book of the Flower," in which the flower, or "most precious thing," is the approbation of the audience.

Zeami had been trained not only in performance but also in the tradition of Zen Buddhism, and this sensibility is everywhere in his writing. The

Fushi-Kaden opens with a brief inquiry into what he calls "the hoary past" to trace the origins of Nōh in India, the land of the Buddha. Zeami identifies Nōh as a religious rite but notes that former princes employed the art "either to promote peace in the nation or for public entertainment."[13] William Scott Wilson notes that Buddhism at the time, with its emphasis on *mandalas* and public performances of "secret" rituals, was already heavily invested in artistic expression. But in the more secular Zen Buddhism, most of these trappings are swept away, and the practitioner is taught to focus inward. As Zen rose in popularity in Japan, the aristocratic Nōh drama developed into an extremely sophisticated and beautiful performance form that Zeami deepened through his own exposure to "itinerant Buddhist monks, warriors, and likely some dodgy travelers on the road."[14]

The book walks the reader through the stages of training a Nōh actor, beginning at age seven. The training is extremely exacting; not until age twenty-four will an actor merit the title of "beginner." While the *samurai* class regularly practiced Nōh movement and recitation in addition to weapons, calligraphy, and other aristocratic pursuits, Zeami forbids the Nōh artist to pursue any other discipline except poetry and also forbids "sensuality, gambling, and heavy drinking" while exhorting his students to "put strength into your practice, and avoid conceit."[15] Zeami demands intense discipline and the highest devotion as students work their way through several seeming paradoxes towards *myōsho*, the "moment of peerless charm," which arrives only after the actor has acquired *yugen*, or "grace." This is intensely difficult to achieve:

> The aesthetic quality of Grace is considered the highest ideal of perfection in many arts. Particularly in the Nō, Grace can be regarded as the highest principle. However, although the quality of Grace is manifested in performance and audiences give it high appreciation, there are very few actors who in fact possess that quality. This is because they have never had a taste of the real Grace themselves. So it is that few actors have entered this world.[16]

Replicating one's teachers precisely is a process of strict adherence to one's teachers and study of those who have come before. What the student gains from this training is almost superhuman self-control and unification of mind and body. The student learns to operate (on stage and in rehearsal) at 100 percent capacity but only to show the audience 70 percent, and the result creates a sense of fluidity and perfect grace. When the student achieves *myōsho*, he won't know it himself because he will be concentrating on maximizing every aspect of his art and skill, but the audience will perceive it, and the artist will achieve a level of unique perfection. Like Aristotle, Zeami seeks to achieve in theatrical performance a transcendent emotional experience for the audience, but in Nōh, the source of this transcendence is the beauty of the performance as opposed to the tragic quality of the plot.

Zeami's dramatic theory emerges from a tradition that blends the ideals of Buddhism with a deeply poetic aesthetic and the rigor of a martial-arts training academy and has become the touchstone for a tradition of dramatic art that has persisted for centuries. But the impact of Zeami's approach was not limited to Japanese theater—particularly in the last thirty or so years, Zeami's once-secret treatises have become standard reading in theater training programs all over the world.

Lodovico Castelvetro (1505–71)

In 1453, the armies of Sultan Mehmet conquered Constantinople, effectively bringing an end to the Byzantine Empire. Scholars of Greek literature, philosophy, and drama fled the ruins to Western Europe, bringing with them many classical texts and scholarly traditions that had hitherto been almost unknown in the West. A passionate hunger for classical texts and ideas proliferated across Europe. By the sixteenth century, Aristotle and Horace had become the unquestioned standard-bearers of dramatic aesthetics in Europe, and their popularity set the stage for some bitter battles concerning the emergent "humanist" (non-theological) drama. Castelvetro was an aristocrat from Modena, Italy, who led an extremely eventful life. Educated in law and literature, he traveled across Italy for his studies, finally winding up in Rome where he earned a reputation as an author and teacher. He later returned to his hometown of Modena, where he joined a notable circle of literati and became involved in a critical imbroglio when he panned the canzones of the poet and translator Annibale Caro. Caro infamously denounced Castelvetro to the Inquisition as a translator of the works of Philipp Melanchthon, a Lutheran reformer, into Italian. Under house arrest in Rome, Castelvetro learned that the Inquisition had obtained a copy of the translation supposedly in his own handwriting and had to flee for his life. He was declared an impenitent heretic on November 26, 1560, and lived as a fugitive in France and Austria, where he penned his greatest works.

Chiefly of interest for dramaturgs is Castelvetro's 1570 book *On Aristotle's Poetics,* in which he interprets Aristotle very rigidly to create a highly disciplined approach to writing drama. Here he formulates and cements the concept of the "Three Unities"; that is, a mandate that drama should have a single plotline (unity of action), take place in a single location (unity of place), and represent action that takes place in a single day (unity of time). The concept draws upon the notion of *verisimilitude* (authenticity of representation) that differs from Aristotle's notion of *mimesis* in some important ways. For Aristotle, such a notion of authenticity was applicable primarily to the play's action (not to its tone); for Castelvetro the notion is an ironclad sine qua non of every element of dramatic expression. But Castelvetro challenges the authority of Aristotle in many ways; he contends, for example, that Aristotle had no interest in any practical social or psychological utility from the drama (such as teaching) apart from *katharsis*, which Castelvetro sees as a "bitter medicine" for purifying the psyche of irrational emotions.

Castelvetro's work marks a critical moment in the history of Western dramaturgy because it signals, if not the beginning then, at least the ascendance of *neoclassicism*, essentially a movement of aesthetic criticism that sought to establish an ideal form for all the high arts based largely on models gleaned from the infusion of classical texts and ideas in the West. In the service of this ideal, philosophers strongly advocated the establishment of strict rules and codes, and governments backed these ideas. Rigid laws for the creation of art, laws based on sixteenth- and seventeenth-century readings of the classical texts, became the critical standard. These laws had a profound impact on the development of playwriting in Europe (particularly in France), although Spanish and English playwrights remained largely unconcerned with them until the eighteenth century. Shakespeare's plays sometimes explicitly disregard these notions, preferring instead to theatrically engage the audience's own imagination. Consider, in light of these arguments, this excerpt from the famous "O for a Muse of fire" prologue to *Henry V*, written in 1599 (twenty-eight years after Castelvetro's death):

> Suppose within the girdle of these walls
> Are now confin'd two mighty monarchies
> Whose high upreared and abutting fronts
> The perilous narrow ocean parts asunder.
> Piece out our imperfections with your thoughts.
> Into a thousand parts divide one man,
> And make imaginary puissance.
> Think when we talk of horses that you see them
> For 'tis your thoughts that how must deck our kings.
> Carry them here and there, jumping o'er times,
> Turning th' accomplishment of many years
> Into an hourglass.[17]

(19–31)

Shakespeare here calls attention to the artificiality of the theatrical experience, but rather than seeing it as something to be avoided, he embraces it. For Shakespeare, theater is not meant to be "realistic" but a realm of imagination, where the audience and the actors work together to create entire worlds of the mind. The success and amazing diversity of the theater of Shakespeare and his contemporaries would be held up as a powerful argument against the narrow readings of Aristotle provided by Castelvetro, and thus began an argument that shaped theater practice for the next four hundred years.

Lope Félix de Vega y Carpio (1562–1635)

In the late fifteenth century, a period known as the *Réconquista* ("reconquest"), Christians finally succeeded in wresting political control of Spain from North African Muslims, who had dominated it for centuries. The ensuing period was one of tremendous growth and cultural output in Spain, known as the Golden Age. Because of the very strong Catholicism of the Spanish culture, medieval theatrical forms persisted as the products of "folk culture" while university-educated playwrights experimented with humanist dramas. Whereas in most other parts of Europe, the two forms (one associated with Catholicism, one with Protestantism) were ideologically incompatible, in Spain they existed side-by-side and often informed and enriched one another.

A dominant dramatist of the era, Lope de Vega wrote his first play at the age of fourteen. His astonishing production of literary works aside, Lope de Vega was at various times in his life a naval officer, a priest, an actor, and, according to some accounts, a playboy and even a procurer for his patron. Under a sentence of banishment from Madrid for events entangling him to an actress, Lope wandered Spain for a time of almost unbelievable literary output. He wrote epic and mock-epic poetry on serious and frivolous topics, inspired by religion, history, mythology, or his own imagination, and sonnets, ballads, and romances, epistles in verse, elegies, sacred prose, and odes of all descriptions. But his surpassing accomplishment was his theater. Estimates as to the number of his plays varies, but Lope himself claimed to have composed fifteen hundred comedies and hundreds of shorter pieces. Some five hundred are extant. The topics and structures of his plays are immense, running from short scenes to full five-act dramas and including pastorals, history plays, biblical dramas and saint's plays, dramas of romance and chivalry, comedies of manners, *capa-y-espada* ("cloak-and-dagger") intrigues, mythic tales, forms unique to Spanish drama like *loas* and *autos*, and some unusual abstract works that seem more appropriate to avant-garde experiments of the twentieth century than to a Spanish Renaissance humanist.

Lope de Vega's contribution to dramaturgy, apart from this amazing corpus, is largely his extended essay *El arte nuevo de hacer comedias* (*The New Art of Writing Plays*). In this witty essay, presented originally in 1609 as an address to the Spanish Academy, Lope conceals beneath a wash of self-effacing comments an incisive critique of the neoclassical guardians of "high culture." In a tongue-in-cheek manner, Lope ridicules their attempts to restrict the taste of audiences and the proliferation of dramatic innovation. He writes, "Nobody can I call more barbarous than myself, since in defiance of art I dare to lay down precepts, and I allow myself to be borne along in the vulgar current. . . . But what can I do if I have written four hundred and eighty-three comedies, along with one which I finished this week?"[18]

By appearing to condemn his own writing as "artless" and the demands of the Spanish audience as "crude," Lope actually provides an elegant justification for the liberation of drama from overbearing rules and decorum of the kind insisted upon by Castelvetro. Such rigor is impossible, Lope argues, because of the demands of the "uncultured" crowd for novelty and variety, for "customs can do more among those who lack light of art than reason and force."[19] But beyond these facile excuses is an insightful commentary on the state of popular culture in Spain and an erudite defense of his own creative explorations and his immense body of work.

Lope de Vega's influence on the great playwrights who came after him, like Calderón, was immense. Like English drama of the same period, Spanish drama of the Renaissance shows little impact from French dramaturgy (which influenced most of the rest of the continent strongly). Possibly, Lope de Vega, combined with the dynamic energy of the Golden Age, helped to inoculate Spanish drama from the more extreme effects of neoclassicism. Lope's followers would set the tone of Spanish drama for centuries, and his plays are still performed regularly in the Spanish-speaking world.

Pierre-Augustin Caron de Beaumarchais (1732–99)

Born to a watchmaker and raised in the trade, Pierre-Augustin Caron as a young man developed a watch that could be fitted into a ring for Madame de Pompadour, one of the mistresses of Louis XV, King of France. Another watchmaker attempted to pirate the design, but when the matter was resolved in Caron's favor, the young watchmaker (the future Beaumarchais) came to the notice of the king.

Louis was one of the most powerful monarchs in the world. In Europe, France was second only to Russia in terms of size and commanded a mighty influence around the globe. French architecture, interior design, furniture, painting, sculpture, poetry, and drama were considered the gold standard across Europe, assiduously studied and shamelessly copied. French drama held the neoclassical ideals articulated by Castelvetro as the highest form of theatrical expression, and these ideals were rigorously enforced. However, as the century progressed, antimonarchism would rise in France, and with it would come a questioning of all of these ideals. Louis XV, increasingly unpopular, would leave a conflicted legacy, including extended internal unrest, secret police forces, and an assassination attempt on his own person.

Like Lope de Vega, Caron led an astonishing life of high adventure and social mobility. In this world of transforming political fortunes, patronage, and intrigue, Caron did extremely well. Enjoying the patronage of the influential Madame de Pompadour (who did much to advance the artistic, philosophical, and political life of France), Caron was a court favorite, teaching music to the king's sisters and making fortunes in international business speculations. He rose quickly, purchasing the noble title of Beaumarchais for himself. His first foray into playwriting came in 1767 with his *Eugénie*, which was a largely biographical account of his dispute with José Clavijo y Fajardo, a Spanish journalist, naturalist, and theater director who was responsible for a successful campaign to have the *autos sacramentales* (medieval Spanish Eucharist plays) banned. Clavijo had been involved in a love affair with Beaumarchais' sister and then reneged on his agreement to marry her (the story was revived by the German playwright Johann Wolfgang von Goethe in his 1774 play *Clavigo*).

Beaumarchais' success made him some bitter enemies, and after the death of Louis XV in 1770, Beaumarchais came under accusations of forgery, adultery, and even of poisoning his wives. Imprisoned, Beaumarchais became a victim of the corrupt justice system and wound up losing his fortune and his civil rights. Afterwards, he joined the secret intelligence service of the new king, Louis XVI, and was sent around the world to destroy documents that attacked the king and his court affairs. These missions, according to Beaumarchais himself, resulted in some wild adventures and derring-do (if he is to be believed). In his capacity as an intelligence operative, Beaumarchais became deeply involved with the fortunes of the American Revolution and secretly inveigled Louis XVI to provide significant amounts of money and arms to the colonists, making possible their armed insurgency against Great Britain.

During this period, Beaumarchais created his greatest contributions to the drama: his *Figaro* trilogy: *The Barber of Seville* (1773), *The Marriage of Figaro* (1778), and *The Guilty Mother* (1792). These comedies were deeply controversial, partially because of Beaumarchais' own scandalous reputation and partially because the plays themselves provide a ruthless (and hilarious) criticism of the absurdities and excesses of the French nobility. In *The Barber of Seville* is perhaps his most famous line: "I hasten to laugh at everything for fear of being obliged to weep at it" (1.2).

In retrospect, it seems that Beaumarchais' dependence upon the king's favor is at odds with these antimonarchical sentiments, which indeed were seen by some (including the later Napoleon) to sacralize and hasten the revolution that would result in the execution of Louis and his entire court. But Beaumarchais' political experiences had led him to become committed to the principles of an emerging philosophy that came to be known as the Enlightenment.

The Enlightenment is really not one particular line of thought but several, not limited to philosophy but also growing out of developments in science, logic, ethics, and theology. The basic tenets of the Enlightenment are the privileging of rational thought over emotional reaction and superstition, of empirical research to guide the formation of deductive theories, of tolerance and openness, of systematic doubt and skepticism of authority, of increasing the liberation of all peoples, and, above all, of protecting the free exchange of ideas through reasoned discourse. Influences from this movement were eagerly welcomed by Europeans and the new Americans eager to break free from centuries of social, political, and religious oppression. Some leading thinkers of the Enlightenment included René Descartes, Francis Bacon, Isaac Newton, Jean-Jacques Rousseau, David Hume, and Baruch Spinoza. Such thinkers helped form the concepts of natural law, self-evident inherent human freedoms, the right to self-determination of creed and religion, and the necessity of open exchange of ideas to the freedom of human thought and action that were so important to the founding fathers of the United States of America. Thanks to Beaumarchais, the King of France fostered that Enlightenment Revolution, an act that may have inspired his own destruction in the French Revolution of 1789. As for Beaumarchais, no sooner had he battled his way back up the ladder of French high society and seen his rights and privileges restored than that regime would be violently overthrown. Despite his revolutionary ideals, he was declared a loyalist to the nobility and imprisoned in 1791. On his release in 1792, he worked for the revolutionaries to secure weapons from Holland but was again declared an enemy of the state. He was unable to return to France until 1796 but afterwards lived out his remaining years in Paris more or less peacefully.

Beaumarchais' important contributions to dramaturgy rest not only in his progressive use of plays as tools for social change but also in his body of theatrical criticism. His Enlightenment aesthetic consciousness was evident as early as 1767, when he crafted his *Essai Sur Le Genre Dramatique (On Serious Drama)*, in which he attacked the most fundamental principles of neoclassical dramaturgy:

> The inevitable blows of fate do not offer the mind any moral lesson. When one can only shudder and be silent, is not the act of reflection the worst thing one might do? If a morality were extracted from this genre of play, it would be a dreadful one which might lead many souls toward crime, since its fatalistic vision would provide them with a justification; it would discourage many from following the ways of virtue, and all such efforts,

according to this system, would be for naught. If there is no virtue without sacrifice, so too there is no sacrifice without hope of reward. Any belief in fatalism degrades man by depriving him of the freedom without which his actions reveal no sense of morality to him.[20]

The fatalism of tragedy is the engine of its ability to generate *katharsis*. The tragic protagonist must be skewered by his own greatness, doomed by his own commitment to high ideals or sacred duties. But Enlightenment philosophy takes two premises as central: that it is within human power to improve the human condition and that nothing is inevitable except progressive transformations. These assumptions underpin all Enlightenment accomplishments in science, social policy, and philosophy. Tragedy, Beaumarchais observed, is incompatible with this notion and "degrades" humanity by robbing it of this most fundamental principle. Beaumarchais' writing would remain important to those playwrights of the nineteenth and twentieth centuries who wished to subvert the dominance of tragedy and to those social thinkers who wished to subvert the sense that tyranny and inequality were equally inevitable. As the Enlightenment swept Europe in this period of widespread political unrest, new dramaturgies would develop to bring theater into accord not only with aesthetic ideals but also with important new principles of philosophy and social progress.

Gotthold Ephraim Lessing (1729–81)

Like Aristotle educated in theology and medicine, Gotthold Ephraim Lessing was attracted to the theater as a hobby at an early age. In 1748, he studied at the University of Wittenberg and later, penniless, moved to Berlin, a bustling metropolis where he was exposed to the writers and thinkers of the Enlightenment.

Lessing would become deeply influenced by this philosophy of liberation and progress. Living by his writing alone (he is said to be the first German of letters to achieve such a feat), Lessing began to build a reputation as a minor playwright and brilliant dramatic critic, hostile to neoclassicism, and published several articles in quarterly literary journals. At that time, he struck up a deep friendship with a Jewish philosopher, Moses Mendelssohn, with whom he collaborated extensively. After receiving his master's degree in Wittenberg, Lessing returned to Berlin in 1752, where he produced his first great "bourgeois tragedy," *Miss Sara Sampson*. He continued to write plays for production and criticism with Mendelssohn but was beset with troubles, central among them an unfortunate rivalry with Voltaire.

In the 1760s, Lessing engaged his crusade against neoclassical aesthetics in earnest. He attacked Horace and argued that aristocratic value systems and rigid aesthetic rules ought not to substitute for an author's erudition, imagination, experimentation, and honest critical engagement with society. His works grew in popularity, and in 1767, Lessing was invited to help establish the Nationaltheatre in Hamburg. The managers of the theater hoped that Lessing would act as a sort of in-house critic who would praise the German drama and the Enlightenment values and perhaps write pithy plot summaries and give historical notes in the programs. The Nationaltheatre got more than it bargained for; what Lessing delivered was an immensely erudite, deeply engaged, witty, ironic, and often quite scathing indictment of German aesthetic culture and what he saw as its uncritical, unexamined, myopic devotion to neoclassical (specifically French) drama and criticism. Lessing did not disregard Aristotle; on the contrary, he considered the *Poetics* to be "as infallible as the *Elements* of Euclid."[21] But he wrote that in their slavish devotion to neoclassical interpretations of Aristotle, French dramatists had created a stultified, conformist theater culture. Of course, some French playwrights and critics like Beaumarchais and Voltaire were busy subverting that conformism (and suffering for it). But because of the devotion of the German theatergoing public to traditional notions of French drama, Lessing felt a compelling need to work to develop a counterculture that would better reflect what he felt were Enlightenment ideals. He closes his collected essays with the following:

> I should be vain enough to deem I had done something meritorious for our theatre, if I might believe that I have discovered the only means of checking this fermentation of taste. . . . No nation has more misapprehended the rules of ancient drama than the French. They have adopted as essential some incidental remarks made by Aristotle about the most fitting external division of drama, and have so enfeebled the essential by all manner of limitation and interpretations, that nothing else could necessarily arise therefrom but works that remained far below the highest effect on which the philosopher had reckoned in his rules.[22]

Lessing honored the plays of Elizabethan England, in which a playwright's invention was less restricted. Even the minor plays of Shakespeare, Lessing argues, were more faithful than Voltaire's greatest dramas to Aristotelian dramaturgy.

After the Nationaltheatre's collapse, Lessing collected his 104 publications into a single book, the *Hamburg Dramaturgy*. This witty, erudite text defines the parameters of dramaturgy as we think of it today; a tool for diagnosis of plays to maximize their aesthetic and social values. Aristotle, scientist that he was, would surely have preferred this empirical, deductive approach to dramatic analysis over a servile devotion to a single critic's ideas (even if that critic is Aristotle himself). This sequence of historical dramaturgs concludes with

Lessing because his work most effectively and clearly articulates the role of the dramaturg as thought of it today: an expert in play analysis and theater history who is profoundly committed to the notion of theater as a tool for dialectical self-improvement and social change. Lessing's notable accomplishment is to judge a piece of theater not on its adherence to abstract ideals but on its effectiveness within its immediate culture. After Lessing, the position of "dramaturg" becomes essential to the practice of the great German theaters, and the office's utility becomes swiftly apparent to the rest of Europe and later to America.

This brief survey is meant only to give the student of dramaturgy a sense of the progress of particular important threads of dramaturgical thought and innovation from around the world and various points in history up to the eighteenth century, after which the character of dramaturgy undergoes some significant changes. As it views theater as a dialectical tool, dramaturgy shifts its engagement from abstract aesthetic idealism to the development of certain practical philosophical models of interpretation. But the above condensation of a few influential dramaturgs should get you thinking about dramaturgy as an important historical phenomenon that takes the form of an ongoing conversation between playwrights and critics about how the theater works, or should work, or could work, or must work, and why. This should give the groundwork needed to begin developing your own dramaturgy, appropriate for the discourses that are important in your experience. The following chapter picks up the thread from a different angle and examines instead of individuals movements of critical philosophy that have dominated the powerful dramaturgy of the last two centuries.

Exercises

Go deep! Select the most intriguing of the dramaturgical writers above, and write a continuation of the entry provided. First, read one or two of their dramaturgical essays in depth. Then do the following:

- Find two or three commentaries on their work written in the past fifteen years. You might look at the introductions of new translations, scholarly essays, or dramaturgical casebooks. How are their theories being employed by theorists and dramatists today? Do they stand up?
- Find a play (or festival) from the general era and region of this dramaturg (the writing could be one authored by the dramaturg). Write a short essay that answers the following questions:
  - Can you find examples of what the dramaturg is advocating/complaining about?
  - What would the dramaturg have thought of the play? Or, even better, did the dramaturg comment on the play him- or herself?

- If the dramaturg is also the playwright, how well does he or she live up to his or her own ideals?

Go wide! Below is a chronological list of some more of the most important big names in theater criticism and dramaturgy prior to the nineteenth century and the titles of some of their most important writings. Using the entries above as a guide, create short dossiers on three of them. Include:

- A brief biography that gives the reader some context for the dramaturg's ideas, particularly including any triumphs or reverses that the dramaturg enjoyed or suffered for his or her ideas. Good things to include are the dramaturg's birth and death dates, country, social class and line of work, and his or her relationships with people (and institutions) of power.
- A summary of their most significant works on dramaturgy—don't stop with the one or two listed next below!
- An encapsulation of their work that contains their impact on later playwrights and critics or indeed on social movements.
  Note: Remember, if these are playwrights as well as dramaturgs, you may try looking at their scripts for clues to their dramaturgy but also explore their own prefaces to their plays, any critical writings, or letters that survive.

Marcus Tullius Cicero, *About the Best Kind of Orators*
Longinus, *On the Sublime*
Quintus Septimius Florens Tertullianus (Tertullian), *On the Spectacles*
Augustinus of Hippo (Saint Augustine), *City of God*
Giovanni Boccaccio, *On the Geneaology of the Gods of the Gentiles* (Book 14)
Giovambattista Giraldi Cinthio, *Discourse on Comedy and Tragedies*
Julius Caesar Scaliger, *Poetics*
Stephen Gosson, *The School of Abuse*
Sir Philip Sydney, *The Defense of Poesy*
Ben Jonson, *Timber*
Pierre Corneille, *Apologetic Letter*, *Discourses*
Georges de Scudéry, *Observations on the Cid*
Jean-Baptiste Poquelin (Molière), *Critique of School for Wives*, preface to *Tartuffe*
Jean Racine, preface to *Phaedra*
Nicholas Bolieau-Despréaux, *The Art of Poetry*
Denis Diderot, *Paradox of Acting*, *On Dramatic Poetry*
Jean-Jacques Rousseau, *Politics and the Arts*
François-Marie Arouet (Voltaire), *A Discourse on Tragedy*
John Dryden, *An Essay of Dramatic Poetry*

Samuel Butler, *Upon Critics Who Judge of Modern Plays*
Jeremy Collier, *A Short View of the Immorality and Profaneness of the English Stage*
William Congreve, *Amendments of Mr. Collier's False and Imperfect Citations*
Joseph Addison and Richard Steele, *The Spectator*
Samuel Johnson, preface to the *Plays of William Shakespeare*
David Hume, *Of Tragedy*
Friedrich Schiller, preface to *The Robbers*, *The Stage as a Moral Institution*
Johann Wolfgang von Goethe, *On Truth and Probability in Works of Art*
Georg Wilhelm Friedrich Hegel, *The End of Art, Dramatic Poetry*

Go long! Having become familiar with the writings and philosophies of one of this chapter's dramaturgs (in the entries or in the list above), select a popular play written in the past five years and analyze the text against the expectations/fears of the dramaturg in question. What would he or she have thought of this play?

Power Plays

> I really do inhabit a system in which words are capable of shaking the entire structure of government, where words can prove mightier than ten military divisions.
>
> —Vāclav Havel, "Words on Words"

> The unexamined life is not worth living.
>
> —Socrates, *Apologia 38a*

In 2006, I sat in on a graduate class on Greek drama taught by dramaturg and scholar Brian Johnston. Frustrated by the professor's analysis of the *Oresteia*, which brought together a wide spectrum of political, religious, and historical observations, a student remarked, "Excuse me, professor, but don't you think you're reading too much into this?" The professor replied, "Well, since Aeschylus was a genius and I'm not, I rather think I'm not reading enough into it."

The professor's reply contains, of course, an admonition that we dramaturgs particularly should always keep in the forefront of our minds, which is "Have I *really* asked enough questions of this play?" The answer to this must always be a humble "not yet." It is a reminder not to rest on our laurels and not to cease exploring the darkened terrain just because we found one possible way to cross it. A play is a garden of forking paths: it is sheer madness to think that after a month, year, or decade of study, we can exhaust its dramatic possibilities. But Johnston's reply also is a reminder that in theater, the biggest limitations we ever encounter are the ones we construct ourselves when out of laziness or obtuseness we fail to use our imaginations to their full extent. Why *should* we put limits on our explorations and our curiosities? The next great idea (maybe the one that would make Aeschylus sit up in his grave and say, "Finally they get it!") might be just outside the current pool of ghost light, waiting for an intrepid dramaturg to stumble across it.

At the end of the day, it's really not possible to "read too much" into a good play, not if you approach the process of reading with integrity and rigor. If it were, there would be a finite number of times that a play could be performed afresh. Some very courageous dramaturgs risked derision, isolation, exile, imprisonment, torture, and even death for their ideas; some dramaturgy changed whole worlds and started aesthetic or philosophical movements that affect choices to this day; some dramaturgs are honored with monuments and buildings. That should indicate that this kind of work is important and that the right words at the right time in the right place, as Havel says, can be as powerful as an army.

This chapter explores the dramaturgy of ideas and interpretations. The primary tool for this exploration is *critical theory*, a broad collection of techniques for interpretation grounded in various philosophical movements that scholars jokingly call "the isms." Taken as individual movements the isms provide powerful precision tools for perceiving the meanings, both intended and unintended, of a piece of drama. Some artists are initially a little suspicious of this kind of writing, partially because of a tendency among theater practitioners to prefer "practice" over "theory." These prejudices need to be combated directly, because working with critical theory is what makes contemporary dramaturgy so central to the artistic process. Theory provides interpretive strategies that have been specifically developed to transform dramatic literature into moving, socially relevant artworks and to keep artists open to new interpretations and new ideas. It is productive to think of critical theory as a variety of tools for a variety of jobs. But it all begins with developing an understanding of drama as a form of *dialectics*.

Drama as Dialectic

Georg Wilhelm Friedrich Hegel (1770–1831) made a profound contribution to philosophical thought in his use of *dialectics*. The word stems from the Greek διαλεκτική and was a technique employed widely, in many Athenian social fora, for coming to a rational conclusion. Fundamental to any logical process, dialectics begins when one debater proposes an idea (or *thesis*), then an opponent proposes a counteridea (or *antithesis*), and they argue it out, with the ideal result being not necessarily that the strongest idea triumphs but that what will emerge is a third idea that's better than either of the two initial ones (a *synthesis*). A perspicacious dramaturg will remark that this is a dramatic model, because it is grounded in dialogue and relies on conflict.

Hegel's writings, particularly *Phenomenology of Mind*, are largely concerned with illustrating the potential of dialectics to direct the evolution of human thought and action towards a more perfect, just, and harmonious condition.

Human individuals and societies, like organisms, *evolve*, adaptively discarding old useless ideas in favor of new useful ones in response to oppositional forces, both from within the society and without. Every new social or psychological state of being, Hegel observed, contains in it contradictions and shortcomings that will sooner or later necessitate its destruction and replacement with a new state of being. In Hegel, progress is a series of productive conflicts that refine and strengthen society and the individual until humanity achieves what Hegel thought of as the ideal social state of being: a constitutional government in which order prevails but not at the expense of freedom. Hegel also observes such productive struggles in philosophy and aesthetics, between knowledge and faith, between mind or spirit (*geist*) and nature, and so on. Hegel's philosophies were immensely popular among philosophers, moralists, and political revolutionaries and were picked up and heavily employed by both conservative, orthodox, authoritarian thinkers (the so-called Right Hegelians) and by liberal, freethinking, and democratic thinkers (the so-called Left Hegelians). In the current world, it is common to identify almost every political platform as "right," "left," or "centrist," and those positions are in reference to Hegelian dialectics.

Hegelian dialectics make possible the aesthetic movement now called *romanticism* and thus lay the foundations for a dramaturgy of tremendous social importance. On his Web site, "Ibsen Voyages,"[1] Johnston notes that in a Shakespearean tragedy, we are introduced to a moral universe that is "closed"; that is, the social order is nondialectical, ordained by God, whose will is manifested in things like who gets to be king. The villain is someone who seeks to be more than he or she was ordained to be and violates the natural order for selfish reasons. Because of an Elizabethan worldview that viewed all the elements of the universe as connected in a rigid hierarchical system, this disruption of the human social order actually affects the entire universe. In the various plays, this results in earthquakes, bad weather, riots, and odd animal behavior and occasionally causes the metaphysical barriers between this world and the next to become weak and permeable, permitting the presence of supernatural nasties like witches and ghosts in the material world. This state of affairs persists until a hero arises to *restore the order* (which he can only do by dint of tremendous personal sacrifice). In romantic tragedy, which appears in the works of Lessing, Friedrich Schiller, and Goethe, for instance, the universe is morally "open." That is, there is no hand on the cosmic tiller directing the course of human events, and humans are therefore capable of dialectics, progressively creating their own fates by the choices they make. The hero in this case is the transgressor, standing up to the antiquated, stultifying order and causing tragic but much-needed disorder. As a result of this disruption, a new order arises that is better (in the sense that it allows humans more freedom to explore their own paths to righteousness and harmony) than the one it replaces. The Shakespearean hero is one who lays down his life for traditional order; the romantic hero is a rebel.

Romantic drama illustrates that plays (like any cultural product or social institution) are dynamically engaged with the culture that creates them, influenced by some ideas, influencing others in a streaming and evolving discourse (a garden of forking paths). In a society that is dynamic, open to dialectical thought, and reliant on scientific principles and technological innovations and whose rulers do not resort to censorship, it is possible to employ drama (the most dialectical of all arts) as a critical, even essential component of human self-discovery. This is drama as staged philosophy and the playwright and dramaturg as *thinkers*.[2]

Of course, such an amazing tool is not always used for the best ends. Drama can also be silly, escapist, nostalgic, narcissistic, intellectually unchallenging, or self-congratulatory. Sometimes, productions shore up their shallow dialectical content with big-budget spectacle in the form of the designer's magic and up-tempo song-and-dance numbers. Of course, strong production values are not always at odds with strong thinking, but plays become less useful, in a Hegelian sense, when they become mere fluff. Such plays can even be damaging if they distract audiences from serious problems by creating the false sense that "everything is okay." In light of the potential of the drama to act as a Hegelian tool for dialectical self-discovery, producing this kind of drama is like using a supercollider particle accelerator to toast a marshmallow and produces a very sanitized theater: commercial and from a dramaturgical point of view uninspiring.

When working on drama that is dialectically rich and intended as a tool for self-discovery and social progress, the dramaturg should be at least as skilled at critical philosophy as the playwright. It is necessary to "read into" such plays as deeply as possible, and critical theories provide excellent tools for doing just that. This is the kind of skill that takes a lifetime of study to achieve, and its importance is probably the greatest argument for the centrality of the dramaturg to the theatrical process. Actors act, designers design, directors direct, and dramaturgs ask questions; critical theory is a set of tools for the shaping and answering of questions.

Theory Capsules

What follows is a series of short capsules that describe the major threads of dramatic critical theory since 1800. Each capsule describes the basic tenets of the theory, its philosophical foundation, and its utility in terms of the interpretation of dramatic literature and performance. The capsules also look at some of the criticisms or shortcomings of the theories, so that you can develop a sense of which tool might work best for different kinds of dramaturgical problems. Where it is helpful to do so, the capsules provide examples of playwrights whose work is directly informed by the theory. At the end of the chapter are exercises that help build the skills necessary for employing these ideas in the service of creating vital, relevant theatrical productions(see appendix B for a list of further reading). The current chapter is only meant as a practical and very basic introduction to critical theory's application in production dramaturgy; students should consult Mark Fortier's *Theory/Theatre: An Introduction* (2002), and more advanced scholars should become familiar with *Critical Theory and Performance: Revised and Enlarged Edition* edited by Janelle G. Reinelt and Joseph R. Roach (2007).

One further caveat: any attempt to methodize or categorize philosophical movements cannot avoid giving short shrift to the full range of ideas in the movement, to crossovers and hybridizations between movements, and to internal disagreements within movements. For the purpose of this book, which is to provide an introduction to the practice of production dramaturgy, summaries and broad strokes are required. It is not at all my intention to efface these mergers and divisions but only to group philosophers into some understandable traditional frameworks that dramaturgs can use to begin their own philosophical work. Studying critical theory is the work of a lifetime, and I urge all readers new to the field to pursue any and all of these ideas that intrigue them, because all have great potential to guide and enrich work as artists.

Historical Criticism

The study of the theater is very old (much older than the documents that remain in the historical record), and the most time-honored approach for critical engagement with the theater has been that of the historian. The term *Theatrewissenschaft* ("theater science") was coined by scholars around 1900 to describe a rigorous, objective analysis of the historical contexts and production conditions of plays and periods. Traditional theater history is an endless search for origins and useful sources, documents and artifacts that provide evidence of the conditions of a lost time that surrounded the production of a dramatic text, performance, or movement.

Historical research (which encompasses biography, ethnography, sociology, and anthropology) is the cornerstone of humanistic inquiry for the simple reason that *history is identity*. History is, after all, presentable only as a series of stories that communities tell about their own origins and developments, triumphs and struggles, and together these create a sense of the society and the individual's role within it. What is an individual identity except a collection of such stories (national, tribal, religious, familial, and personal)?

The philosopher George Santayana (1863–1952) wrote famously in his 1905 book *The Life of Reason* that "those who do not remember the past are condemned to repeat it." This notion drives home the importance of historical research to the production of drama. Often, theater artists believe they are innovating new forms when they are just rehashing old ones and so will fall into the same traps the older revolutionaries did. Understanding one's own artistic work as part of an ongoing movement is critical knowledge; without it, the best an artist can hope to do is mimic his predecessors or flail desperately with blind experimentation. History, done well, can provide a map of the past that indicates possible paths to the future. Historical understanding both broad and deep of one's art is often the determining factor between a great artist (one who makes a mark on that history) and one who is merely interesting for the moment. Theatrical artists are unwise when they reject the information a dramaturg provides in terms of production histories, biographies of authors, and other salient pieces of historical information that are essential to understanding what a play is supposed to mean.

The problem (and what makes history a "theoretical approach" rather than a hard science) is that the search for origins and sources is one that must always be incomplete. Historians are tragically aware that the historical record is fragmentary, full of misdirection, and even lies. Theater historians furthermore must always operate with the permanent loss of that one event that would render the greatest store of understanding: the performance. The incompleteness of the record and the importance of history to concepts of identity give historians much more influence over human affairs than most people realize. This realization led British satirist Terry Pratchett to quip in 1997, "History changes all the time. It is constantly being reexamined and reevaluated, otherwise how would we be able to keep historians occupied? We can't possibly allow people with their sort of minds to walk around with time on their hands."[3]

Furthermore, the discipline of history is permeated with notions of teleological progressions from "primitive" to "sophisticated" societies, which can be very damaging to objective analysis of cultures in their own contexts. Also, historians of art have had a tendency to view documents like laws, records, and other histories as of a different category than aesthetic works. Histories and laws are thought to reveal "truths," while aesthetic works are believed to encode that truth within untrustworthy fictions. The idea is that the study of the one will reveal the hidden secrets of the other, and sometimes historians have not taken into account that laws, records, and histories are also human products that are influenced by the same (often perverse) social forces that shape a drama or a poem. But conceiving history as a science holds the historian up to an ideal of rigorous engagement with evidence and an ethical mandate to be as objective as possible in its analysis and evaluation; unfortunately, this mandate is not always enthusiastically followed.

In the past four or five decades, there has been something of a territorial battle between "traditional theater historians" and "theater theorists" in the academy. This is partially because critical theory, following Karl Marx, sees all language, documents, and artifacts (especially histories) as inherently ideological and so has often set itself against traditional historical methods. Historians, on the other hand, sometimes feel that their own work is unscrupulously raided by theorists with a political axe to grind and so taken out of context or misapplied. However, it seems that new bridges are now being formed between these camps, as theorists have become more rigorous and empirical, and historians have developed more flexible methods of inquiry that expose ideological assumptions.

The dramaturg's intellectual arsenal must contain shots from both of these lockers. This cannot be emphasized too strongly. Historical research is the bread-and-butter of dramaturgy that provides the basis of understanding that any production needs to succeed. But developing "theoretical lenses" for looking at historical information as well as scripts makes the dramaturg flexible and responsive and, above all, effective as a guide for the rest of the company or for an adaptation or translation in the endless struggle towards new relevance. The best dramaturgs are rigorous historians, sharp theorists, and visionary artists, and they move fluidly between camps at academic conferences and in rehearsal.

Structuralism

Like all philosophers, Swiss linguist Ferdinand de Saussure (1857–1913) was interested in getting at what is really going on, why we think what we think, and why humans cling to certain concepts that seem to have no referent in reality. Unlike Plato or other philosophers who pursued *ontology* (the metaphysical study of essential being), Saussure felt that the answers to questions like "What is beauty?" or "What is truth?" could not begin to be answered until we could actually determine what it is we mean by *beauty* or *truth*. Words, he felt, were a barrier to knowledge. His focus then was on *linguistics* and the structures of meaning that humans employ every day but that we understand incompletely or not at all.

Saussure conceived of semiotics (or "semiology") as a tool for describing the structure of human language, that is to say, as a model for describing *how* "signs" (in Latin, *semae*, human tools for the conveyance of meaning, which include words, gestures, and other forms of communication) mean what they mean. Signs are actually composed of two formal elements, a *signifier* and a *signified*. The signifier is that part of the sign that is perceived in reality: the utterance of a word, the wink of an eye, or what-have-you. The signified is the concept or abstract that is indicated by the signifier. Since critical theory is directed toward the interpretation of sign systems (like scripts and theatrical productions), semiotics is the basis of all other forms of critical exploration. *Semiosis* (the process by which signs create meaning) is the medium for the communication of all human information, ideas, and emotions. If we think of critical theory as a meal, semiosis is the plate upon which the rest of it is served.

Saussure's writings are significant because they reveal that although most people think of the process of meaning as a "fixed" system, one in which signifiers and signifieds are connected by eternal logic, the link between these two elements is actually fairly arbitrary. What exactly a given gesture or grunt actually means is determined not by anything definite or material but by social conventions and linguistic contexts. That is to say, signs are defined not in relation to objects or concepts but in relation to other signs within larger systems of producing meaning. Because the signs do not actually connect to their material referents, they establish systems of meaning that are sometimes based on wild assumptions and omissions and often produce meaning in entirely unintended ways.

Semiotics is sometimes quite disturbing in its facility for revealing the networks of illusions that constitute our lives. It reveals that semiosis is a rather perverse and unpredictable process, dependent on contexts and histories, and that the process can be hijacked by those who understand the mechanisms so that new meanings can be established, and old ones discarded. Many students have a difficult time initially wrestling with these concepts, but by and large, it is actually easier for theater practitioners. Because the process of making theater is self-consciously aware of its own semiosis, and the theater itself is a site of what semiologists call "thickness" or "density" of signs, many theater practitioners see semiotics as a language for describing what they do every time they walk onto a stage. Semiotics makes theater "readable." An actress who plays Joan of Arc, for instance, knows that she is not really Joan of Arc but is employing a system of signifiers (including the script, her body, her gestures and actions, her costume, and the lights, sound, and scenic elements of the production) all of which put together *mean* Joan of Arc. The character on stage is not the actress, nor is it a function of the script but a separate entity composed entirely of signs. The audience is aware of that, too, and comments on it when leaving the theater: "Wow, I really believed she was Joan of Arc!" So semiotics is very useful for describing how each individual signifier that makes up this entity works and how an individual change (in the color of a sash, or the direction of some blocking, or the intensity of a particular lighting instrument) affects the whole system. It is also useful for helping determine how a theatrical production could communicate across social barriers, how the audience itself produces signs that affect (and potentially can enrich) the production, and how to condition the audience to be maximally receptive to the artistic vision.

One of the most interesting concepts in theater semiotics is *ghosting*, articulated by theater theorist Marvin Carlson. Imagine that actress playing Joan of Arc, who holds a wooden prop that *signifies* a sword. Onstage, she slays an enemy with the sword and then turns the sword upside-down and kneels before it, giving prayerful thanks for the victory. The prop has now taken on new significance, that of the Cross. But it is not a clean transformation. The old *signified*, the sword, *persists* in the audience's memory and thus enters into a fascinating dialectical relationship with the Cross, making the audience draw parallels between Joan's militarism and her piety.

Saussure's work in semiotics incited the development of a philosophical school called *structuralism*. With applications in many fields, structuralism describes a broad territory, but its common characteristics are: a focus away from misleading surface elements towards the underlying structures of meaning, an awareness that the meaning of any part of the system is determined in relation to other parts of the system and not to some transcendent "truth," and an assumption that such structures underlie all systems that produce meaning. Structuralist criticism has had an enormous impact on theater; examples include the school of Russian Formalism—which included Viktor Shklovsky (1893–1984), Roman Jakobson (1896–1982), and, later, Mikhail Bakhtin (1895–1975)—which had a profound effect on the shape of the massively influential Russian theater of the twentieth century, and the Prague School—which included Jakobson as well as Vilem Mathesius (1882–1946)—which was particularly concerned with problems of aesthetic criticism.

Marxism

Karl Marx (1818–83) admired Hegel's devotion to dialectics and agreed with him that history is the product of the collisions of social forces. However, Hegel attributed the evolution of society to an idealized concept of a "spirit of the age" and felt that changes in this zeitgeist determined the way people think and act, the culture that they create, the politics they follow, and so on down to the day-to-day choices of an individual's life and the material conditions people experience. Marx felt that this idea was correct in every respect except that it was upside-down; it was the material conditions of life that determined how people think, feel, and act. As opposed to Hegel's "dialectical idealism," then, Marx offers "dialectical materialism."

The problem, as Marx saw it, was that the Industrial Revolution had generated a state of economic affairs that was deeply unfair to its workers. Say you want to create a factory that makes widgets. You need two elements: capital (to invest in the factory) and workers to make the widgets. The widgets cost three shekels to make; one for materials, one for labor, and one for overhead, and the owner sells them for four (because he or she provided the capital, he or she takes the one-shekel profit). In this model, everyone is making one shekel per widget. Now, if demand for the widget increases to the point where the owner can charge five shekels, does the owner give the workers raises? Or does the owner take the profits and invest in more factories, paying the workers one shekel per widget like always (or even less, if he or she can)? The owner turns the profits to becoming richer and expanding his or her economic empire, while the worker languishes at the same level because the worker's pay is connected not to the value of a widget but to the perceived value of his labor. This worker is *alienated* from the product of his labor. Meanwhile, lawmakers come from the owner class (they're the ones with the leisure time and the fiscal resources to be the rulers), so they make laws that are designed to protect this state of affairs, both to keep the value of labor artificially low and to keep the workers from being able to do anything about it. Individual workers who resist could be fired, arrested, even executed for messing with the system. In this model, the worker cannot enjoy the fruits of his or her labor and so becomes essentially a slave, unable to act to improve his or her own condition no matter how hard he or she works.

Marx felt that this state of affairs encouraged oppression, hunger, poverty, violence, and social chaos and envisioned a different society that was just and therefore harmonious. He noted that it was the workers who controlled what he called the *means of production*: the farms, the mines, the factories, the shipyards, and all the infrastructure of the industrialized West. If a single worker refused to capitulate, he or she could be dealt with, but what if all the dockworkers decided to halt their activities? Or all the garbage workers? Or all the farmers? Or all the industrial line workers? If they act collectively, Marx observed, the workers could bring the wealth-generating process of industry to a screeching halt. This discovery reconfigures the whole power relationship and acknowledges the creation of new social factions, or political "classes," whose interests are diametrically opposed; and it is the conflict between industry own-ers (the *bourgeosie)* and workers (the *proletariat)* that generates the dialectics of post–Industrial Revolution politics. In order to have a controlling hand in these dialectics, all the workers need to do is act collectively. Why, Marx wondered, do people not see this?

Because, he argued, the entire purpose of culture in a capitalist society is to obscure that injustice; to create myths and distortions that make this unequal power split seem perfectly right and natural. In an 1844 essay, Marx wrote that art ought to strive to work against this distortion, to expose the workings of this unjust system, to foster a consciousness of class issues, and to rouse the anger of the proletariat against the bourgeoisie. In order to do this, Marx suggested, art should provide a counteralienation, a disconcerting vision of the world in which the "normal" state of affairs is revealed to be abnormal and unjust.

Marx's writings had a profound affect on global politics, philosophy, and aesthetics. Almost all of the political movements of the twentieth century were reactions either for or against his theory, and Marxism is the foundation for many of the modern critical theories used everyday by theater artists and thinkers. Marx is critically important to the current study because his writings became fundamental to dramaturgy in Europe and America and had a tremendous influence on important national theatrical discourses, which in turn had tremendous impacts on the lives of millions of people. Marxist criticism of art is designed to accomplish the following tasks:

- Expose the narratives of obfuscation that illegitimately naturalize the dehumanization of and violence against oppressed peoples
- Provide counternarratives of resistance and liberation
- Act as a base of educating "hearts and minds" to make proper social changes that increase justice and equality

Walter Benjamin, a member of the prestigious "Frankfurt School" of materialist aesthetic philosophers, provides powerful examples in his essays of these pernicious forces in operation and what can be done about them. He views traditional drama as one of the many products of the "triumphal procession" of a society that is made possible by the bloody destruction and oppression of others. To disguise this, he writes, drama and other arts are infused with a kind of aura of transcendent beauty that at once illegitimately disconnects art with material reality and erases their true identity as artifacts of exploitation. But, he argues, radical drama can be just as effective at clarifying wicked social conditions as traditional drama is at disguising them.

Significant playwrights and dramaturgs who require a Marxist critical context to fully understand are:

• *Bertolt Brecht* (1896–1956), one of the most important playwrights, directors, and dramaturgs of the twentieth century. In 1926, when he was assistant dramaturg at the Deutsches Theater in Berlin (one of the world's most prominent theaters), Brecht went so far as to say, "When I read Marx's *Kapital*, I understood my plays."[4] Building on the work of other directors like Erwin Piscator and Vsevolod Meyerhold, Brecht developed a radical political dramaturgy that he named "epic theater." Brecht developed "dramaturgical collectives" with other playwrights and theater theorists (many of them female) with whom he generated his most celebrated works. After many political reverses, Brecht in 1949 founded the Berliner Ensemble, a company dedicated to developing his Marxist dramaturgy. There he meticulously documented his productions and workshops, leaving a rich legacy of radical leftist theatrical experimentation that continues to massively influence theater production today, more than fifty years after his death.

- *Hallie Flanagan (1890–1969), who studied with some of the great Russian dramatists in Moscow and developed a "ripped-from-the-headlines" dramaturgy focused on increasing the social relevance of American theater, particularly to the most disenfranchised members of American society. In 1935, Flanagan took over the Federal Theatre Project, part of the Works Progress Administration that employed thousands of artists (including Orson Welles, John Houseman, Leonard Bernstein, Marc Blitzstein, and Arthur Miller), and presented to millions of Americans. Among the most interesting products of the FTP was the "Living Newspaper." For these highly Brechtian dramas, which relied on scenic minimalism and nonmimetic acting styles, teams of writers scoured the news wires for stories about pressing issues of the day to dramatize. Some of these, particularly Triple-A Plowed Under, Power, Ethiopia, and One-Third of a Nation, used an overtly Marxist theoretical lens to criticize American economic and political policies. The FTP was shut down in 1939 by President Franklin D. Roosevelt's political opponents, who cited these plays and Flanagan's connections to Russian theater to brand her a Communist.*

- *Augusto Boal (1931–2009), founder of the Theatre of the Oppressed, a politically radical style of producing theater that was associated with an equally radical movement in education. Originally designed as a way to perform politically charged activist theater under the sway of a military junta government in Sao Paolo, Brazil, Boal's theater emphasizes a sort of "guerilla" mentality, developing techniques for performing "under the radar" of the oppressive government censors. Boalian theater could occur anywhere—on the street, in a restaurant, or in a park—effectively ambushing audiences who had little or no warning before they would suddenly be watching a production. In this respect, Theatre of the Oppressed is deeply committed to Marxist principles of alienation, recontextualizing ordinary affairs in the context of these surprise performances. But Boal's theater is also profoundly dialectical, even to the point of inviting the audiences to help the actors revise the storylines of the performances for more harmonious outcomes. For this work, Boal was arrested, tortured, and exiled, but his dramaturgical texts were distributed outside of Brazil and became foundational to international movements of radical political theater. His "gamesercises" have become part of the development of community theaters and even mainstream acting training all over the world.*

Psychoanalysis

Psychoanalysis is an attempt to explain human behavior through a description of the structure of the mind, or *psyche*. The field is strongly associated with Sigmund Freud (1856–1939), an Austrian psychiatrist. Freud famously mapped the psyche as three separate regions in constant, tumultuous, and dialectical relationships with one another. At the base of human consciousness is the *id*, the animalistic urges toward pleasure and away from pain that drive all human action. In conflict with the id is the *superego*, the repository of ideals, laws, and taboos that make existence in human society possible. These two zones are in a perpetual war in which the id's urges are tamped down and redirected by the superego's restraints, but almost all of this conflict takes place in the "unconscious mind," and the individual subject is utterly unaware of it. All the individual subject is aware of is the outcome of that conflict moment-to-moment, and that adjusted awareness is called the *ego*. In a perfect psyche, the superego channels the energetic urges of the id into productive and harmonious activities, and the ego reaps the benefits of this dialectic.

Unfortunately, the system almost never works like that, because the id and the superego both operate largely in the subconscious realm of symbols, while the ego must deal with what Freud calls the "reality principle." The most important moments in a person's life, those that shape the psyche, occur in childhood when comprehension is incomplete, and coping mechanisms are immature. Coping strategies that were developed in childhood eventually cease to work, but the structures are laid, and the individual persists in rehashing old behaviors, in effect in playing a repeating role with an outdated script. These ineffective coping mechanisms result in the creations of new mechanisms that are similarly ineffective, creating "complexes." Left unchecked, these mental imbalances can cause the individual distress (called "neurosis") or may even result in serious disorders of personality (called "psychosis"). Freud's life work was to develop therapeutic techniques for exposing and manipulating these unseen mechanisms to improve the mental health of his patients.

The recognition that human beings are irrational, often acting against their own best interests and appearing to be divided against themselves in some profound internal way, has been the subject of much drama all the way back to the Greeks; indeed, Freud himself often used dramatic metaphors to describe his observations (such as the "Oedipal complex"). Each era of drama has its own explanations—fate, the Devil, the humors, the passions, what-have-you—but psychoanalysis provides a scientific explanation, grounded in research of observable phenomena, and this proved irresistible to a form of drama that emerged in the latter half of the nineteenth century: social realism.

Earlier playwrights had targeted the relentless rationalism of the Enlightenment, which did not account for what German romantic playwright Friedrich Schiller called the "substratum," that zone of human consciousness that embraces the irrational, the mystic, the symbolic, and the magical. But social-realist playwrights like the influential Norwegian master Henrik Ibsen (1828–1906), found in psychoanalysis a system for explaining the irrationality of human thought and behavior that was rational and above all dialectical, ideal for character development in plays designed to reveal hidden truths about the human condition, without resorting to the mysticism of the romantics.

Ibsen's plays, which also owe something to the emergent humanism of Marx, are dedicated to focusing the audience on real problems faced by real people in real societies. As Marx advocated, Ibsen's plays call attention to the ways in which unjust social forces stunt and poison the human spirit. But while the later plays of Bertolt Brecht would largely focus on the deleterious material effects of bourgeoisie culture on the proletariat, Ibsen's plays look mainly at the deleterious psychological effects of bourgeois culture on bourgeois individuals. With this kind of content, the social-realist playwrights brought plays with the pathos of Greek tragedy into the modern, scientific world but also brought that tragic pessimism and fatalism that Brechtians reject as anti-activist. Nevertheless, Ibsen's plays challenged deeply held middle-class values and social injustice and provided a shock to the theater world of Europe that would displace the sovereignty of melodrama and give strength to the social-realist movement. The movement included some writers now considered to be among the greatest playwrights of all time, including:

- *Anton Chekhov (1860–1904), whose plays, under the direction of Konstantin Stanislavski (1863–1968) at the Moscow Art Theatre, established a powerful tradition of psychological realism in Russian drama. Stanislavski and his company of actors and designers at the MAT, while wrestling with plays like* Uncle Vanya, The Seagull, *and* The Cherry Orchard, *would themselves pioneer important psychologically realistic techniques of directing, design, and acting. Stanislavski's primer on realistic acting,* An Actor Prepares, *remains a central text in the training of actors all over the world. The influence of the MAT on the development of theater across the world would be unparalleled, and throughout the first half of the twentieth century, dramatic writers and dramaturgs would travel to Moscow to study with these legendary figures; in America, his disciples Harold Clurman, Cheryl*

Crawford, and Lee Strasberg founded the Group Theatre in 1931, which would establish Stanislavskian technique in American theater practice.

- *George Bernard Shaw (1856–1950), an Irish socialist playwright and drama- turg whose compelling and deeply literary plays, such as his early endeavor Widower's Houses, launched scathing attacks on the British ruling class and their exploitation and disenfranchisement of the working class and of women. His plays include* The Devil's Disciple, Arms and the Man, Man and Superman, Major Barbara, *and perhaps his most famous,* Pygmalion, *which was adapted into the smash musical* My Fair Lady. *He was also a prolific essayist and engaging drama critic who is thought to have authored hundreds of thousands of letters and other writings. With the British theater critic William Archer (1856–1924), he campaigned to have Ibsen's plays translated into English, making them accessible not only to Britain but also to an emerging native playwriting tradition in the United States.*

- *Eugene O'Neill (1888–1953), whose plays were, according to Sinclair Lewis, so "terrifying" and "magnificent" that they radically altered the theater culture of America, generating a homegrown playwriting tradition that was interested in the plight of the American underclass, particularly including people of color, and was deeply engaged with the inner struggles of men and women. Picking up on Ibsen, O'Neill's brutal realism in plays like* The Iceman Cometh, Desire under the Elms, A Moon for the Misbegotten, *and* Mourning Becomes Electra *defined an era of American history and incited many crucial innovations in American theater (including the casting of black actors). O'Neill became the first playwright to win a Nobel Prize for literature and inspired many followers who reached greatness in their own rights, including the American masters Tennessee Williams (1911–83), Arthur Miller (1915–2005), Lorraine Hansberry (1930–65), and August Wilson (1945–2005).*

- *The Performance Group, a collective of American theater artists who ap- plied a less-mainstream interpretation of psychoanalytic theory (espoused by the European theorists Gilles Deleuze and Felix Guattari in their book* Anti-Oedipus) *to the creation of a series of counterculture performances in the 1960s and 1970s. These performances included nudity, sensual caressing, violation of actor-audience boundaries, and possible drug use. One notable event was an adaptation of Euripides'* The Bacchae *known as* Dionysos in 69, *in which actors moved fluidly between roles during performances, and audience members were brought onstage to join the performance. The Performance Group, following the pioneering work of French radical theater experimenter Antonin Artaud (1846–1948), sought to make their performances a form of psychological and social therapy not only for the audience but for the performers as well. How well they succeeded is still hotly debated, but there is no doubt that they pushed the boundaries of what is possible in the theater remarkably far and left an indelible mark of liberation on experimental theater.*

Feminism, Gender Theory, and Queer Theory

One of the best known (and least understood) schools of critical thought, "feminism" as thought of today, is really an outgrowth of Marxism, pioneered by women theorists who felt that Marxism's humanitarian agenda did little to liberate women from oppression within the chauvinist social systems that have dominated human cultures for millennia. But few schools of thought have proliferated so rapidly and taken on so many forms, some of them vehemently or even violently opposed to others. It is better to speak of "feminisms," but it is possible to articulate what these various branches of thought have in common to some degree.

All feminisms turn their critical lenses more or less on the function of "patriarchy," which is a system of power characterized by the dominance of the interests and values of men over women. Within patriarchal systems, women are systematically and institutionally isolated from positions of power and enslaved to a second-class citizenship. As Marx observed of capitalist cultural products, patriarchal cultural products are largely engaged in making the oppression of women seem normal, usually by asserting that women are somehow "less than" men in terms of physical and mental capability. Patriarchy is widespread; most (if not all) cultures practice it in some form or another; and there is no indisputable evidence of a significant lapse in patriarchy at any point in human history. Feminist thinkers present as evidence for this, among other things, the absence of women thinkers and artists from the historical record, which they argue is the result of a misogynist process of validating the contributions of men more highly than women. Semiotically speaking, these male-dominated millennia have resulted in a way of thinking that so devalues women that even our language is stacked against female liberation, and almost all characteristics culturally associated with women are considered weak and ineffective when compared to male-associated traits.

These days, particularly in the United States, the term *feminism* has come to be associated with a (largely imaginary) female, radical, man-hating, political underground that is chaotic and irrational (thus, in itself, reinforcing a patriarchal stereotype). But by definition, a feminist is someone who asserts that women have been systematically excluded from systems of power and representation.[5] Furthermore, while there are many branches of feminisms, some more radical, some more liberal, all feminist critics employ their interpretive tools to expose and dissolve systems of patriarchal oppression. Where feminisms depart from one another is in how best to bring these states of being about.

The task facing feminist critics is indeed daunting. The lack of a feminist perspective in the historical record means that almost all representations of women have been male representations, which has eliminated the canonical works of "high art" from feminist analysis except insofar as exposing their misogyny (although, recently, feminist theorists are developing ever-more-subtle models of critique that are revealing covert messages of subversion even in these works). Furthermore, women are a heterogeneous group, with as many cultural differences (and different privileges) as men. Poor black women and rich white women might come together for specific tasks, as they did to campaign for the Nineteenth Amendment to the U.S. Constitution, which granted voting rights to women, only to find they have little in common afterwards. Because of these differences and others, different feminisms arise.

These can be grouped, loosely, into three broad categories, as Jill Dolan does in her 1993 book *Presence and Desire*. "Radical" or "cultural" feminism assumes that men and women are fundamentally different, with irreconcilably different ways of seeing the world and that the feminine viewpoint is fundamentally better than the masculine. Such feminists see the problems of sexism as inherent in any system guided by a masculine perspective, and the only solution is to tear down these systems completely and replace them with female-dominated ones. Radical feminists look for (and seek to create) forms of cultural expression (like drama) unique to women and, in the case of the drama, often reject Aristotelian and other dramatic structures as patriarchal, developing new models according to principles of feminine representations. The second broad category is "liberal" feminism, which sees patriarchy as a problem of the system but not of any fundamental, essential quality of men and women. Radical action is not needed to create equality between men and women, merely a process of enlightening both men and women to the pernicious effects of sexism and creating a new, more harmonious political sphere free from patriarchal influence. Liberal feminist dramatists often employ mainstream dramaturgy, retooling the content but keeping the structures to generate better representations of women in classically structured plays. A third broad category is "materialist" feminism, which sees the entire identity of femaleness itself as a social construct, like other identities, inscribed expediently in the service of the wealthy and powerful. Instead of looking for an "authentic" femaleness, materialist feminists focus like Marxists on the material conditions of reality that create false expectations and illusionary realities at the expense of women and men both.

Feminist criticism finds particularly fertile ground in the study of drama for at least three significant reasons. First, feminism is particularly interested in the representation of women, and the dramatic record provides a rich diversity of female characters to examine. Second, feminism is particularly interested in what is called the "male gaze," a socially conditioned process of "seeing" women represented that guides a sexist interpretation, and theater provides ample examples of that gaze and of opportunities for subverting and redirecting it. Finally, feminist criticism is deeply concerned with matters of the body (since, after all, the body provides the unreliable semiosis through which an individual is identified as male or female in the first place). Because all performances are grounded in the physicality of the performers, feminism blends very productively with other techniques of performance analysis. Furthermore, because theater art is highly contextual (its semiosis fundamentally altered by the time and place of its performance), scripts take on new meanings each time they are performed. This means that even very ancient performance texts can be adapted to a more modern sensibility about women's rights, sending messages of female liberation in plays (for instance, in Aristophanes' fifth-century BCE sex comedy *Lysistrata*) the authors may not have intended. Feminist theory is likewise useful for analyzing female playwrights and actors, like tenth-century German medieval playwright and dramaturg Hrosvitha of Gandersheim or English Restoration comedienne Aphra Behn (1640–89), when they do emerge in the historical record. Furthermore, and perhaps most saliently, feminist criticism can be used to create a feminist dramaturgy that guides the productions of the kinds of plays feminists would like to see.

Feminist theory as adopted by lesbian theorists took on certain unique characteristics and directed itself to applying the basic principles of feminist criticism to the question of sexual identity in a larger sense. The discipline of Queer Theory is now a strong school of its own, which has appropriated the formerly pejorative label "queer" and made it a battle cry. Queer Theory in the drama is dedicated to applying critical interpretive tools to retrieve lost narratives of homoeroticism in traditional plays and aesthetic value systems and to expose homophobic (queer-hating) and heteronormative (making queerness seem wrong or abnormal) narrative tropes in existing cultural objects. Queer Theory also fosters a "queer-conscious" tradition of playwriting and dramaturgy that liberates homosexuals from the typically denigrating representations they have historically suffered. Queer Theory, particularly as it is applied to the drama, has been enthusiastically receptive to postmodernism (see the section "Poststructuralism and Postmodernism").

Playwrights and dramaturgs who have employed these theories in their works include:

- *JoAnne Akalitis (1937–), an American director who founded the celebrated experimental-theater group Mabou Mines in New York City in 1970. Although Akalitis has explicitly resisted the labeling of her work as "feminist,"[6] her groundbreaking work, notably in her Obie-winning 1984 production of F. X. Kroetz's* Through the Leaves *and her 1994 restaging of Behn's* The Rover *at the Guthrie Theatre in Minneapolis, has been cited for its liberating treatment of female characters.*

- *Caryl Churchill (1938–), a British dramatist whose work is associated with Brechtian Epic Theatre. Churchill's plays originally critiqued bourgeois value systems, but as her career developed, she began to experiment with less-traditional structures and techniques of storytelling. Workshopping her plays with feminist improvisational troupe Monstrous Regiment resulted in her celebrated 1979 play* Cloud 9. *This strangely fragmented play, where unexpected cross-gendered and cross-racial casting creates a network of dialectical relationships, provides a multilayered exposé not only of sexuality and gender politics but also of capitalism, colonialism, and psychological abuse. Churchill's other plays include* Vinegar Tom *(1976),* Top Girls *(1982), and a dark fairy tale called* The Skriker *(1994), compelling dramas that employ high theatricality to critique gender roles in modern society.*

- *Tony Kushner (1956–), a celebrated American playwright, dramaturg, and theater historian, who is also an influential gay-rights activist. In his much-lauded* Angels in America: A Gay Fantasia on National Themes *(completed in 1992), Kushner unravels complex networks of assumptions about homosexuality, gender, and AIDS and reveals that they are tied to fundamental American identity crises at the end of the twentieth century. As a dramaturg, Kushner has fostered much new play development in America and worked on several adaptations of Brecht (with translator Wendy Arons and others).*

Reader-Response and Reception Theory

All dramaturgs back to Aristotle are engaged to some degree with the effect that performances have on audiences. Traditionally, the artistic process has been seen as one of *transmission*, in which an artist viewing the world develops an idea and expresses that idea through the artistic medium. In this model, the audience or reader or viewer is a more or less passive receptor of the idea, and the work's value was assessed largely on its effectiveness as a medium for transmitting the idea. Audiences, then, should strive to be the ideal receptors for the "truth" of the piece, revealed by the author in the process of viewing. Reader-response and reception theories, developed in the 1960s, are concerned with both the impossibility and the undesirability of being that "ideal audience." First of all, these theorists argue, can we really determine the authorial intentions of a piece written thousands of years ago for another culture when we can barely determine what's going on in the heads of authors living now in our own cultures? Secondly, such an approach puts stark limits on interpretation that strip the piece of rich fields of potential meaning. The ideal audience is a fiction, which is a good thing, because such a theory frees the viewer from the dictatorship of the author, permitting a "readerly" approach to art that allows and even encourages multiple interpretations and multiple meanings.

Although this approach seems to threaten traditional forms of interpretation, for theater makers, this is in many ways a no-brainer. A truly historically accurate production of a play like the *Oresteia* would likely be alien and incomprehensible to a modern audience. The play's longevity stems not from the impact of the original production but rather from its facility in speaking to many audiences in many cultures over many periods. But this is true on a microscopic scale as well—once a play has been produced, it will never be produced exactly the same way again, even in the very first revival. New dramaturgies are necessary for every production. Directors and designers (unless they are thieves) push the boundaries, not content with replicating previous designs, to find new ways of communicating to new audiences. Actors must adapt the roles to their own bodies and proclivities. Times change. Plays are presented publicly, where the reactions of audiences can actually change the facts of the piece's production, and on a semiotic level, no two audiences members really see the play the same way. Theater is really all about reception and the ways in which it can alter the production of artistic meaning. Mark Fortier notes that these theories are particularly relevant to dramaturgs who are engaged in adaptation projects.[7] Many dramaturgs see the process of adaptation as one of rescuing a script from a stultifying traditional interpretation and re-presenting it in a new, liberated context that renews its relevance. This can be a political project (exposing class, race, or gender prejudices) or a philosophical one (much postmodernist art, for example, is designed specifically to complicate notions of authorial control over meaning and to proliferate interpretations).

Playwrights and dramaturgs who have employed reader-response and reception theories include:

- *David Mamet (1947–), an American playwright whose work is known for its stylized manipulation of meaning and brutal critique of American society. His 1992 play* Oleanna, *in which a college student accuses her male professor of sexual harassment, is often cited as an example of the necessity of reception theory. The play spawned a massive controversy as to its meaning (whether it was meant as an indictment of political correctness or an exposure of the abuse some women are made to suffer by men in authority). Mamet steadfastly refused to clarify his intent, and the slogan on the poster for the 1994 Bay Kinescope film adaptation reads "Whichever side you take, you're wrong."*

- *Maria Irene Fornés (1930–), Cuban-born playwright whose work experiments with subverting of traditional audience reception. In the first production of her important 1977 play* Fefu and Her Friends, *the audience was physically divided into separate groups, and each group saw the scenes of the second act in a different order. As a result, people's perspectives were weighted differently, and each group effectively saw a different play than any of the others. No single individual's perspective could be wholly trusted nor wholly discounted; therefore, the interpretation of the acts of the powerful, violent final scene was impossible except through sharing perspectives with members of other groups.*

- *Harold Pinter (1930–), British Nobel laureate, whose plays are stripped of definitive meaning in many critical areas, leaving the interpretation up to the audience. In Pinter's plays like* The Birthday Party *(1957) and* Betrayal *(1978), human psychology (especially in such crucial areas as character and memory) operates perversely in accordance with unseen inner forces and desires. "What happened" is entirely dependent on whose perspective the viewer is following, and even that can change suddenly and radically. Language is meaningless—silences, however, are pregnant with potential. An air of menace surrounds this ambiguity; its consequences are dire. The reception of Pinter's plays by audiences around the world exemplifies the importance of reader-response theory: Pinter is celebrated in certain quarters, vilified in others, categorized alternately as "absurd" and "Leftist." Like Mamet, Pinter refuses to clarify, so it is up to the viewer to determine meaning for him- or herself.*

Poststructuralism and Postmodernism

The term *modernism* broadly describes social and cultural movements of the nineteenth and twentieth centuries that put a strong emphasis on the ability of humans, through logic and diligence, to eliminate barriers to progress towards superior states of being. In modernism, the past is usually examined, found wanting, and discarded in favor of the next big thing, while a classical sense of "high art" is preserved and even sacralized. Popular culture is denigrated. Modernist theater, like that of Italian futurist F. T. Marinetti (1876–1944), was interested in technology, speed, and a sometimes reckless dash into the future. In the 1960s, many philosophers and critics looked back upon the horrors of World War II and the exploitations of colonialism and saw them as the inevitable and logical result of this blind, sometimes amoral pursuit of "progress" that schizophrenically employed a narrow (usually elitist and often racist) view of the past as a guide for advancement into the future. These thinkers, beginning perhaps with Friedrich Nietzsche, forecast that this way of life would in violence, decadence, and nihilism.

A new form of critical theory, deconstruction, emerged to deal with these problems as early as the 1920s. Deconstruction theory enables a new school of thought, *poststructuralism*, of which postmodernism in art is thought to be a product. Poststructuralism, like its forebear structuralism, is concerned with the systems that underlie everyday interactions, but it does not adhere to the idea that such systems are closed and unchanging. It sees them instead as chaotic, founded on nothing much but illusionary connections, an observation that enables poststructuralists to interrogate systems of authority and reconfigure their interpretation to respond to new questions, without the traditional pious regard of institutionalized readings. The result is the revelation of what German theorist Martin Heidegger (1889–1976) called "concealments," strategic erasures and amnesias of motives and origin events that, when revealed, undermine the legitimacy of the very institutions that constitute our social and cultural value systems. This deconstruction is very liberating for those who are on the short end of the social and cultural stick, so poststructuralism is generally concerned with, to paraphrase Dan Latimer, the shish-kebabbing of every sacred cow it can find.[8] After the philosophical revolutions of the 1960s, these tools would be widely employed by writers like the influential French-Algerian Jacques Derrida (1930–2004) to utterly discredit the modernist worldview as exploitative, racist, sexist, and locked into a navel-gazing narcissism that threatened peace and stability around the world.

Postmodernism, then, is what replaces the deconstructed modernism. It is a conception of social and cultural processes as perverse operators that are generated not from any underlying reason or truth but from capricious human desires alone. Hearkening back to Saussure, postmodernists observe that there are words, and there are the emotions and images evoked by those words but that there seems to be no underlying truth that links those two; what is between them is pure chaos. But Saussure believed this to be a closed system, relationally fixed in place, while for postmodernists the whole shebang is totally up for grabs. Particular emphasis is placed on the subject of identity, which is understood by postmodernists to be grounded not in any real, material truth but constructed by social processes. Gender, for instance, is a vast system of signs interpreted by dominant social forces and has only a superficial relationship to actual biological sex; race is a system of exclusion and persecution that is only vaguely tied to actual skin color. Concepts of "truth" can change radically and suddenly. There is no actual "truth," only a chaotic sea of changing terms upon which we bob like a dinghy in a hurricane.

In abandoning the search for truth, postmodernism dissolves hierarchies of all kinds. If "truth" is merely a perverse, expedient notion, then no particular point of view is worth more than any other. This has resulted in some critics accusing postmodernism of frivolity and an obsession (a "fetish") with surface reality, with no attempt to find deeper meaning (many postmodernists embrace this accusation). But this same fetish with surfaces has generated a voracious critical omnivorousness that has allowed many previously unheard voices (those of women, homosexuals, racial subalterns, and other oppressed groups) to gain prominence in cultural and social discourses. This fetishism, argue postmodernists, finally enables the true freedom of thought and action that Marx struggled to achieve with his social criticism.

Postmodernism has proven popular because it provides what appears to be an excellent description of modern life, particularly in the West (where mass consumerism, the privileging of the viewpoint of the "regular Joe," the chaotic representations of reality provided by the electronic media, the Internet, a general suspicion of elite institutions like universities and the government, and the facility that public figures have for "spinning" facts to fit their agendas all appear to confirm the futility of the search for "truth" and the joy available in the fetishization of surfaces). In the drama, postmodernism has incited the explosive proliferation of varied and exciting performances that shatter traditional boundaries. Some theater artists who emphasize postmodern ideas include:

- *Naomi Iizuka (1965—), a Tokyo-born multiethnic American playwright whose work is celebrated for its attacks on "authentic experience" and its collapse of periods, places, and characters. Her 1998 play 36* Views, *the story of a wheeler-dealer in the art world who comes upon a hoax Japanese pillow-book and exposes and entangles so many layers of deception that it becomes impossible for the viewer to tell fact from fiction. Her work also emphasizes the Japanese aesthetic concept of mono no aware, an ancient idea that synchs well with postmodernism: the realization of an object's beauty at the same moment as the realization of its impermanence.*

- *Anne Bogart (1951—), an American director and adaptor who was one of the primary developers of the Viewpoints technique. Viewpoints is actually a body of techniques for actors and directors when approaching a play, notable for its deprivileging of the text, which becomes subservient to notions of space, emotion, movement, and time. Actors are encouraged to do their own research, without limits on their curiosities, to bring in other texts to enhance or alter the meanings present in the original script.*

- *Robert Wilson (1941—) an American designer and director whose boundary-shattering work is notable for its austerity, slow pace, and sometimes astonishing scope in terms of place and time. Wilson's work emphasizes the postmodern view of language as a site of crisis, beautiful yet always on the verge of collapse, by including images and sounds (like screams, a baby's "crib poetry," or animal vocalizations) or calling attention to the constructedness of language with visual verbal graffiti.*

Postcolonialism

The sixteenth century heralded a four-hundred year era of expansion of the territorial controls by European nations over the planet. Effectively, the European nations became empires with political dominion over lands far across the world. Europe could reap the benefits of those colonies, which were measured in commodities like slaves, rubber, and rum and in strategic importance; the native inhabitants of those colonies, however, could not participate in the political processes that determined the conditions of their lives, nor could they enjoy the fruits of their own labors as the wealth of their nations was siphoned off to line the coffers of their European (and, later, American) masters, who battled one another for control of colonies and trade routes. This state of affairs began to dissolve in the mid-twentieth century, as European nations lost control of their colonies either through political action or uprisings. The world now may be said to be in a postcolonial period (although the dominance of nations over one another has certainly not ceased and is even taking on new characteristics and seeing non-Western imperial powers on the rise).

Postcolonial theory is applied to make sense of events and cultural products in this context. Possibly, its founding text is *Orientalism*, a 1978 book by Palestinian literary critic Edward Said (pronounced sah-EED, 1935–2003), who built on the Marxist notion that discourse (like all human social and cultural products) is inherently ideological. He wrote that the study of the Eastern world by Western academics, which at that time was called Orientalism, was guided in large part by institutionalized prejudices about Easterners as culturally inferior in a variety of ways. But, Said argued, Orientalism did not really *describe* the conditions it purported to analyze; it actually *created* them by using a language that was preemptively weighted against the East. In effect, the prejudices were built around vague notions that had no referents in reality, and the goal of Orientalist studies was to justify the prejudices (thereby legitimizing Western colonization of those peoples) by finding evidence to support them. The entire thing is a dangerous fiction that not only erases the histories and identities of the oppressed peoples but also becomes a self-fulfilling prophecy as the colonized subjects learn they can gain approbation and substantial rewards from their Western rulers by behaving in ways that confirm the stereotypes. All of this has a terribly enervating effect on the psychologies of the colonized, who find the tropes of their own inferiority repeated and reinforced in their own communities while the empire continues to strip them of their political rights and material necessities of life. The result is an unending stream of violence and political chaos.

Said's writing provides a new language of resistance to these circumstances, and other writers who followed him not only deepened his ideas but also applied them more widely: for instance, to Jews during the European medieval period, to the Irish under the dominance of the British, to Native Americans following the Great Westward Expansion, and to African Americans living in the post-Reconstruction United States. Postcolonial theory has also been widely applied across the disciplines of the academy but has a particular home in the criticism of drama. Drama, with its emphasis on dialectics, its wide accessibility for many audiences, and its ability to be performed cheaply, has a special appeal for writers from colonized communities. Postcolonial criticism works not only to expose the mechanisms of "othering" and psychological abuse that imperial culture has on the colonized but also provides a site of resistance to imperialism. Often, this kind of writing takes the form of postcolonial adaptations of well-known texts that have a rich production history in the West, as by the following writers:

- *Wole Soyinka (1934–), a Nobel Prize–winning Nigerian dramaturg, playwright, political figure, and theorist whose work specifically addresses the problems of colonialism in Africa, although his critique is not limited to Europeans (he wrote that the color of the man who wears "the oppressive boot" is not relevant). A prolific writer, Soyinka's most celebrated plays include* The Bacchae of Euripides, *a powerful highly theatrical adaptation of the classical play to the modern themes of material and psychological oppression, that exposes the hidden links between colonizer and colonized.*

- *Aimé Césaire (1913–2008), born in Martinique, a powerful influential political figure and one of the founders of the Négritude movement, a community of resistance against French colonialism. He was the mentor of the psychiatrist Frantz Fanon (1925–1961), who described the deleterious psychological effects of colonialism and is hailed as one of the foremost postcolonial critics. Césaire was dedicated throughout his life to the problems of cultural alien-*

ation under colonialism and developed a dramaturgy of resistance against it, the most well-known product of which is his A Tempest, *his 1969 racialized adaptation of Shakespeare's* The Tempest *that emerged with the American Civil Rights movement and has been performed all over the world.*

- *Guillermo Gomez-Peña (1955–), the Mexico City-born, U.S.-based dramatic theorist, performance artist and "reverse anthropologist" who is known for darkly funny and innovative performance/installations that playfully subvert traditional notions of empire, race, gender, and language. Gomez-Peña's performances cross borders (of nations as well as ideas), emphasizing hybridity and interconnectedness to expose the inevitable violence, absurdity, and unsustainability of cultural imperialism. His controversial dramaturgy includes notions of "gringostroika" and "amigoization." His 1992 performance* The Couple in the Cage *featured two exotically dressed "savages" presented freak-show style to gaping audiences, who were then invited to write down their impressions: these documents exposed a pervasive ignorance and irrational race hatred. His best-known dramaturgical text is* New World Border: Prophecies, Poems, and Loquera for the End of the Century *(1992).*

Once again, these small capsules represent only the tip of the iceberg. Critical theory is a lifelong study, but in the end, it will give the emerging dramaturg an edge that will not only make the dramaturg seriously competitive in the market but also give him or her the tools needed to look beyond the circumstances of his or her own experiences and consider what life is like from another point of view. That, after all, is what philosophy is all about, and the better a thinker can put him- or herself into someone else's shoes, the more effective that thinker will be as a cultivator, innovator, and creator of a vibrant and important theater culture.

Exercises

Go deep! Starting with the short descriptions of the theoretical models above, pick the one that seems most ridiculous, abhorrent, or difficult to you. Start by reading up on this model, perhaps in an encyclopedia or online. With that information, find three authors who have written this kind of criticism, and read one essay from each. Note that some of these essays will use a lot of specialized language (or, less charitably, "jargon"). That's something you will have to get used to, but for this exercise, try to find essays from these authors that have less jargon and are easier to understand (your professors can help). Condense these articles into three or four main points each, and compare them. Then make a ten-minute presentation to your class on this form of criticism and these authors. What are the common goals of this school of thought? What are these authors trying to accomplish? In so doing, you will need to suspend your own judgment until you've completed your overview.

Go wide! Having sorted out the basic principles of the theory you found most difficult, find a play that has been self-consciously written to the ideals of the theory, and write a short summary of the play (say, fifteen hundred words or more) that exposes how the theory works within the text. Remember, the plays may resist! Don't force the issue, just attempt to glean how the principles of the theory inform the creation of the play.

Go long! Having familiarized yourself with the principles of one of these critical models and seen how a playwright self-consciously generates a theoretically aware piece of drama, you are well on your way to developing a "critical lens" for that theory. Now, go see a performance of a play, and apply this critical lens. Write an essay that is at least two thousand words long that addresses these questions about the play:
- Is the production (not necessarily the play) aware of the principles of this theoretical model (is it overtly feminist, for instance)?
- If yes, how well does the production express the fundamental principles of the theory? Do they succeed? Or are they in opposition to the theory, trying to produce a counternarrative?
- If no, then how does the play succumb to the pitfalls that the theory warns about? Does the play convey a message that is unintentionally (or intentionally) racist, sexist, homophobic, capitalist, colonial, psychologically immature, structuralist, or what-have-you?

TWO

Analysis

4

The Twelve-Step Program for Script Analysts

> Genius is only busied with events that are rooted in one another, that form a
> chain of cause and effect. To reduce the latter to the former, to weigh the latter
> against the former, everywhere to exclude chance, to cause everything that oc-
> curs to occur so that it could not have happened otherwise, this is the part of
> genius that works in the domains of history and converts the useless treasures
> of memory into nourishment for the soul.
> —Gotthold Ephraim Lessing, *Hamburg Dramaturgy #30*

Gotthold Ephraim Lessing's profound meditation above is a reminder that the
work of genius is characterized not by those sudden flashes of insight that sometimes come but by a process of engaged, humble, and methodical discovery and
refinement that eventually results in something good and useful. In dramatic
writing, this is a process that has remained astonishingly uniform throughout
the historical record. In 2004, the Greek playwright Elias Malandris assembled
Aeschylus's tragedy *Achilles*, hitherto believed lost, from some papyrus fragments that had been discovered serving as cavity fillers in recently excavated
Egyptian mummies. That summer, the Cyprus National Theatre (THOC)
mounted a production of *Achilles*, the first in over two thousand years. How is
it possible to bridge the gap to a lost civilization so quickly and smoothly? How
can *Achilles* have meaning for us, who live millennia after Aeschylus died?

The answer is that a play is a machine, one that manufactures *meaning*. It's
a staggeringly complex machine, and many of its moving parts are invisible to
the untrained eye, but it is a machine nonetheless, and it operates on certain
principles that have gone essentially unchanged for thousands of years. These
principles can (and must) be taught, because despite their antiquity they continue to produce significant and meaningful art. We still have a lot to learn from
those ancients and their tools. I'm reasonably proud of the laptop I'm using to

write this book, for example, but bury it with a dead Pharaoh for a thousand years and see how useful it still is.

When a dramaturg reads a play, he or she does so with the expectation that pretty soon someone, probably an artistic director, is going to come up and ask, "So, what's that play about?" That's a question about the *meaning* of the play; that is to say, about the *thematic* elements of the play. Deriving a theme from a script is an intense process of deep critical engagement and strict attention to detail. Before we can even begin to talk about themes, we must subject a play to a rigorous analysis. Here that process is broken down into twelve steps that should provide a road map for navigating most, but not all, of the plays you will encounter in your dramaturgical career.

The Steps
Step 1. Admit That You Don't Know Everything

In his famous 1758 "Paradox of Acting," French Enlightenment philosopher Denis Diderot observes, "In order to move the audience, the actor himself must remain unmoved."[1] But this is as true for all theater professionals as it is for actors. In the years that I have been involved with academic theater programs, one thing that the faculty agree upon is this: that the *art* of theater cannot be taught, only *experienced*. The art of the theater does not occur in the script but rather in *performance*; that horribly brief moment when months of study, training, collaboration, rehearsal, budgeting, and planning meet a live audience head-on. No, we can't teach that, but what we can teach is the *technique* of theater. As Diderot said, we must move the audience, and the only way we know to do that is to drill our technique so long and so hard that we are able to create the illusion that there is no technique at all.

All the skills of the theater begin with reading; that is, with understanding the fundamental mechanics of dramatic literature. It is the bread-and-butter of dramaturgy, but it is equally fundamental for directing, acting, and design. It is the common point to which we all must return continually when we collaborate on a production. In many ways, the dramaturg's main task is to be the custodian of the script and its meaning (which means, also, its context, its philosophy, its spirituality, its sexuality, its theatricality, and any part of it that can be mined by the company to create meaning).

The total extent of that meaning is always unknown, as are the total possibilities of a performance to unveil it. The dramaturg must remain committed to the sometimes onerous task of perpetual critical engagement. It is our job to ask questions, constantly, of the script, the director, the cast, the design, the audience, and most important, ourselves and our own preconceived notions. Developing an ability to read plays *critically* means looking at the mechanisms that shape and drive the play and figuring out how the playwright meant them to work in their original contexts. Then, and only then, are we prepared to try and make them work in our own contexts. This process requires a serious acceptance that we cannot know everything, we cannot divine exactly what the playwright meant or how the audience was (and will be) affected. But asking questions is the beginning of a process that has as its goal the creation of a true artistic connection. Though it may be nothing more than a quick flash of "I get it" that passes between audience and performance, it is the experience we seek in the theater and one of those moments that make life worth living.

Step 2. It's All about the Performance

The second vital step in being a critical reader of drama is the recognition that the script is *not* the finished work of art. To any practitioner of dramatic art, this seems like a pretty obvious observation, but very few people really understand what this means. A poem, for instance *Dry Salvages* by T. S. Eliot, can sit printed in a book in a library for decades without anyone looking at it, static, frozen, and waiting. But when I pull down that book and read:

> The sea has many voices,
> Many gods and many voices.
> The salt is on the briar rose,
> The fog is in the fir trees.
> The sea howl
> And the sea yelp, are different voices
> Often together heard: the whine in the rigging,
> The menace and caress of wave that breaks on water,
> The distant rote in the granite teeth,
> And the wailing warning from the approaching headland
> Are all sea voices. . . .[2]

You are transported by the language immediately into Eliot's poetic seascape. The poem is activated by your reading of it, and the complex processes that generate meaning and pleasure and everything else we read poems for are all right there. The poem needs you, the reader, and only you in order to become art.

It would be a different story, of course, if the work you pulled down was a musical score, like Mozart's *Requiem*. First of all, it's not written in "music," it's written in a complex code, a graph of dots and dashes, which is actually a series of instructions for the musicians. Can you even *read* it? If you can, what has to happen before this page of weird symbols and grids can become a work of art? It has to be played by a musician. Then, many x-factors come into play to influence how it becomes art: the quality of the instrument, the skill of the player, the acoustics in the room, and so on. In the case of the *Requiem*, what you've got a hold of is a symphony, so it requires the collaboration of many musicians, all working in harmony, which requires rehearsals, and a conductor, and a hall, and a stage manager; all of that requires money, which means fundraisers, accountants, security; and if you want to have an audience, you're going to need ushers, administrators, ticket sellers, advertisers . . . you get the idea.

A dramatic script resembles sheet music more than it does any other form of writing. Although it's not readily apparent to a casual reader, a dramatic script is actually written in a complex code, and it requires a lot more than the imagination of one reader to activate. It's not a work of art. It is rather a blueprint; a plan, or if you are of a more devious frame of mind, a *plot* for creating a work of art (more on that later).

The problem we often encounter when we are learning to read dramatic scripts is that we are usually trained to treat them like poems. Take, for example, this famous line from Shakespeare:

> Is this a dagger I see before me,
> The handle toward my hand?[3]

Macbeth here is asking a question which is unanswered by his prose. If you're in an English class reading this, you can go where your imagination takes you. If you're in the theater, you have to find some answers: "Well, is it a dagger, or isn't it? Can he actually *see* it? Can the *audience* see it? Is it flying in? If it is, we're talking about a pretty sophisticated stage effect . . . How did Shakespeare's company do it? What did it *mean* for his audience to see a dagger appear like that?" and so on.

Another problem emerges when it comes to speech, which is a lot more than merely mouthing words. Imagine Shakespeare's young King Henry exhorting his troops to near-suicidal heroism:

> Once more into the breach, dear friends, once more,
> Or close the wall up with our English dead![4]

In the classroom, we are taught that iambic pentameter is spoken in a clear, proscribed rhythm, which suggests to the uncritical eye that the line sounds like:

> Once MORE inTO the BREACH, dear FRIENDS once MORE

This would sound ridiculous on stage. Any actor worth his salt is going to make choices and might speak it much more like this:

> ONCE MORE into the BREACH, dear friends, ONCE MORE!

The violation of the regular heartbeat of the iambs calls attention to the line, enhancing its power; the heart of the listener races in arrhythmic sympathy.

Can we seriously doubt that Shakespeare intended that to happen on stage? But it's something we miss if we don't read with performance in mind.

Playwrights count on the cohesive operation of many, many systems of meaning in order to bring their vision about: space, sets, lights, sounds, gestures, vocal stress and intonation, costumes, and theatrical conventions, for instance. In order to read a play *critically*, as much of this as possible must be taken into account. Ronald Heyman, in *How to Read a Play* (1977), expands this idea:

> We do well to think of the text as a score for a series of theatrical impacts, many of which are not verbal. This encourages us to read more slowly, considering each new development in relation to the effect—or complex of effects—it could have on the audience.[5]

Without such a reading, it's easy to miss the humor of Samuel Beckett's bleak masterpiece *Waiting for Godot* or the tragic gravity of Tom Stoppard's black comedy *Rosencrantz and Guildenstern Are Dead* and therefore to make serious errors about those plays' potential impacts. It's not easy to read this way, but it is absolutely central to the dramaturg's work (as it is to the director's, actor's, and designer's), and the good news is it gets easier with practice and experience. One strong exercise you can do is to get in the habit of reading (and rereading) the script of a play just before going to see a production of that play.

Step 3. Action

A play is composed of actions in the same way that a flame is composed of fire; that is, utterly. In *Playwriting: The Structure of Action* (1971), Sam Smiley details this:

> All human activity, to some degree, is action. It is not merely movement, but change. Action in life ranges from the simple, when a person blinks his eyes or scratches his neck, to the complex, such as a man's decision to kill or not to kill his enemy. The continuing actions, from birth to death, of each human being are infinite and perpetual. A person's actions are the most fascinating things about him.[6]

Drama, in Smiley's view, is "structured action." In this observation, Smiley is revisiting Aristotle, who was passionately concerned with human action both on and off stage.

As noted in the previous step, the lines of text on the printed page are the script are not actions but instructions for actions; some specifically described, some apparently only when staged. When speaking of dramatic actions, we are actually referring to anything on stage that produces meaning, including spoken words, inflections, entrances, exits, crosses, swordfights, and the thousands of tiny choices that add up to the total theatrical experience; the flip of a fan, the wink, the kiss, the cocking of a pistol, or the horrifying speech from the Second Messenger in Sophocles' *Oedipus Tyrannos*, who describes what has just happened just offstage. These are all actions, and they are all equally important. As an example, Smiley describes the scratching of a neck as "simple," but how significant does it become when it is Osvald Alving in Henrik Ibsen's *Ghosts*, scratching a sore on his neck as his inherited syphilis finally makes itself known?

Dramaturgs do not ask, "What's this play about?" when what they really want to know is, "What happens?" The answer to that question is what we refer to as "*the* action" of a play (it's also called the *spine* or the *arc* of the play), which can usually be articulated in a single, active sentence:

- A city afflicted with plague turns to its charismatic leader for help (*Oedipus Tyrannos*).
- A young prince seeks to solve the mystery of his father's death (*Hamlet*).
- Two men wait desperately for a third who never appears (*Waiting for Godot*).

But, of course, the action of the play is made up entirely of smaller units of action, which nowadays we usually group into, appropriately, acts. Each act, furthermore, is broken down further into scenes, and each scene into beats, which, thanks to the nature of theatrical action, can really only be understood backwards.

Step 4. Reading Backwards

What a beat is exactly is subject to a great deal of debate, but for our purposes here a *beat* is as the smallest actable unit of action. That means that it is the shortest possible section of a play that can have its action clearly articulated on stage by an actor. Furthermore, each beat describes an action whose result is actually the beginning of the next action. In his indispensable book (1983). David Ball calls these units "forwards" because they propel the action of the play itself. Ball's book is particularly useful in the way it exposes that the "big" actions of a play are made up of tiny overlapping "little" ones, which push each other forward like the intermeshed gears of a clock.[7]

An example of this overlapping is in Paul Henning's 1962 "The Ballad of Jed Clampett," which was the theme song of a famous sitcom, *The Beverly Hillbillies*:

> Come and listen to my story 'bout a man named Jed
> A poor mountaineer, barely kept his family fed
> But then one day he was shootin' at some food
> And up through the ground come a-bubblin' crude.[8]

This little ditty describes four separate actions, each one initiated by the resolution of the previous one:

1. Because Jed's family is hungry, Jed goes hunting.
2. Because Jed goes hunting, he sees a rabbit.
3. Because Jed sees a rabbit, Jed fires his gun.
4. Because Jed fires his gun, Jed discovers oil.

And he loaded up his truck, and the rest is history.

In his book, Ball asks this question, "Why does Hamlet kill his uncle Claudius?" It is not because a ghost in act 1 told Hamlet that Claudius is responsible for his Hamlet's father's death. It is because Laertes confesses in act 5 to conspiring with Claudius to kill Hamlet, which is the last piece of evidence Hamlet needs to solve the mystery of his father's death. Now, people are always talking about Hamlet as a man who cannot act. As Matt Gray, my colleague and professor of acting, says, "How interesting would that be to watch? An actor up there not acting! Try and sell tickets to that one." Actually, Hamlet, from the moment he meets the ghost, is on a quest to solve and avenge his father's death. The testimonial of the ghost is suspect; as a man of reason, Hamlet explains that he needs to corroborate this with real evidence. And thus he launches on a series of extremely complex actions (including many theatrical devices such as pretending to be mad and putting on a play) that eventually result (however unintended) in Laertes' confession. Once he has that, Hamlet immediately slays his uncle. There's no hesitation at all, as far as the critical eye of the dramaturg can see. Each action has seamlessly and smoothly provoked the next one, and together they add up to a compelling drama.

Another powerful example is in Sophocles' *Oedipus Tyrannos*. The very first action of this play, the absolutely first beat, has the priest of the city asking Oedipus to help his people by curing the plague and results in Oedipus promising to do whatever it takes to save the city. Until we reach the last beat of the play, we cannot understand the terrible significance of that answer. We have to read the script backwards.

Now, there is only one way to read a script backwards, and that is to read it forwards, twice. Try this experiment: read the next six plays you come across twice, and see how your comprehension is magnified.

Step 5. The Agonists

Characters, like everything else in a play, are composed entirely of actions. Actors will tell you that characters are composed of traits, but we have to deduce those traits by interpreting their actions. It is not Mother Courage's name that makes her courageous, but her refusal to succumb to the horrors of war in Bertolt Brecht's *Mother Courage*. We may make certain assumptions about Sir Fopling Flutter, but we confirm them by his rakish actions in Sir George Etheredge's *The Man of Mode*. Sky Masterson asserts himself to be a womanizer early on in Frank Loesser, Jo Swerling, and Abe Burrows's *Guys and* Dolls, but his loyalty to Sarah reveals that he's not at all the cad he pretended to be.

In Greek plays (and plays structurally modeled on them, which most of the plays in the Western canon are), it's profitable to identify a protagonist and an antagonist. People often make the mistake of thinking that the protagonist and the "hero" are the same person. Nothing could be more obfuscating. *Hero* implies the character that is the most virtuous, the most selfless, the most moral, or who has the most to lose. These are traits, not actions. Instead, we should look at the structure of the drama and what actually happens onstage. As an example, consider Stephen Sondheim, Burt Shevelove, and Larry Gelbart's 1962 Broadway smash, *A Funny Thing Happened on the Way to the Forum*, where there actually is a character named Hero. And he is a hero: forthright, handsome, amorous, and stupid. But he's a minor character at best; the play's thrust is derived entirely from the actions of Hero's slave, Pseudolus.

The term *protagonist* derives from the Greek root *agon*, which means "ordeal" or "struggle." It's also the root of the English word *agony*. *Agon* was a term that the ancient Greeks used in reference to things that involved the opposition of two discursive forces, most notably a legal or political case. For instance, the Assembly might have an *agon* over whether to punish Sicily with a military invasion for seizing control of the western sea lanes. One senator would make speeches in favor of (or "pro") the invasion, another would speak against (or "anti") the idea. Ideally, these agonists, through their discursive (and dialectical) struggle, would either prove the best idea or bring forth a third idea that might be even better.

The terms *protagonist* and *antagonist* transferred to the Athenian theater sometime in the sixth or fifth century BCE. When we seek to identify the protagonist of the play, it becomes (like everything else) a question of action. Who is at the center of the action of the play? Whose choices are most important to the development of the action? At the end of the play, who has undergone the most change? Typically, the protagonist is this person, and the rise and fall of the play in general is also the rise and fall of this character's personal story. The antagonist is the character impelling all this action and change in the protagonist. The protagonist is not always the hero, nor the antagonist the villain. Consider the *Star Wars* films: if you watch merely the first film, you will see that everything hinges upon the actions of Luke Skywalker, who changes from a farm boy into a warrior. But look at the first three movies as three acts of one plot, and your focus shifts away from the choices of the heroic Luke and concentrates on the villainous (and tragic) Darth Vader, who undergoes a much more profound transformation and who is the protagonist of the trilogy.

Once you establish the protagonist, you must begin to analyze his or her choices very carefully. Let's consider Sophocles' *Antigone*. In this tragedy, our sympathies are obviously with Antigone from the beginning. Powerless and alone, she is willing to die to protect the burial rights of her dead brother. Creon, her uncle the politician, knows that burying her brother could destabilize the political situation in a city torn by civil war and before that plague. He forbids her to act. But act she does, in defiance of him. She argues that spiritual truths are more important than human ones. He locks her in a cave. She kills herself, causing a cycle of deaths that leaves Creon alone and broken. But does Antigone change at all, even one iota, in terms of her character traits? She started the play ready to die, and that she died only confirms her heroism. It is Creon who learns a tragic lesson, it is he who changes, and it is Creon's story that Sophocles wants us to watch.

One caveat: when looking to see who changes most in a drama, note that the change from "alive" to "dead" is usually not very significant: a character that dies for what he or she believes in (like Antigone) hasn't really undergone any significant character change. After all, she'll be back when the curtain rises tomorrow night. But in Ibsen's masterpiece *A Doll's House*, a loyal, middle-class wife who has never rebelled against patriarchy in her life decides to leave her husband and children, and the drama produced by that choice is so compelling that the play continues to fascinate us more than a hundred years after its creation.

Step 6. Given Circumstances

Given circumstances is an important term used by directors, actors, and designers when they are trying to determine the shape of their ideas about characters, sets, costumes, and so on. When reading a play, given circumstances are derived from the actions and from the stage directions. They include the "who, what, where, when, why, and how" of the action of the play. This information can be revealed by the setting, the time of day or year, the dispositions and qualities of the characters, or whatever information the playwright gives to direct our analysis in a particular direction.

To return to *Oedipus*, when the play opens, we get some critical information from the short opening conversation between the Priest and Oedipus. We learn that the setting is Thebes; that Oedipus became king via a heroic feat of intellect; that he's a good king; and that the city is afflicted with a horrible plague. But we should also learn very early on, through his onstage actions, that Oedipus walks with a limp (even though it is not mentioned until much later).

All of these are given circumstances, and we mine these tidbits of information as thoroughly as we can.

A lot of analysts of dramatic literature talk about a sense of "stasis" or "balance" that exists at the beginning of the play and gets disturbed, and the disturbance incites the action, but this is a misleading way to think about drama. There can never be stasis on stage: the action begins when the curtain rises, and every new piece of information impels the next. At the opening of *Hamlet*, Denmark's king lies dead under mysterious circumstances, his brother seems to have usurped the throne, the Norwegians are massing to invade, and on top of that, there's been a ghost sighted recently. So we begin by meeting some guardsmen at Elsinore who are scared out of their bloody wits. Their fear impels them to bring Hamlet to meet the ghost and so on. When *Oedipus* opens, the city is wracked by a plague, the people are desperate, the king has begun his investigation already and is merely waiting for Creon to return from the oracle. A play is like a shark: it has to keep moving forward at all times, or it dies.

It is not a sense of lost stasis but, rather, the given circumstances of a particular play that determine its internal logic and by extension the various paths that the action can take. Theatrical conventions that guide interpretations are also part of the given circumstances. In a farcical world, we can expect characters to ignore asides delivered by other characters; in a melodrama, we can believe a magical elixir has rendered a character completely unrecognizable to the others even though he hasn't even changed his hat; in opera, it is possible for characters to confuse two men even though one of them weighs two hundred pounds more than the other. *Romeo and Juliet* might appear to be a lighthearted love story in the first act, but Shakespeare has warned us from the opening lines and from the prince's actions early on that this is a serious world in which violence is certainly possible, if not tragically inevitable. A skilled dramaturg must constantly probe the text and ask pointed questions of it as the reading progresses. What are we meant to be seeing? What theatrical conventions are in play? What kind of action is the audience prepared to accept at a given moment?

Sometime after the opening beat comes a point in the development of the action that presents a choice to the protagonist that will irrevocably shape the rest of the drama. Playwrights and dramaturgs call it variously the "point-of-no-return," the "inciting incident," or the "attack." This can come early (Oedipus's second speech in the play contains his fatal promise to do whatever it takes to lift the plague from the city) or later on (Hamlet does not "swear on his sword" to avenge his father until act 1, scene 5) or much later (Romeo kills Tybalt in act 3, scene 1) but when it comes, it marks the last chance that the protagonist can turn aside from the course of action the play lays out. That is to say, the action of the play now leads inevitably and irrevocably towards the ultimate resolution of all the actions, and the protagonist must now suffer all the obstacles the playwright has invented.

Step 7. Needs, Obstacles, and Conflict; or, "Gee Whiz! Thanks, Dad!"

When an actor approaches a script, he or she looks very carefully at how the given circumstances of a story give rise directly to the character's needs. A designer does exactly the same thing. Everyone in the theater should be looking at the script with the same critical framework and coming to the same conclusions about the nature of the play's action (otherwise, we will have a pretty silly-looking end product). Take *Oedipus* for example; the actor and designer should both deduce the same thing: that the suffering of his people has incited Oedipus to seek divine guidance—and that same suffering will compel him to push to find the horrible truth about himself even when he knows it may result in his own destruction. Antigone wants to bury her brother. Romeo and Juliet want to be together. The needs give rise to actions, as the characters attempt to get what they want.

But, of course, it's not that simple. Imagine this act 1 closer for *Romeo and Juliet*:

JULIET: Daddy, I'm in love with Romeo Montague.
CAPULET: Smashing! Call the caterers. We'll have the wedding here on Sunday!
JULIET: Gee whiz! Thanks, Dad!

And curtain call is 8:30 P.M. This is great if you are paying for a babysitter but not if you are seeking some kind of substantial emotional or intellectual reaction to a profound piece of drama. Imagine this final scene in Arthur Miller's *Death of a Salesman*:

WILLY: I think I'll go for a drive.
LINDA: Wait! I know you had an affair, and I forgive you.
WILLY: What a lucky man I am! By the way, I'm proud of you boys, and I love you a lot. Can you forgive me?
BIFF AND HAPPY: Gee whiz! Thanks, Dad!

As an ending it's lacking pathos, isn't it? One more, from August Wilson's *Fences*:

TROY: I wasn't allowed to play professional sports because I'm black, so you don't get to pursue your dreams either, Cory.
COMMISSIONER OF BASEBALL: (*entering*) Mr. Maxson! We're really sorry! We need you to pitch for the Yankees this afternoon!

TROY: Hot diggity! Go ahead and play football, son.
CORY: Gee whiz! Thanks, Dad!

What Shakespeare, Arthur Miller, and August Wilson knew is that if plays are machines that are made of actions, they are fueled 100 percent by conflict.

The process by which playwrights create conflict is mechanically very simple. Given circumstances give rise to needs; needs incite characters to action. Obstacles appear that block the characters from getting what they want. That generates conflict that is emotionally or intellectually compelling to an audience (but only when the audience cares whether the characters get what they want). The characters develop tactics and strategies to get around those obstacles, and that process puts flesh on the skeleton of the play's action. How characters act to resolve conflicts reveals their traits: is a character willing to kill to get what he wants, like Macbeth? Does he resort to trickery, like Puck from Shakespeare's *A Midsummer Night's Dream*? Does he turn his back on his family, like Tom in Tennessee Williams's *Glass Menagerie*? Conflict, in its many flavors, is the essence of drama.

Step 8. Lines of Conflict: Peer Gynt's Onion

There was a trend a while ago for basic literature textbooks to identify the "themes" of drama and other written narratives as things like "man versus man" or "man versus nature." But the term *theme* comes from Aristotle, and that's not even remotely what he meant. We are still not yet ready to establish themes for our readings at this point in the process. But we are ready to start making some larger assessments about what the playwright had in mind.

What those old literary textbooks were actually describing were lines of conflict. It is critical to identify the various nexus points of conflict in the drama, because how they play out will give us our most important clues to the themes of the piece. Brian Johnston in *The Ibsen Cycle* (1992) calls attention to the scene in Ibsen's *Peer Gynt* in which the protagonist dissects an onion, only to find that like Peer Gynt himself, the onion has only layers upon layers and no true core.[9] Plays (and certain pop-culture ogres) are like that. Playwrights can generate conflict on multiple levels of awareness simultaneously, each one resting on the other and supporting yet another like Russian nesting dolls, and each one with a different observation about the human condition to divulge. At least seven of these lines of conflict are evident, moving from most internal to most external:

Line of psychic conflict. Here is where the subconscious battles of the individual ego take place, the eternal war between our drives and our sensibilities that create (and disturb) our sense of self.

MACBETH: Methought I heard a voice cry "Sleep no more! Macbeth doth murder sleep. . . . "

Line of personal conflict. This tracks the conscious awareness of our proclivity to be our own worst enemy (the protagonist and antagonist are the same character).

OEDIPUS: By my own sentence I am cut off, condemned
By my own proclamation 'gainst the wretch,
The miscreant by heaven itself declared
Unclean—and of the race of Laius.
Thus branded as a felon by myself,
How had I dared to look you in the face?

Line of individual conflict. This is the most commonly seen line of conflict, that between two people (the protagonist and antagonist are two distinct characters)/

CLYTEMNESTRA: Bring me an axe with which to kill a man.

Line of social conflict. Conflict here deals with institutions, responsibilities, bonds of family and tribe, class and other political identities, and history (the antagonist is not a character but a social institution, a norm, or a group).

HJELMER: No man would sacrifice his honor for the woman he loves.
NORA: That is a thing hundreds of thousands of women have done.

Line of natural conflict. Here are fought battles that deal with larger perspectives than human societies encompass: weather, extreme temperatures, time, distance, light, and darkness (the antagonist is not a human thing but something found in nature).

LEAR: Blow, winds, and crack your cheeks! Rage! Blow!

Line of supernatural conflict. Metaphysical concerns are in play: here the protagonist's struggle is against gods, fate, ghosts, devils, space aliens, witches and also abstractions, ultimate values, and recognitions that lie beyond the scientifically knowable universe.

GHOST: I am thy father's spirit,
Doom'd for a certain term to walk the night,
And for the day confined to fast in fires,
Till the foul crimes done in my days of nature
Are burnt and purged away.

Line of supertextual conflict. These aesthetic concerns involve other plays, traditions of playwriting and production, common symbolism or allusion, or dialogues with other cultural forms. This is not a question of contention between a protagonist and antagonist but about the relationships between streams of cultural products.

This last line of conflict cannot be left out. Plays derive a significant portion of the meaning they produce through their (sometimes obscure) relationships with other plays (as well as with music, novels, philosophy, poetry, art, and other forms of expression). This can be profoundly obvious (Stoppard's *Rosencrantz and Guildenstern Are Dead* is gibberish if the audience isn't already familiar with *Hamlet*, while Sondheim's *Sunday in the Park with George* relies on at least a rudimentary awareness of George Seurat's painting *A Sunday Afternoon on the Island of La Grande Jatte*), but it can also be very subtle. Historian Andrew Sofer notes in *The Stage Life of Props* (2003) that whole eras of dramatic literature might employ the same symbolic object, like a skull or a fan, so the use of such a prop specifically taps into a discussion that is greater than the scope of the play itself. Sofer argues, for instance, that the seeds that sprout in August Wilson's 2001 *King Hedley II* are, in a way, the same ones sown by Willy Loman in Arthur Miller's 1949 *Death of a Salesman*.[10] Understanding this level of connection is the work of a lifetime, but the dramaturg who can make such fine distinctions can perceive the vast networks of aesthetics that make up our ideas of what theater is and does in our society.

Of course, good plays make use of multiple lines of conflict at any given time, but only a very few plays, those that fully exploit the possibilities of theatrical dialectics, "slice the onion" by hitting all seven of them: *Oresteia*, *Rosmersholm*, *King Lear*, *Fences*. There are a few more. This dramatic Septuple Crown generally occurs only with the great masters and only at the heights of their powers.

Step 9. The Climactic Plot

Now we can finally begin to look at the total structure of our play. Literary critic Hayden White notes that *plot* is a juicy little term; it can refer to an area of land, like a grave, but it can also refer to a secret plan made by shadowy conspirators.[11] What these things have in common with the action of a drama is that they can literally be plotted, as on a graph. The structures of individual dramas vary, of course, particularly between cultures or eras when aesthetic traditions begin, end, or radically change. But the "Aristotelian" or *climactic* plot, which dominates Western dramatic literature, tends to follow a basic parabolic shape that is easily recognizable (techniques for plotting nonclimactic dramas will be dealt with explicitly in the following chapter).

It is necessary to distinguish between *plot* and *story*. The *plot* is the sequence of actions that appears on stage. The *story* is a narrative concept that the playwright uses to frame the plot and make sense of the actions in a larger context. Consider, for instance, the story of Oedipus (which begins at his birth when his father seeks advice from the oracle and ends with Oedipus's exile) and his wanderings, his death, and his ascension to heaven (which happen in another of Sophocles' plays, *Oedipus at Colonus*). The story of Oedipus contains all the details of his life, including his battle with the Sphinx. Consider the plot of *Oedipus Tyrannos*, which consists largely of Oedipus standing in front of his palace, methodically assembling all the pieces of the mystery of the death of King Laius until he learns his own horrifying secret. Where in the plot of *Oedipus* is the stabbing of his eyes? Nowhere! In the plot of the play, a messenger enters and describes the deed, then Oedipus returns, already blinded.

When we are plotting the play, we are concerned exclusively with *what happens*. For a climactic graph (see fig. 1), the x-axis (the horizontal line) denotes the time that passes as the play unfolds, and the y-axis (the vertical line) denotes the level of emotional intensity experienced by the audience, with 0 being "completely bored" and 100 being "psychotic episode" (see aesthetic distance, step 10). In keeping with our penchant for reading backwards, we likewise create our graphs from end to beginning. The major "fixed" plot points are the following:

1. *Closing beat.* This is the last complete action of the play. Where have we wound up? What's been resolved? What was the aftermath of the resolution? Who was rewarded, and who punished? What lessons about the human condition have been learned and by whom and how?

2. *Climax.* The climax is defined in this model as the beat that incites the highest intensity in the *audience*. If it is a classically constructed piece, this moment is usually when the central conflict of the play is resolved, for good or ill, and the chain of actions that began with the attack (which is major plot point 3) has concluded. The whole play has looked forward to this point, and the remainder of the play looks back at it; this is why we refer to this kind of plot as "climactic."

3. *Attack (or inciting incident).* This beat is the moment when the protagonist makes a choice that irrevocably leads to the climax.

4. *Opening beat.* This is the first complete action of the play—often the source of given circumstances. Where are we? What's going on? What has happened already?

Given that the audience's level of excitement is slightly higher just before the curtain rises than it is in normal everyday life, our climactic plot now looks like

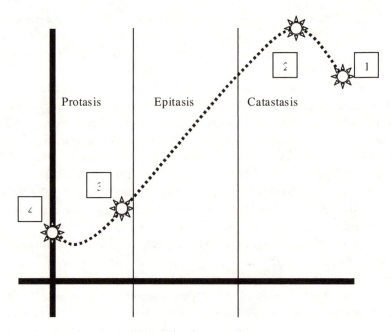

Fig. 1. The climactic plot

figure 1. The characteristic parabolic shape is why we often refer to the "arc" of a play or the "arc" of a character.

The actions in the section of the play encompassing points 4 and 3 were called *protasis* by the Roman dramaturg Aelius Donatus, or the moments when the given circumstances of the play are revealed. Donatus called the beats between 3 and 2 *epitasis*, or "intensification," when the circumstances laid out in the protasis interact and raise the emotional pitch of the action. Because of the rising slope of the plotline between points 3 and 2, it is also called "rising action." Donatus referred to point 2, the climax of the play, as the *catastrophe*, literally the "downturn," and called the beats between and including points 2 and 1 the *catastasis*, literally the "settling," because the intensity of the play drops off after the climax as we assess the consequences of the plot's resolution. Another name for this segment is the *dénouement*.

Other points to be plotted are "floating," that is, they may occur multiple times anywhere on the plotline described by the four major beats, but they contribute to what Donatus would call the "intensification" of the plot. They include:

Discovery beats. Also *anagnoresis.* These are beats in which some critical information necessary to the plot development is revealed, such as when Oedipus discovers that he himself is the murderer of Laius. Practitioners refer to "*the* discovery" of a play as the beat when the most critical, life-changing information is revealed.

Reversal beats. Also *peripeteia.* These are beats in which the flow of action in the play is radically altered, such as when Oedipus's search for Laius's murderer becomes a inquiry into his own history. "*The* peripety" is usually a reference to the point at which the character is at his or her lowest ebb, because that's the moment at which the character's fortunes either radically turn around or drop precipitously into total ruin.

Expository beats. These beats reveal "backstory," that is, all the things that happened before the plot began. In *Oedipus*, almost the entire play is expository, but most plays deal quickly with exposition, as it can really drag down the forward motion of the plot if it's not handled well. The worst example is *featherdusting*, referring to the practice of having the servants in the manor house discussing the events of the day while dusting the armoires, such as "I can't believe it's been exactly seven years to the day since Lord Ramsbottom mysteriously disappeared while hiking on the moors" or having a character address another saying, "As you know, I am your father."

MacGuffin. This term may have originated with Alfred Hitchcock, but it refers to the age-old practice of creating beats in which something more or less random happens to "hook" the protagonist into the storyline: a letter arrives with the news of a death in the family, a stranger appears holding a tribal fetish and mysteriously dies, Jason must find something called the Golden Fleece. It is distinct from other plot points in that the MacGuffin itself, whatever it might be, is not intrinsic to the plot—it could be anything. Jason could just have easily been sent to seek the Holy Kumquat.

Students of social psychology and cultural anthropology will recognize that this "arc" structure repeats itself quite often in human events—we tend to organize religious and social rituals along the same lines from bar mitzvahs, revivals, and faith healings to political debates and courtroom procedures. Even sporting events tend to resolve themselves in arcs (if they don't, we say they are "anticlimactic"). There is a rhythm here that humans find very familiar—its absence, particularly in a play, can be disorienting and disturbing (see chapter 5).

Step 10. Aesthetic Distance

In "Sense and Senility," an episode of the BBC comedy series *Blackadder* by Richard Curtis and Ben Elton, a witless Prince George goes to the theater. Appalled by the murder of one of the characters, the prince summons his guards. Soothed by his footman, who explains that what happens on stage is make-believe, the prince is the picture of calm when suddenly an anarchist storms the stage and lobs a bomb into the prince's box. Now thinking himself the worldly sophisticate, the prince applauds while everyone else runs for cover, and he gets blown up. The prince in this hilarious scene has been guilty of two lapses in discernment; first he has too little aesthetic distance, then too much.

Aesthetics is a cognitive, evaluative process by which humans assess abstractions like beauty, sublimity, profundity, horror, and other matters of what we call "taste." Dramatic events are capable of generating all kinds of aesthetic responses. These can be purely visceral, as in the horror plays of the early-twentieth-century Grand Guignol theater in Paris; these gore-soaked plays, many written by "Prince of Terror" Andre de Lorde (1871–1933) in collaboration with his psychoanalyst, featured necrophilia, eye-gouging, throat-slashing, baby-strangling, and acid-hurling and shocked the conservative Parisian culture mavens. Some plays are designed to titillate and feature pornographic stimulus but are nevertheless works of brilliance from a dramaturgical perspective; plays like this might include the works of John Wilmot (1647–80), Earl of Rochester, under England's Charles II in the Restoration period (Wilmot's brilliant but obscene works include *A Satyr on Charles II* (1674), which depicted Charles as a sex-obsessed, neglectful ruler), and of the notorious philosopher-pervert Marquis Donatien Alphonse François de Sade (1740–1814), whose *Count Oxtiern* (1800) continues to shock readers two centuries later.

However, plays of visceral or pornographic aesthetics rarely have a prominent place in posterity either because they offend official sensibilities, or they outlive their historical immediacy. This is not to say that such plays are not worthy of intense study and revival—far from it! Indeed, sometimes one generation's fringe play becomes middle-of-the-road Broadway fare for the next, such as Richard O'Brien's 1973 science-fiction transvestite melodrama *The Rocky Horror Show.* Rejected by mainstream critics, the play, after two successful runs in London and Los Angeles, was adapted into a film that engendered a cultish live-performance phenomenon that continues to be performed thirty years later and was revived in a popular production in 2000 at New York's Circle in the Square Theatre. But such plays are not the everyday fare of most professional dramaturgs in the United States.

Plays that dramaturgs are most likely to handle on a day-to-day basis are usually designed to elicit aesthetic responses either from the head or the heart. Playwrights focus on intellectual aesthetics to communicate complex ideas that they want the audience to consider; this group may include plays as diverse as Euripides' 415 BCE *Trojan Women* (a political tragedy about the destruction of Troy), Bertolt Brecht's 1930 *The Exception and the Rule* (one of his best-known "epic" theater pieces about the dangers of economic inequity), and Stoppard's

1993 *Arcadia* (a complex meditation on the nature of science, time, and human relationships). Plays that aim to elicit an emotional response, such as Aristotelian *katharsis*, are far more common, running the gamut from classical tragedy to melodrama to romances. But the best plays in the canon do not exist exclusively in one category or another. Masterful writers cause the aesthetic responses of a viewer to shift around during the course of the performance, ranging from intellectual scrutiny to emotional connection.

Generally, when the audience's connection to the action onstage is extremely intense and emotional, we say that there is little aesthetic distance between the action and the audience (this reached a historical nadir, we are told, when pregnant women in the audience of the first production of Aeschylus's 458 BCE *Eumenides* were allegedly so affected by the appearance of the monstrous Furies that they spontaneously miscarried). When the audience is in a more critical frame of mind, evaluating the action more dispassionately, we say there is greater aesthetic distance. Staging effects, rhetorical tropes, costume, set, lighting, sound; all of these things can be employed to manipulate the audience's aesthetic distance. A rule of thumb is that any event on stage that calls attention to the illusion of the play (exposure of the theatrical mechanisms, self-conscious references, violation of the "fourth wall," and so on) will *increase* aesthetic distance, while powerfully emotional moments and captivating effects that tempt the audience to "suspend its disbelief" (that is, to get caught up in the action) *decrease* aesthetic distance.

Step 11. Theatricality, or, "the Unseen Shark"

In his "Spring Bulletin" (*Getting Even*, 1972), Woody Allen asks, "Why is a play about a loveable old character named Gramps often not as interesting in the theater as staring at the back of someone's head and trying to make him turn around?" We could argue, if it didn't kill the joke, that the play to which Allen refers is lacking in *theatricality*. Smiley called this quality "a play's capability, as a staged performance, of interesting and entertaining an audience" (51). So, we call something theatrical if it pulls the audience's attention away from the backs of the heads of their fellow patrons; this can include a variety of things that attract human attention, like violence, suspense, fun, skill, relevance, passion, titillation, fear, combat, surprise, sex, speed, novelty, mystery, and conflict. Unquestionably, the most theatrical thing is *change*.

However, it is important at this point to discuss the difference between *theatrical* and *cinematic*. We often get these two concepts confused in our hypervisual, hyperstimulated times. Awed by the Big Screen's ability to pan back to reveal the Sinai Desert or cut to a ferocious laser battle between space-ships, it seems that the stage has spent much of the twentieth century either retreating into living-room realism (you, me, our couch, and our problems) or trying to steal cinema's thunder with colossal, big-budget sets and technical proficiency. Tony Awards aside, the problem as I see it with the amazing, un-believable, wonderful helicopter-set piece in *Miss Saigon* was that as astonished as they may be, the audiences are no longer concerned about Kim, abandoned to the Viet Cong and her desperate, uncertain fate. Instead, all they can think about is the helicopter. That is the danger of applying cinematic solutions to theatrical problems.

Theatricality specifically takes advantage of those qualities of the theater that no other medium can reproduce. As the old theater aphorism goes, "Theater is life, film is art, television is furniture." Unlike the action of film and TV, theatrical action exists in space and time along with its audience. The audience can actually shape the performance with its reactions. Unlike any other art form except live music and dance, theater is *present.* A theatrical imagination looks for solutions that enhance the theatergoing experience, not distract from it. The dramaturgies of Brecht and Kurt Weill are keenly directed towards enhancing this quality. Theatricality is reflected in the work of Maria Irene Fornés, Caryl Churchill, and more recent shows like Greg Kotis and Mark Hollman's *Urinetown!*

Furthermore, a master playwright will save the most theatrical moments for his most structurally important beats. For instance, the attack in *Hamlet* occurs when he and his friends swear on his sword. Consider this beat from act 1, scene 5:

> HAMLET: Never make known what you have seen to-night.
> HORATIO, MARCELLUS: My lord, we will not.
> HAMLET: Nay, but swear't.
> HORATIO: In faith, My lord, not I.
> MARCELLUS: Nor I, my lord, in faith.
> HAMLET: Upon my sword.
> MARCELLUS: We have sworn, my lord, already.
> HAMLET: Indeed, upon my sword, indeed.
> GHOST (*BENEATH*): Swear.

(158–74)

Stage this in your mind. Hamlet is desperate and wild from his unearthly visita-tion. Horatio and Marcellus are terrified, both of the specter and of their crazy-looking friend. Hamlet insists that they swear, shaking his sword in their faces. They resist, seeking sanity. Hamlet grows almost delirious, repeating himself. In the midst of this madness, a ghostly voice suddenly resounds through the theater from *beneath* the stage! It's a supremely theatrical moment, one that probably scared the original audience right out of their Jacobean hosiery.

The implications of this understanding are critical to the dramaturg's science. The most powerful emotional moment in *Oedipus* is, of course, the self-gouging of Oedipus's eyes. This is a moment of amazing power: humans generally spend a lot of energy *protecting* their eyes and become quite distressed at even the mere thought of any injury to them. Oedipus's self-mutilation goes so deeply against our instincts and reason that we are cathartically struck by how profound his grief must be. Why would Sophocles put this intense moment offstage? Our traditional answer is, "Well, the Greeks' sense of decorum forbade acts of violence on stage." How unsatisfying is that? Are we to imagine Sophocles coming to, say, his *choregos* with an early draft in which the eye-gouging does take place on stage, only to have the *choregos* say, "Sophie, you know I love your work, baby, but this just ain't gonna play with the *ephebes* and the blue-hairs. You're gonna have to use a messenger." No. Let us assume for a moment that Sophocles knows what he's doing and that he is not surprised by the convention against violence. He takes advantage of that, manipulates it expertly. By putting the eye-gouging offstage, he accomplishes two powerful feats of theatricality. First, he removes the need for any onstage effects that would distract the audience from the emotional impact of the act: no one can say, "Wow, what an amazing blood-spurting effect!" or "Hey, I can see how they did that with a sheep's bladder." Instead, a powerful actor, in describing the act, causes the audience members to create the scene *in their minds*, where it is far more impactful (and far more realistic) than it could ever be on stage. The second feat of theatricality Sophocles achieves here is that because the scene is being created in words, he can carefully direct the audience's eye to the goriest details and steer them towards interpreting the vision in a way most conducive to his goals as a playwright.

The downside, of course, is that Messenger has to be a pretty darn good actor. But think about it: what's *really* scarier? Seeing a big shark attacking a helpless swimmer? Or showing the swimmer surrounded by darkness with horrifying music playing? We don't see the shark, so the one we create in our minds is scarier than the one they could come up with in the effects lab. When we *do* see the shark, all rubber and robot, we're a little disappointed. The unseen shark is, ultimately, a theatrical effect rather than a cinematic one.

Step 12. Thought and Theme

Okay, at this point we are finally ready to begin talking about themes. Aristotle's term in the *Poetics*, translated as both "theme" and "thought," is actually διανοια (diánoia), a concept he learned from his own teacher Plato. Plato used the term specifically to emphasize that true knowing is a dialectical process (as opposed to the then–more commonly used term "noesis," or mere "understanding").

So when Aristotle talks about the *diánoia* of a play, he is talking about the dynamic, dialectical wisdom that lies at the heart of all this production of meaning. Is this something that can be stated simply? Aristotle explains in *Poetics* that dialectical knowledge has to be expressed dialectically: "What were the business of a speaker, if the Thought were revealed quite apart from what he says?" Some kinds of knowledge can't merely be written and transmitted; they need to be spoken out loud, in public, so others can speak back. If plays are supposed to be dialectical tools for self-discovery, then the process only works if the audience participates in the discussion and therefore in the creation of artistic meaning.

The thought or theme of the play is the intellectual, spiritual, mystical, psychological, visceral, or emotional cargo it carries—some artists like to speak of the "truth" of a play. The great playwrights used drama as their chosen medium because the dialectical nature of theater was the best possible way for them to publicly express their (often unpopular) religious, social, political, or humanitarian ideas. We should tread warily when we try to nail such writers down to something that can be summed up in a single pithy statement. Nevertheless, it is our job as dramaturgs to come up with an approach to a text that a director can build a performance upon.

Let's consider *Oedipus*. Often the first impulse in seeking a theme for *Oedipus* is something like "Don't sleep with your mother!" This is not a lesson that Oedipus needs to learn: he already knows that. When he suffers the discovery that he has slept with his mother, he plunges needles into his eyes. That's part of his punishment. But what is he being punished *for*? What was his horrible crime? Some analysts will say "hubris," which is part of the answer, but it stops too short. Oedipus may be a little proud, but he is a genuine hero. He said he'd save the city and punish the murderer no matter what, and he did, even though it meant his wife's death and his own ruin. He is just, good, brave, and civic minded. What is his crime? Trying to help when he could? Using his great intellect to serve the public trust? For this, he is punished so horribly? This cannot be what Sophocles wishes us to glean from Oedipus's tragedy. The truth of the matter is that Oedipus is being punished for his father's crime, infanticide. The vengeance Oedipus rightfully took on his father, however unwittingly, has become a fresh crime demanding fresh vengeance, and there is no one left to exact retribution on Oedipus, except Oedipus himself. So we're not done yet.

This play is a sea of conflicting forces. Everyone strives to do the right thing, but the blood guilt of a long-dead king is inevitably crushing them. There's not a thing anyone can do, as Queen Jocasta realizes in the play's most poignant anagnoresis:

JOCASTA: May you never know who you truly are!

OEDIPUS: Go, fetch the herdsman, and let this woman glory in her blue blood.

JOCASTA: Oh! You're doomed! You're doomed That is the last word I will ever speak to you.

And, finally, we have the chorus's pessimistic summation of the king's life: "Count no man fortunate 'til he ends his days, free of pain at last." How uplifting is that? So where can we turn for a theme? What knowledge of benefit to our species can we wrest from this blood-soaked house of horrors?

Well, we do have a city that has been saved by the selfless actions of a man, a man who brought the contagion with him. There is something Sophocles might wish to observe here about the relationship between the physical health of the state and the moral or spiritual health of its ruler. But Oedipus is a creature from a time when Greek heroes fought one another to decide the contests of kings, and Sophocles is a citizen of Athens, the golden democracy, whose military supremacy derives from the phalanx (which relies on everyone doing his part for his neighbor, neither more nor less: a hero inside a phalanx is deadlier than any enemy). No more kings, Sophocles is perhaps saying, because we can't tolerate them, and no more heroes, because we can't survive them. The shaking fist of the small-*r* republican revolutionary is replaced with this sad supplicant, who not without some regret chooses social equality as the only sustainable path forward.

Is that right? Well, to paraphrase Brian Johnston, Sophocles was a genius, and I'm not, so I may yet be missing something. The point I'm making here is that the theme of any great play is meant to be a discussion of its truths, not a pat moral aphorism suitable for a fortune cookie. The best I can do, as a dramaturg, is to read deeply, engage critically, deduce my conclusions, and present them as clearly as I can to my production team. Then we can wrestle our way through them together in a manner that hopefully makes for a night of entertaining, even important, theater.

And that is the twelve-step program for play analysis. But when it comes to aesthetic questions, no single answer is ever sufficient. Remember that from a dramaturgical perspective, the *right* answer is the one that produces the most interesting things on stage. So there is no one-size-fits-all plot diagram to be designed, and there is no single model of play analysis that's going to work in every case. This is only one way to look at scripts with climactic plots, a way that was incited by wiser dramaturgs than I and adapted by me for my own dramaturgy. I find it works admirably well as a starting point for *most* of the plays I read.

No doubt you will develop your own systems as your skills progress, but the two most important qualities of any dramaturgical approach are *critical engagement* and *flexibility*. The first quality is the ability to see when your method of analysis is insufficient.

The second is the ability to do something about it.

Exercises

Go deep, wide, and long: WOYZECK! *Woyzeck*, written by Georg Buchner, represents one of the greatest mysteries in modern-theater history. Buchner died while writing it, and the pages of the script lay undisturbed in his desk for decades. When they were finally rediscovered, the script was composed only of pages that could be divided into discrete scenes, but to this day, no one has any idea of the order of the scenes, and it is unlikely that anyone ever will. It is impossible to even begin a production of this powerful, popular play until an order of scenes can be established.

Dramaturgy to the rescue! Go find a copy of a translation of *Woyzeck*—any will do, but make sure it has all of the scenes in it. DON'T READ IT! Copy the scenes, and arrange them into separate piles, removing any indication of the order the editor arranged them. Read each scene carefully and in random order. Using your analytical skills, arrange the scenes into an order that generates a climactic arc. You may eliminate up to five scenes. Compile a document that begins with your dramaturgical approach: why you've chosen to arrange the scenes in this particular order, what you hope to emphasize, why you cut what you did, and the reassembled script. NOTE: You can do this even if you've already read the play or seen someone else's adaptation of it, but try to examine a variety of ways these scenes can come together.

There's no right or wrong answer—the only criteria for evaluating your work is in how effectively you achieve the goals you set out to accomplish. What kind of stories can you tell with this kind of material?

5

Form Follows Function

No mask like open truth to cover lies,
As to go naked is the best disguise.

—William Congreve, *The Double Dealer*

If you stand on a soapbox and trade rhetoric with a dictator you never win.
That's what they do so well; they seduce people. But if you ridicule them, bring
them down with laughter—they can't win.

—Mel Brooks

A play is a machine that produces meaning. As the blueprint for that machine,
the script of the play has to actually work—in other words, it has to be performable. All good scripts have that characteristic in common. Outside of that,
however, a script can take as many forms as the human imagination allows,
and not all of those forms are well served by a classical Aristotelian analysis.
Aristotle wrote his *Poetics* primarily for the analysis of Athenian tragedy and
only peripherally for other forms. It is true that the great majority of successful writers intentionally imitate Athenian tragic structure, and so Aristotle's
analysis is widely useful from neoclassicism to romanticism to realism. But
humans are complex creatures and produce complex art forms. Where free
experimentation is valued, form follows function as playwrights try new ways
to reach audiences. As a result, there is a lot of drama out there for which
climactic analysis is not going to be useful, and for those texts, we need to
have other tools in our toolbox. Below are three broad generalizations about
genres of scriptwriting that confound (sometimes intentionally) traditional
Aristotelian analysis, and some suggestions about how, as a dramaturg, you
might approach them.

Comedy

It is possible that Aristotle wrote *two* books of *Poetics*; the one on tragedy we know, the other, on comedy, is presumably lost forever. But we do have a sense of Aristotle's ideas on the topic of comic drama from references, tantalizingly fleeting, that he makes in *Poetics*. He notes that comedy has great versatility and employs all kinds of poetic devices (book 1); that it is mimetic (although tragedy represents men as better than they really are, and comedy as worse, as said in book 2); that is was invented and developed in the outlying villages (*kommai*) of Greece by wandering troupes who were not sufficiently sophisticated for the city audiences (hence, comedy was played for the *kommoi*, "commoners," book 3 relates); that it is for poets who prefer satire and lampooning, and like tragedy it was initially improvisational (book 4); that the nature of comedy is the mocking of "low persons," ugliness, and defects that are not painful or destructive, and that it has no clear recorded history because it was never taken seriously (book 5); that it is more artificially constructed than tragedy (which is based on history), because it deals more primarily with the *probable* rather than the *possible* (book 9); and finally, that comedy may have multiple plots and different catastrophes for different characters and that everything is resolved in the end (book 12).

Aristotle's writings lead to the conclusion that the different pleasures of tragedy and comedy both result from watching a character violate an important social rule. Of course, they do so for very different reasons. In tragedy, the characters know the rule is inviolable, but they violate it anyway (consciously or unconsciously) because they must—something in their noble nature demands it, and then they must pay the terrible consequences. The Aristotelian view of comedy suggests that its pleasure derives from watching a character violating an important rule after succumbing from ignorance, lust, greed, or some other human failing to a low, bestial nature. The *katharsis* of tragedy, he says, is a result of the spectator's fear that he or she, too, could be profoundly affected by the tragic protagonist's choices; in comedy, for Aristotle, the stakes are a lot lower, so we are free to enjoy it without fear.

To a modern eye, it seems that Aristotle is really missing a lot of comedy's potential for engaging in dialectics, at least in this writing. But Aristotle's lifelong project was to set down "first principles" for the study of human and natural things, and comedy, by its very nature, *resists* reduction into first principles. The most important aspect of comedy, as a very old vaudeville joke goes, is *timing*, and this is as true for the delivery of an individual joke as it is for jokes that traverse the millennia. The struggles and travails of Oedipus are as relevant now as they were in the fifth century BCE, but Aristophanes' hilarious zinger about the sexual promiscuity of Senator Lycaon's wife in *Lysistrata* falls flat in front of a twenty-first-century audience, no matter how well it's delivered. On the other hand, ancient problems of warmongering, nationalism, and sexual politics are still prevalent, so most of *Lysistrata* does continue to be relevant and hilarious. comedy depends utterly on *context*, and context is always changing.

So what exactly *is* comedy? This can get confusing because the term may refer to either *structure* or *content*. Structurally, a comedy's plot is often arced like a tragedy's, with a protasis, epitasis, and catastasis including a climax. As opposed to tragedies wherein the resolution of the conflict is often even worse than the conflict itself, comedies end comparatively happily or at least with harmony restored. In terms of *content*, this means that "comedy" applies correctly to texts like medieval cycles, in which the deaths of saints and martyrs (painful though they may be) are releases from pain and the consummation of divine providence, or even like Dante's *Divine Comedy*, in which after very serious, horrifying, and enlightening episodes, Dante comes to understand that in terms of the total cosmos, everything ultimately works out okay. These kinds of comedies are not particularly *funny*, although they may have some comic moments.

When it comes to *funny*, we are talking about *performance that engenders laughter*. Like *katharsis*, laughter is a release of tension. Aristotle observed that both tragedy and comedy rely on the violation of some rule—such a violation causes tension in those who witness it—and laughter is one way to release such tension. Any of the following things presented to an audience might generate the right kind of tension that incites laughter:

- Insufficiency, inferiority, and/or lack
- Superfluity and/or unnecessary things
- Illogical juxtaposition of things not normally compared
- Irony
- Caricature, exaggeration, and the grotesque
- Understatement and/or minimization
- Things of the body: violence, food, farts, excrement, sex, even death
- The breaking of any kind of social rule (including insults and cracking wise about someone's mama)

Aristotle felt that it was the lowering of personal stakes that made laughter possible in drama and so gave it short shrift in the *Poetics*. But many great theorists since (including Freud, Bakhtin, Brecht, Baudelaire, and Eco) have investigated the potential of comic performance to influence people's hearts and minds in meaningful ways. So meaningful is laughter that it is often considered politically or spiritually *dangerous* because the pleasure we get from laughter is so great that we will sometimes value it more highly than the rule that was broken. We will permit certain kinds of language and actions to exist where otherwise they might be inappropriate or even forbidden, if they are funny. When it comes to politics (from global to playground), laughter can be a weapon. When employed by powerful people against the weak, laughter is derisive and humiliating, but when employed by the weak against the strong, laughter is an equalizer. The Russian formalist critic Mikhail Bakhtin (1895–1975) wrote, "Laughter presents an element of victory not only over supernatural awe, over the sacred, over death; it also means the defeat of power, of earthly kings, of the earthly upper classes, of all that oppresses and restricts."[1] Laughter is extremely good at bringing the mighty low, which is why in so many totalitarian regimes, certain types of public laughter are outlawed, punishable by imprisonment, torture, exile, and even death.

Comedy depends on context. Looking at medieval drama alone, we can see (sometimes even within a single play) certain actions, like sex and death, depicted as tragic and sinful but also as comic and silly, or we can observe that the same action committed by two different people (such as the sacrifices offered by Cain and Abel in the medieval English passion play *The First Murder*) can be in one case sacred, in the second ludicrous.

Many, many subgenres of comedy use laughter and humor: some of the more prominent ones are detailed below. These are merely broad categories that serve well only when we are speaking of generalities. Comedy is boundary blurring, so naturally it is often very difficult to describe its structure except on a case-by-case basis. Where exactly does satire end and farce begin? One answer is, "Who cares?" The function of these terms is merely to provide some landmarks for navigating. When analyzing comedy, be prepared for any kind of structure or combination of structures, because the structure serves the joke. Direct your analysis less toward the cause-and-effect of Aristotelian plot structure and more toward the social context of the event—who is the butt of the joke? What secret truth is revealed in the laughter? Why laugh instead of cry?

The answers are as varied as the times, but do not make Aristotle's mistake of underestimating this immensely slippery and powerful tool for social change.

- *Old Comedy refers to a genre of Athenian comedies dating to before the end of the Peloponnesian Wars, of which only the plays of Aristophanes survive. These plays are, like Athenian tragedies, highly ritualized with large choruses and musical numbers.*

- *New Comedy refers to plays written in Greek and Latin from the era of Alexander onward into the Roman period. These are markedly different from Old Comedy, with far less emphasis on ritual and a much more naturalistic "situation comedy" feel to them. The Dyskolos, by Menander, has even been called the first comedy of manners (see "Comedy of Manners" below).*

- *Satire is thought to descend from the Athenian Drama Festival, in which the playwrights always closed their tragic trilogies with one play featuring satyrs (mythical half-man and half-goat creatures) on the same theme. The clownish satyrs were symbolic of the bestial tendencies of humans, and the Satyr Play was thought to give the playwrights a chance to explore their themes in a more lighthearted way. Satire pokes fun at human failings and usually is used in plays that are critical of political figures in some way.*

- *Farce,* a cousin of satire, describes a frenetic, sometimes violent form of comedy in which fabulous plot contrivances are brought to bear in the service of exaggerating some peccadillo or weakness of human nature. Farce places a heavy emphasis on sight gags, one-liners, witty banter, and physical comedy.

- *Commedia dell'Arte, a Renaissance form of comedy, relies on stock characters that date back to New Comedy and probably even earlier, to the Greek comic form that Aelius Donatus called "commedia attellana." The characters, easily identified by their ritualized movements, specific masks, signature props, and catch phrases, get in and out of funny situations that are improvised by the actors around lazzi, loose microplots developed around a single comic premise or line of stage business. Commedia is practiced in its original form, but its influence is widespread and can be easily recognized in the work of Shakespeare, Carlo Goldoni, Pierre Corneille, and many others up to modern cartoons, clowning, and films.*

- *Black Comedy, which takes particular delight in finding the humor in things that are horrific or taboo, reveals that attraction and repulsion are really two sides of the same psychological coin.*

- *Parody is a term that refers specifically to drama (and other art forms) created to mock through imitation a subject usually treated with seriousness (this could be a person, an idea, an institution, or another work of art, for instance).*

- *Kyōgen is a highly specialized form of comedy that shares a common ancestor (sarugaku) with the tragic tradition of Nōh. Like Nōh, Kyōgen is extremely ritualized and focused on gestures, but while Nōh illustrates sacred Buddhist teachings, Kyōgen often parodies Buddhism, with an emphasis on slapstick and stock characters.*

- *Comedy of Humours refers to a comic form popular in the Renaissance that capitalized on the idea (which dates back to Hippocrates) that human personality varieties were generated by bodily substances known as "hu-mours." An excess of blood made a person sanguine, an excess of choler (yellow bile) made one angry (choleric or bilious), an excess of black bile (in Greek, "melas khole") made one melancholy, and an excess of phlegm makes one uncaring and apathetic (phlegmatic). "Humourous" comedies create comic archetypal characters based on these principles.*

- *Comedy of Manners, popular in the Restoration, is a form of satire (often sexual in nature) mocking the dominant social class in which witty, edu-cated, and sophisticated people attempt to politely destroy each other.*

- *Dada deserves its own place in this discussion. A form of artistic avant-garde that sought to mock culture itself into nonexistence, Dada was part of the theatrical experimentation of the early part of the twentieth century. Performance was part of the experiments, and Dadaists devised pieces meant to call attention to the cracked and crumbling institutions that constitute our civilization and even to the ridiculousness of art itself.*

- *Theater of the Absurd, while undeniably possessing comic elements, is dif-ferent from other forms of performance in that its laughter appears to be a kind of desperate reaction to the realization that existence appears to have no innate purpose or goal. "Absurd" performances tend to showcase the meaninglessness of human activity, and although the realization is bleak, the performances of meaninglessness are often quite funny.*

Ovidian (Episodic)

In a 2008 *New Yorker* interview, the playwright Sarah Ruhl gave readers a clue into her non-Aristotelian dramaturgy:

> Aristotle has held sway for many centuries, but I feel our culture is hun-gry for Ovid's way of telling stories. . . . His is not the neat Aristotelian arc but, instead, small transformations that are delightful and tragic. . . . The Aristotelian model—a person wants something, comes close to getting it but is smashed down, then finally gets it, or not, then learns something from the experience—I don't find helpful. It's a strange way to look at experience.[2]

Ruhl is referring to *Metamorphoses*, the most famous work of Publius Ovidius Naso (43 BCE–17 CE). Ovid was a celebrated (and vilified) poet who lived in the time of Caesar Augustus. Ovid's poetry covers many subjects but is largely concerned with the erotic and the amorous. *Metamorphoses* is actually fifteen books of poetry of immense beauty, taking as their subjects stories from Greek mythology that feature transformations of one thing into another and illustrate Ovid's take on the many flavors of love.

Metamorphoses is often called an "epic" poem (or a "mock-epic"), which places it in the same category as poems like the *Iliad*, the *Odyssey*, and the *Aeneid*. Certainly, Ovid intended such comparisons to be made, as he wrote in dactylic hexameter (in which Roman heroic poetry was always constructed). But the term *epic* is actually one more we inherit from Aristotle, so, once again, it is profitable to begin a discussion of dramatic structure with the *Poetics*.

In his *Poetics*, Aristotle defines "epic" writing in opposition to tragedy, as an alternate form of mimesis. Here he is referring to the poems of Homer and his many imitators who provided material for the popular *rhapsodes*. The epic, Aristotle says, is like tragedy (and unlike comedy) in that it imitates "characters of a higher type" but differs in verse form and narrative style. One major difference, he says in book 5, is that tragedies tend to confine themselves to a single event that unfolds in "a single revolution of the sun," but epic plots have no such limits. In book 24, Aristotle describes epic poetry in more detail—it holds much in common with tragedy in terms of its adherence to the six constituent elements, but the lack of tragedy's narrow temporal scope enables epic poetry to follow multiple plot lines at once. Epic poetry does not unfold as a single action but as many different actions in separate *episodes*. Aristotle conceded that this gives epic poetry a slight advantage over tragedy in terms of charming its listeners, but on the whole, he gives epic poetry scant respect (saving the presence of Homer, of course), because of its facility with irrational characters, themes, and actions. In book 24, he concludes that tragedy is a "higher" art form than the epic (in the face, apparently, of popular sentiment at the time).

Aristotle's dismissal of epic poetry did not deter Ovid in the slightest, nor did the Elizabethan playwrights seem to give it much thought: Shakespeare's plays can, usually, be analyzed effectively with an Aristotelian arc in mind, but they occur in episodes, follow multiple subplots, and freely mix serious with lighthearted content. Gotthold Ephraim Lessing applauded such freedom, and Shakespearean writing became a model for the humanist romantic playwrights who argued that Shakespeare was nevertheless more true to Aristotelian dramaturgy than, say, the neoclassicists. But Aristotle's rejection of the epic would actually give ammunition to Bertolt Brecht and other Hegelian thinkers whose dramaturgy was more explicitly utilitarian than Aristotle's. Dramaturgy influenced by Enlightenment thought seeks to magnify theater's potential as a tool for dialectical self-discovery and the improvement of society as a whole and thus is not content with Aristotle's *katharsis* as a supreme goal because of the sense of fatal inevitability of the protagonist's downfall. Drama critics following Karl Marx would strongly associate tragedy with "false consciousness" generated by the ruling elite. It is in the interest of the powerful to promote fatalism among those it oppresses, Marx wrote; it is their most powerful tool because it utterly undercuts the will to resist. Of course, this sentiment originated previous to Marx and continues independently of specific adherence to Marxism, but in the intervening centuries, a distinct branch of dramaturgical thought would generate plays that wanted nothing to do with Aristotelian climactic arcs and their allegedly intellect-numbing emotionalism.

The dramaturgy of twentieth-century radical German playwright and dramaturg Bertolt Brecht is dialectical materialist theater, explicitly Marxist. He called his dramaturgy "epic" specifically to invite comparisons to Aristotle. Epic theater is structured in episodes rather than in a single arc, follows multiple storylines, has a clear leftist social agenda, and focuses on the lives of real people instead of dimly remembered figures from history or fictional monarchs. Designed to increase aesthetic distance, epic plays make no attempt to create an illusionary world. Instead, they call attention to their theatrical nature. Whereas Aristotelian theater is mimetic or representational of real life, epic theater, as devised by Brecht, is nonmimetic or *presentational*, with no attempt to create a "theatrical illusion" of a false reality. Instead of a closed world of highly moralized storytelling, epic theater is designed to be dialectical and open, with the audience included in the creation of meaning. For instance, epic characters routinely break the "fourth wall," stagehands conduct special effects in full view of the audience, and actors break character to discuss the scene; also, words and gestures are often at odds in Brechtian theater and the music jarring or inappropriate (take, for example, "Mack the Knife," a toe-tapping ditty about a brutal serial killer, written by Brecht's collaborator Kurt Weill for their 1928 *Threepenny Opera*). Epic dramaturgy argues that life does not actually unfold in the neat arcs described by climactic plays; instead, our lives are a series of events that seem only peripherally connected, at best, and we struggle to make sense of them. Therefore, instead of a single, unified, grand narrative, epic theater employs an episodic structure following multiple stories at once. All of this is designed to encourage a thoughtful intellectual response and a responsible, measured critical engagement, rather than the total loss of emotional control represented by *katharsis*. This gives epic theater the potential to be politically revolutionary.[3]

This is not to say that all Marxist dramaturgies must necessarily reject the tragic arc. The major American social realists of the twentieth century were very moved by the humanitarianism and egalitarianism of Marxist thought and struggled to incorporate them into their work. As Americans, these writers were particularly challenged by Aristotle's insistence that tragedy's emotional force depends on its characters being of high social "magnitude." Eugene O'Neill, for instance, was unable to shake the need for his characters to be socially prominent in *Mourning Becomes Electra*, his 1931 adaptation of Aeschylus's masterpiece *Oresteia*, in which the Greek king Agamemnon becomes Ezra Mannon, a general of the civil war. Arthur Miller, however, argued in his 1949 essay "Tragedy and the Common Man" that even the fall of an "everyman" type of character could generate sufficient fear and pity for *katharsis*. This essay provided a dramaturgical backdrop for his landmark play *Death of a Salesman*, which premiered that same year. This play features Willy Loman, his "lowness" being what renders his tragic fall meaningful for an audience of, ostensibly, democratic Americans, who feel represented by his ordinariness far more significantly than they would by a royal figure like Oedipus or Hamlet. At the end of the century, the characters of August Wilson's ten-play series *The Pittsburgh Cycle* (written between 1979 and 2005) take this even further, being not only from the social underclass but also victims of institutional race prejudice. But in the work of all of these playwrights, there is a sense of inevitability in their destruction, a sense that they are doomed no matter what choices they make. This fatalism seems to be what gives tragedy much its emotional force, and it is the problem Epic dramaturgs find irresolvable.

Epic theater is explicitly Marxist and revolutionary, but the efficacy of this kind of dramaturgy need not be limited to such a specific agenda. The religious plays of the European Middle Ages are also episodic in structure, employ non-mimetic staging, make no attempt at illusion, and suggest a dialectical approach not unlike Brecht's. Substitute Christian ministry for socialist revolution as the end goal, and you begin to see some stark similarities. Shakespeare's utter disdain for the neoclassical debates is refreshingly liberating, but his work resides with one foot in his medieval heritage and the other in the emergent Renaissance classical humanism, so he can be the hero of both Aristotelian Lessing and anti-Aristotelian Brecht.

In light of the many forms of drama that are not well served by an Aristotelian analysis, perhaps we might inaugurate (following Ruhl) a concept of "Ovidian" as opposed to Aristotelian dramatic structure. Ovidian plays would then be those that, for whatever reason, adopt episodic rather than climactic structures in order to reflect a less-rigid approach to the theatrical experience. When subjecting an Ovidian play to analysis, keep firmly in mind that the fluidity of the play's structure is not a weakness of the writing but a sign that the play's form is subservient to its content and its larger social goals. Our analysis, then, focuses on how well the play's construction serves those goals, not on how well it adheres to whatever this century's fashionable take on Aristotle happens to be.

Diffused Crisis

Since the 1950s, playwrights have also experimented with alternate structures in ways that cannot be grouped in either Aristotelian or Ovidian categories. Feminist writers perceived the Aristotelian arc as not only aristocratic but also chauvinist but felt that Marxist dramaturgy didn't work explicitly to represent women in authentic or liberating contexts, either. Postmodernist playwrights like Naomi Iizuka (*Polaroid Stories*, *36 Views*) and those of the American neo-avant-garde like the Living Theater (*Paradise Now*) and the Performance Group (*Dionysos in 69*) rejected both approaches as well, preferring more-fluid models that represented their own sense of the impermanence of institutions and ideas. Other writers have taken Brecht as a starting point to expand on his principles; for instance, the Theatre of the Oppressed, a movement that emerged from the political turmoil of São Paolo in the 1970s (begun by the Brazilian radical playwright and dramaturg Augusto Boal), is not only episodic but also dialectical to the point that the audience is invited to rewrite the script, which is then reperformed to create a different outcome. What these kinds of plays have in common, structurally speaking, is that instead of one clear climax or catastrophic beat that resolves the play's issues, the play's moments of crisis are diffused throughout the plot. These plays take many forms and innovate in many styles, but they seem to share a sort of common ancestry with a single groundbreaking play, Samuel Beckett's 1953 *Waiting for Godot*.

Waiting for Godot presents a thorny problem for dramatic analysis. After an early performance in Paris, critic Vivian Mercier wrote in the *Irish Times* that Beckett had "achieved a theoretical impossibility—a play in which nothing happens, that yet keeps audiences glued to their seats. What's more, since the second act is a subtly different reprise of the first, he has written a play in which nothing happens, twice." Mr. Mercier is pleased to jest, but *Waiting for Godot* is not, from a dramaturgical view, a play in which nothing happens. A lot happens. There is a great deal of *action*, much of it funny, some of it violent, a good deal of it tragic. There are plenty of expository beats, MacGuffins, anagnoreses, and peripeteias. What's missing is what David Ball called *forwards*, actions that move the plot along. The actions of the play do not logically lead to new actions, nor do they grow from previous ones. If you were to plot this play, it might look like an electrocardiogram of someone having a heart attack—arrhythmic spikes of intensity that just drop off and go nowhere. There is no arc. There is no climax. Because there is no climax, there is no way to distinguish protagonist from antagonist, nor is there any way to tell which portions of the play mark protasis, epitasis, or catastasis. The given circumstances are impossible to nail down; we do not know who these men are, how old they are, what country they are in, what year or month it is, how long they have been in this unhappy circumstance, or even what color Gogo's boots happen to be. Nothing is clear. At the end of the play, nothing has been gained, nothing learned, nothing established, nothing destroyed, and even the dialogue is exactly where it was at the beginning of the play. The repetition of the opening phrase "nothing to be done" demonstrates the utter failure of dialectics to produce any kind of progress whatsoever.

The play, obviously, resists traditional analysis, which leads Mr. Mercier and his fellow Parisian sophisticates (who hooted so derisively in early productions that the show was forced to close in midshow one night) to conclude that "nothing happens." But look closely at the play, and you will see that the failures of the actions are not at all random. The audience is very specifically encouraged to expect, for instance, a climax—even the title *appears* to ignite an expectation of the eventual appearance of Godot while actually promising that Godot will never show up at all. The characters desperately try to bring about an improvement in their own lives, and the audience is given no reason to think they won't be successful or at least make *some* progress. But when the first act and then the second end with absolutely no forward motion, we are left with a desolate feeling of futility and despair, and if we are trained only in classical forms of script analysis, a sense that nothing *worthwhile* has happened.

It is tempting to look at the play as a vehicle for answering larger metaphysical questions. For instance, the boy in the play is a goatherd (the goat is a medieval symbol for the devil) and speaks of another boy who is a shepherd (a medieval symbol for Christ, also associated with the lamb). Is Godot God? Beckett strenuously and repeatedly denied that this was the case and vehemently rejected other interpretations that hoped to unlock the play's secret meaning. These rejections did nothing to assuage the hostility of his critics.

However, approach the play as a dramaturg and learn something remarkable. In 1957, *Waiting for Godot* was directed by Herbert Blau with inmates at the San Quentin prison in a theater that had once been a gallows room. The prisoners, Blau found, related deeply to the play and the plight of the characters with their futile, meaningless attempts to improve their lives and with their endless waiting for something better that never comes. An inmate of a German prison had translated the play himself in 1954 with the intention of doing a production. He wrote to Beckett, "You will be surprised to be receiving a letter about your play *Waiting for Godot*, from a prison where so many thieves, forgers, toughs, homos, crazy men, and killers spend this bitch of a life waiting . . . and waiting . . . and waiting. Waiting for what? Godot? Perhaps."[4]

The insights of prisoners gave food for thought to the critic Martin Esslin, who wrote extensively about this play and others like it in his 1961 book *Theatre of the Absurd*. It is not a poorly constructed play, Esslin argued, nor is it a play that has a secret meaning. It is rather a dramatic expression of a stark and extremely bleak worldview. At the beginning of Beckett's life, the Western world was filled with great hope for the future. Advances in science and technology and in democracy seemed to fulfill the greatest dreams of the Enlightenment, and humans would finally be free to devote themselves to self-discovery and self-improvement. But the result of that freedom, it seemed, was a catastrophic global war marked with holocausts and atrocities: cultures and communities snuffed out, cities reduced to hellish ruins. Beckett had witnessed firsthand the absurdities that justified these horrific actions. In addition, Esslin notes that Beckett had suffered personal violence for which he could find no logical originating cause and no purpose. In such a universe, where our best efforts lead to chaos and death, what is the point of human existence? If humans determine what is right for themselves, and there is no larger purpose to life, then any individual action is no better or worse than any other. If there is no hope of salvation or progress, there is no moral order to the universe that guides our actions. Even suicide suggests the possibility for improvement. Without that hope, why bother? What's to be done? The first line of the play tells us: "Nothing."[5]

So, in Esslin's analysis, *Waiting for Godot* is not after all a play in which nothing happens twice. It is a play full of action that was carefully designed to elicit and resist Aristotelian analysis, in order to convey the bleakness and despair of Beckett's worldview. Recognizing that part of this bleakness is humorous, Esslin called this worldview "Absurd" in reference to the work of French philosopher Albert Camus and grouped into this category the plays of Eugène Ionesco, Jean Genet, Arthur Adamov, and (later) Harold Pinter, but the term has also been used to refer to Arthur Kopit, Tom Stoppard, Edward Albee, and Friedrich Dürrenmatt. Whether Esslin's is the right interpretation, his criticism propelled *Godot* to its place as one of the most important plays of its century. In the same critical circles where Beckett was once vilified, he is now honored.

However, many playwrights who were labeled Absurdist by Esslin resisted the term. The Absurd worldview restores that anti-Enlightenment, anti-Marxist fatalism that utilitarian dramaturgy like Brecht's had wished to purge out of Aristotelian drama. If human action is futile, why struggle to make things better? Ionesco felt that his work (although it certainly had Absurd qualities) was deeply political and resisted the label. His 1959 *Rhinoceros*, which depicts an entire town gradually transforming into brutal pachyderms, works very well when seen as an allegory for the spread of fascism in Europe. Many of British playwright Tom Stoppard's plays also have Absurd qualities, particularly in their dialogue, but they also contain subtle parodies and sharp cultural critiques that deny Absurdity's fatalism. The plays of British playwright Caryl Churchill, including *Cloud 9*, also contain structural similarities to Absurd plays, but they are certainly neither apolitical nor uncommitted to a sense of drama as a tool for dialectical self-improvement. To accommodate *Waiting for Godot* and these many descendants, *diffused crisis*" is an attractive term because it groups these plays together by structure, not by content or any presumed authorial intent.

One of the most important effects of *Waiting for Godot* was its effectiveness in widening the expectations of mainstream audiences about what a play can look like and do. Experiments in this form include altering the way structurally that an audience experiences the event. While the avant-garde experimented with forcing direct confrontations with the audience, certain playwrights have written diffused-crisis scripts that actually generate different experiences for different members of the *same* audience. Among them are María Irene Fornés's 1977 *Fefu and Her Friends*. This play is presented in three parts. In part 1, the play's protasis, the audience joins a group of women meeting in 1935 to plan a theater-education project. The character Fefu confesses a deep hatred for her emotionally abusive husband. In part 2, for the epitasis of the play, the audience in the first production is split up into groups, and each of the groups watches the same period of time unfold in the play from different perspectives. That is to say, four scenes are performed simultaneously, with some actors crossing between scenes, but each group witnesses the action in a different order and from a different perspective. For part 3, the audience reassembles to see the final violent scene together, but because of this fracturing of the audience, this scene actually represents the catastasis of several different sequences of action. As Fefu seeks to resolve her own personal crisis, the groups of audience members are forced to draw divergent conclusions. Only from a perspective that involves multiple views and accommodates multiple narratives intersecting, a perspective that no single audience member can achieve alone, can this performance be understood in its totality.

A second play that fractures its audience is Griselda Gambaro's 1971 *Information for Foreigners*. Gambaro's play seeks to disseminate information about real events regarding the clandestine arrests and torture of political dissidents in Argentina. Designed to take place in a house with many rooms, the play requires that the audience be split into several groups, each one with a tour guide. The guide takes each group through the house, and in each room, and in the hallways, the group encounters performances that range from darkly humorous exchanges to vivid depictions of brutality. Throughout, the groups are given information not only about the *desaparecidos* and other victims of state terrorism but also about the complicity of the governments of the United States and other Western democracies. The script suggests the creation of a truly open dialectic, where the audience cannot know for certain which actions are rehearsed and which are spontaneous or who in the group is a spectator and who is part of the show. In this context, it seems likely that the audience will also behave in unexpected ways in this unusual environment, changing the performance even further.

Obviously, in a play like this, terms like *protasis*, *protagonist*, and *climax* have no meaning at all. The effect structurally is that each spectator will have a unique experience of the performance, but on a more profound level, the play works to make the audience feel intimately involved, even complicit in (and therefore culpable for) the horrific events being staged. Such an effect furthers Gambaro's political agenda (to enlist powerful Westerners in her battle against the tyranny of her homeland) far more effectively than a conventional staging and script structure ever could.

It would be ridiculous to claim that the preceding chapter and this one cover the analysis of every play ever written. This is only the beginning of an exploration of certain trends in experimental Western drama. Every play needs its own unique analysis, and a system that works well for a given play may not work at all even for another play by the same playwright. What's more, as new playwrights confront new problems, they will devise new solutions, and new ways of writing will be required to contextualize new forms and bring them to life. But these two chapters at least get the conversation going and reinforce the recognition that a good dramaturg needs both criticality and flexibility to operate well. Keep asking questions, remain open to the answers, and remember that dramatic analysis is, like everything else playwrights do, a process.

Reading is to dramaturgy what inhaling is to lungs—an intake, assessment, and compartmentalization of material necessary for survival. What a dramaturg exhales is discussion, which largely manifests itself as writing. The next chapter describes formulas and techniques for turning an analysis into something clear and useful—written documents that encapsulate dramaturgical ideas for the people who need them most: the cast, the crew, and the audience.

Exercises

Go deep! Select one of the fifteen-book *Metamorphoses* by Ovid that is particularly compelling to you. Do an Aristotelian analysis of its story—find its arc, its climactic moments, its discoveries and reversals, its protagonist and antagonist. Be aware that not all of the books will succumb; if you find one that cannot be so analyzed, find another way to talk about its action. Now, do the same with the books immediately *before* and immediately *after* the one you've chosen. Can you describe the way Ovid transitions from one to the next? How does the placement of this book between the other two books change your understanding of its action and theme? What larger story is being told?

*Go **wide**!* In the news reports of the past ten years, find an account of a comic artist (an actor, writer, or comedian) or other public figure who has gotten in some kind of trouble for telling a joke. What went wrong? Can you articulate why the joke was considered dangerous instead of harmless? What does the rejection of the joke tell about the social context in which it was told?

*Go **long**!* Select another story from the fifteen-book *Metamorphoses* by Ovid, and adapt it into a ten-minute play. Here's the catch: you must retell the story in a *modern* context, set in the twenty-first century, with people and things you would recognize in your everyday life. What replaces the transformative power of gods and magic in our world? What kind of structure will you use to tell your story: Ovidian or Aristotelian? Employ (or develop) a structure that best matches the content of the story and your own goals for its development.

6

Why This Play Now?

Information is not knowledge. Knowledge is not wisdom. Wisdom is not truth. Truth is not beauty. Beauty is not love.
—Frank Zappa, "Packard Goose"

Chapter 1 discussed how Mark Bly answers the question of "What does a dramaturg do?" with "I question." The dramaturg asks a lot of questions, but these are really just derivations of one sort of master-question. That question is the dramaturg's constant companion, and as shown in the final section of this book, it is the question that guides the dramaturg's inquiries, lines of research, and relationships with the rest of the troupe and the audience.

The question is a touchstone that can reliably be counted on to provide a clear focus. No, it's not "Am I getting paid?" It is just this: Why this play now?

In other words, why have we chosen this play to present at this moment in history in front of this audience? Why is it important? To what concerns of ours, and theirs, does it speak? For that matter, who *is* our audience? Who are we? What is it we wish to say? Why is this text the best way to say it? Do we have anything new to say, or are we recapitulating an older idea? How will we make it relevant? How will we make it work? What values do we wish to convey? What values do we *actually* convey? Why are we doing a play and not some other form of art or political action? Why are we doing *this* play and not some other play? Why are we doing theater at all? The clearer your response to this question is, the better you will know what you are doing and what kind of outcome you desire. This chapter looks at how the question "Why this play now?" (WTPN) guides your dramaturgical research and writing processes.

Doing Preliminary Research (and a Web Warning!)

Research is half of the dramaturg's process; the other half is transforming the research into useful ideas and integrating them into the production. Often, that means writing. Research and writing are the particular skills of the dramaturg—the better a dramaturg is at them, the more useful he or she will be to a production process.

Like everything else one does, research and writing are processes and are guided by the WTPN question. Luckily, we are living in the information age, and it is not difficult to get access to all kinds of information, in libraries, bookstores, archives of various kinds, and, of course, the World Wide Web (which is the ultimate garden of forking paths). But therein lay our greatest obstacles as well, because, as Zappa said, information is not knowledge. Like any other specialized tool, the Internet can make our work significantly easier, but it notoriously has three characteristics that impede research:

- *First, it has no way of distinguishing between valuable information and total garbage. Unlike brick-and-mortar publishing, the Internet has very few gatekeepers, few experts on hand to evaluate the quality and utility of a piece of writing before it is presented to you. Not that brick-and-mortar publishing is perfect, but it is able to enforce some standards. Across most of the 'net, anyone can publish whatever, whenever, and change it without warning. Furthermore, although the Internet is very good at tracking information that is emerging right now, it's weaker the further back in time you need to go. There's an awful lot of uncredited copying going on; consume indiscriminately, and you may become guilty of abetting someone else's plagiarism. The good news is that scholars use the Internet all the time, and more-scholarly Web sites that you can trust are coming into existence. Get familiar with them; see appendix E in the current volume for a list of some reliable sources.*

- *Second, the Internet has a tendency to try very hard to distract you from whatever task you are trying to accomplish. It creates a lot of what information technologists call "noise," which means information you don't need or want, and it's usually trying to sell you something. It is most effective when it can make you think that a bit of noise is actually information!*

- *Third, the ease and speed of the Internet have dramatically cheapened the perceived value of information and communication. The upside of this convenience is that the 'net proliferates information—it's much harder to restrict knowledge than it once was, and many more people now have a voice than previously. The downside is that it has created a culture in which there is so much information that people no longer value it as much as they once did, nor do most people respect the work that goes in to producing real knowledge (as opposed to noise). Knowledge, like most things, has become a disposable resource to most people. This is a problem because it takes work and thought to transform raw data into useful knowledge, but most people aren't even aware anymore that such a difference exists.*

These factors make researching on the Web as hard as doing research in the library (or even harder): both require a great deal of discipline and a pragmatic system. I have articulated the basic principles of one approach below—this works for me, but go with what works for you. Again, the better you are at these tasks, the more useful you will be as a dramaturg.

Clarify your topic. Obviously, you have to know what you're talking about if you are going to focus your efforts, but this is deceptively difficult to pull off. It's really a process of sifting the noise from the information, but it also means becoming familiar with your topic (a play, a historical event, an author, a methodology, and the like) enough that you understand how it operates in context (social, political, historical, aesthetic, or what-have-you). The better you contextualize and historicize, the more solid the foundation and the clearer the research. Encyclopedias (in print and online) are a good place to *start* but only to get your ideas in a workable frame—don't rely on them for anything but a jump-start.

Go to the source. To the best of your ability, start assembling as many original texts as you can. Obviously, a lot of the work dramaturgs do is in other languages or with ancient texts, but the more contemporary documents you can find, the better sense you will have of what the context of the event was. These texts will form the basis of a network or a conversation with more modern writings or events.

Listen to the chatter. What are the experts saying about your topic? This is information you will rarely find in an encyclopedia entry or an online brief citation, which are sometimes out of date and always insufficiently short. A modern dramaturg should become familiar with the discourse of scholars, so you have access to the writings of expert thinkers (historians and theorists) on your topic. The best dramaturgs I know participate regularly in scholarly forums like conferences and online list-servs and are as comfortable with academics as they are with artists. The bridge between the production company and the community of scholars is one of the important bridges that a good dramaturg can build.

Contribute. Now that you have a strong sense of your topic, you must ask, "What can I bring to this conversation that's new?" This seems like a daunting task, but your insights and reactions are important. You have a unique set of experiences that have formed in you a unique pattern of thinking, and that's valuable. If you don't believe that, then why are you an artist? But remember, like everything else, this is a process. You will refine this idea in collaboration with the artists of your company as the rehearsal progresses. All in all, your answer will form the basis of your WTPN.

Rinse and repeat. As you progress through the development of your production, you will be required to return to the library and repeat these steps several times. New ideas or information will emerge, and it will be your job to place them into the proper context with an evolving WTPN. In addition, you should think of each production as a sort of laboratory environment in which you are testing your own ideas about what theater is, why we do it, and what it needs to become: in short, in developing a holistic dramaturgy of your own.

Writing a Production History

One way that dramaturgs clarify their topics is by doing *production histories,* which are fairly straightforward research projects. Creating a production history should be the first step in the dramaturgical process for any show you do. In this critical task, you answer the following questions about a given play:

- Has it ever been done before? If not, has something like it been done?
- What did that production look like?
- Who was involved?
- What were its goals (Why this play then)?
- Was it popular? controversial? unnoticed?

Answering these questions is vital to getting the proper context for a show you're doing. I have been constantly amazed at how much great information doing a production history can reveal. Artistic directors, directors, designers, and actors all devour production histories with great relish, not only because it helps them properly contextualize their own work but also because it gives them a sense of being part of theatrical history. A production history is like a record of the intrepid souls who ventured across this territory before; infinitely valuable, especially in dangerous terrain.

To create a production history, I favor the model developed by Pam Jordan, former head of the Yale School of Drama Library. You must discover the what (title), when (date), where (country, city, and theater), and who (author, translator or adapter, dramaturg, director, designers, actors, and production team) of the *first production* (of a contemporary play) or a recent *significant production* (of a classic play). Sources for this include reviews, historical articles, performance reconstructions (theater history articles that specialize in recreating the events as precisely as possible, which you can find in scholarly journals), theater biographies, and specialized periodicals that specifically gather this kind of information (see appendix 4 for a list of some of these sources). Going online can save time, but make sure to confirm in a more reliable source all the information found.

Once you have the basic production information about the production, you need to put it in context by retrieving the reviews of that performance. Begin by writing a condensed summary of the reviews, getting a sense of what the production meant to the author and the people who saw it originally. It's also worthwhile to note if there are any "big names" in the production—how did this project contribute to their overall notoriety? How did their presence impact the work? Can you see any aesthetic trends in the work that these artists would explore later? Did the play win any awards? Did it break any new ground? For a first production, you should also note what major revivals were done of this play; for classic plays, you should note *why* this particular revival is significant. In the end, you will produce a document that looks like this, for a contemporary play:

Production History

What	=	*A Raisin in the Sun*
When	=	1959 March 10
Where	=	U.S.A.—New York—Ethel Barrymore Theatre (Broadway)
Who	=	Lorraine Hansberry (author)
		Lloyd Richards (director)
		Ralph Alswang (sets and lighting)
		Virginia Volland (costumes)
		Sidney Poitier (actor—"Walter")
		Ruby Dee (actor—"Ruth")
		Ivan Dixon (actor—"Joseph")
		Lonne Elder III (actor—"Bobo")
		John Fiedler (actor—"Karl")
		Louis Gossett (actor—"George")
		Ed Hall (actor—"Moving Man")
		Claudia McNeil (actor—"Lena")
		Diana Sands (actor—"Beneatha")
		Glynn Turman (actor—"Travis")
		Douglas Turner (actor—"Moving Man")

Critical Reception

Considered the first naturalistic play featuring African American themes and characters, Hansberry's semi-autobiographical *Raisin* is still acknowledged as a stunningly groundbreaking play in American theater history. In light of a growing discontent and radicalism in the marginalized and disenfranchised black community of the era, who

---

were being excluded from the postwar prosperity the country enjoyed, *Raisin* was hailed as a play that broke the "color barrier" (it was popular among mainstream white audiences and brought new black audiences into the theater) and shattered not only the stereotype of black people as socially inferior to whites but also as incapable of producing realistic, psychologically deep, and powerfully literary drama. Taking its title and themes of black social immobility and frustration from a famous Langston Hughes poem "Harlem" (1951), the play (like the poem) became (and remains) a symbol of the civil rights movement. The production was honored by the New York Drama Critic's Circle Award for Best Play of the Year (Hansberry would be the youngest person, and the first African-American, to receive this prize). Its director (Richards) and many of its stars (Poitier, Dee, and Gossett, in particular) were already pillars of the black theater, but this play would make them iconic figures in American theater history. Upon closing in October 1959, the production moved immediately to the Belasco, where it played until June 25, 1960. It was adapted into a 1961 Columbia Pictures film scripted by Hansberry and including the Broadway cast and into a 1973 musical called *Raisin*, which won the 1974 Tony for Best Musical.

For a significant production of a classic play, the document would look like this:

Production History

What	=	*Nathan the Wise*
When	=	2003 May 1
Where	=	UK—Chichester—Minerva Theatre (Chichester Festival)
Who	=	G. E. Lessing (author)
		Edward Kemp (adapter)
		Steven Pimlott (director)
		Anthony MacDonald (design)
		Hugh Vanstone (lighting)
		Gregory Clarke (sound)
		Michael Feast (actor—"Nathan")
		Jeffery Kissoon (actor—"Saladin")
		Geoffrey Streatfield (actor—"Templar")
		Noma Dumezweni (actor—"Sittah")
		Jonathan Cullen (actor—"Al-Hafi")
		Alfred Burke (actor—"Patriarch")
		Kay Curram (actor—"Rachel")
		Darlene Johnson (actor—"Daya")
		Steven Beard (actor—"Lay Brother")

Critical Reception

Written by Lessing in 1779, the play dramatizes Lessing's own life-altering conflict with Johann Melchior Goeze, a powerful anti-Semitic clergyman in Hamburg, who objected to Lessing's publication of a book on theology that denied the divinity of Christ and the reality of miracles (this book would become popular among many prominent Enlightenment thinkers, like Thomas Jefferson and Benjamin Franklin). In response to the controversy, the Duke of Brunswick (Lessing's employer) forbade him to write theology. Lessing turned to the theater, and transferred the ideological quarrel to twelfth-century Jerusalem. The character of Nathan is modeled on Lessing's friend and collaborator, Moses Mendelssohn, who was one of Germany's greatest philosophers but, being Jewish, still could not enter Hamburg except through a gate reserved for cattle. The play's powerful indictment of blind faith, theological racism, and reactionary politics made it a beacon of the Enlightenment. Banned by the Nazis, it became the first play performed in Germany after the fall of Hitler and is now required reading for German schoolchildren. However, it has fared poorly in English translations, because it had invariably emerged as dense, long, and intolerably didactic (in Eric Bentley's words, "preachy"), and Lessing's masterpiece has been largely uncelebrated in the English-speaking world except by scholars. Edward Kemp's new adaptation, originally considered very risky, is streamlined, funny, and full of action and was hailed by critics as "superb," "deeply moving," and "excellent." Less than two years after the destruction of the World Trade Center by terrorists and in the midst of an explosion of anti-Muslim sentiment in the West, Kemp's play was a voice of tolerance, reason, and the vital necessity of finding a way to live in harmony with those of different beliefs. These events give Lessing's play a profound new relevance, and Kemp's adaptation makes the drama widely accessible to a popular audience.

Along with this document, your production history should include copies of the relevant reviews, any scholarly articles you employed or intend to employ, and if possible, production stills or other images (you can find woodcuts and other records of classic productions in historical archives).

Writing a Performance Review

It is important to remember that besides doing your own research, watching performances (from your own troupe or that of others) is one of the best means of building your own inner library of resources. The dramaturg trades on *practical knowledge*, the ability to apply information in a useful way. So you need more than good library skills and your furious passion for the theater;

you also need to develop methods of figuring out how other production teams have answered WTPN in their own work. You need a dramaturg's eye, and one effective way to develop it is to do write a *performance review* after you go to the theater.

When you are witnessing any kind of production, it is very helpful to habitually employ what is known as "Goethe's 3." Johann Wolfgang von Goethe was a mightily prolific German author, scientist, humanist, and dramaturg of the Weimar classical period, following in the footsteps of Lessing. A dedicated empiricist, he developed these three questions to ask of any production as a prelude to developing a critical review:

Goethe's 3
- What were they trying to do?
- Did they do it?
- Was it worth doing?

You could subtitle these analysis (data collection and decoding), diagnosis (gauging success level and what went wrong or right), and evaluation (setting a "value" on the work itself). These questions are most useful when they are taken as separately as possible and in the proper order.

In order to answer the first of Goethe's 3, "What are they trying to do?" you must have already done some preliminary research before you even get to the theater. At the very least, you have already read the script, if it is available, and executed a preliminary structural analysis. What is the play's action? What kinds of choices do the characters make? What are the lines of conflict? How are they resolved? What is the theme of the play? What moral, spiritual, psychological, cosmic, sexual, social, or intellectual weight does the play carry? Now it's back to the library. Do a production history: find out what you can about the author, the context of the play's writing, and what motivated the author to write the play in the first place. You don't necessarily have to write a full formal document, but the more about the play you know, the better prepared you will be for the next step. Take notes in a small notebook with a good pen, and bring the notebook (and the pen) with you to the theater.

Some students worry that this kind of scrutiny "kills the spontaneity" of the experience, but this is a fallacy. The job of a dramaturg is to determine to the best of one's ability what choices the production team made in transforming the raw material of the script to life. *That's* the interesting part for theater professionals! You will be unable to do that well, if at all, unless you are familiar with the original text beforehand (if it was not a devised or documentary piece). Try it on the next show you see, and decide for yourself whether this enriches your understanding and enjoyment of the production.

When you enter the theater, begin your second round of analysis—on the production itself. Look carefully at the posters outside, the décor of the lobby, the program notes (*especially* the program notes; that's the production drama-turg talking to you), advertising, previews, and any other piece of information that you can identify as an attempt by the production to prepare you for the performance. Everything you encounter between the moment you arrive at the theater and the moment the performance begins is a manipulation of your aesthetic sensibilities. Note the following:

- What's happening to the patrons between the time they enter the door and the time they enter the performance space?
- What does the company want you to be thinking or feeling?
- What's missing?
- What kind of a company is this? What is their overall mission?
- How does that impact their choice of this play?

Because you already have your own analysis of the script, you can begin to guess how the team might approach the text and how they hope you will react to it. It's also wise to listen to what other people in the lobby and the audience are saying about the play, what they've heard or read online. You can break the ice with the person seated next to you by asking, "Have you heard anything about this production?" Later, you can cash in on that relationship by getting your neighbors' reactions and including them in your own analysis.

Now, the show begins. You are still asking question 1, gathering your data like a good scientist. Take notes in your small notebook. Don't make any judgments yet about whether the choices are good or bad. Ask the following questions:

- What *happens* onstage and in the audience? Probably you will begin to see choices the team is making that diverge from your own reading and analysis. What are those choices?
- What are you lead to expect? Are those expectations fulfilled? Are any theatrical conventions established?
- Can you sense the operation of any critical theoretical models?
- Have they changed the script? If they have, are the changes minor cuts or more substantial alterations? Why have they made changes? Is the production faithful to the authorial intent, insofar as you could deter-mine it in your research, or is this a reenvisioning?
- Remember, Aristotle said that the elements of a play (plot, character, theme, diction, rhythm, and spectacle) are *constituent*—they all affect and inform each other. How does the execution of the script in time and space affect your understanding of the piece?

- At intermission and when the show is over, pay close attention to the audience. What are they discussing? How did they react to the show? Are they confused about what they just saw? Angry? Agitated? How is the social ambience compared to how it was when you arrived? Conduct, if you can, polite, informal interviews with the audience and gather any further information you can.
- If there's a postshow talkback, don't dare miss it. If not, hang around and wait for the actors to come out, and eavesdrop on their interactions with the audience and one another. Take notes (discreetly). If anyone asks, tell them you're doing dramaturgical field work.

Data gathered, back in your apartment (or dorm, studio, office, coffee shop, bar, or that corner of the library you've come to think of as "yours"), begin to compile your analysis. Return to Goethe—because you did your preliminary research before seeing the play, you can now answer the first question: What were they trying to do? Take a moment to answer this question before you move on, and include who "they" are. You should be able to state this answer in a single sentence, like:

- The Federal Theatre Project presented the Living Newspaper play *Triple-A Plowed Under* to suggest nefarious connections between government and big business.
- The Carnegie Mellon School of Drama performed a modernized *Lysistrata* as a means of making a political statement against the Iraq War.
- The Palace Theatre on Broadway mounted the premiere of *Legally Blonde* to provide spectacular entertainment to a big audience.
- Miss Spalding's kindergarten presented *Chicken Little* as part of parent's night at Kennedy Elementary.

There is no judgment here—we are merely presenting the data as we found it and accepting the production team at its word about what its goals were (which we deduced from the information we collected earlier). This is very important because it reminds you as the watcher to be as clear with yourself as possible about what exactly you are seeing. It is critical to allow the information to guide the conclusion and not vice versa. When you become more skilled in your work, you can open your reviews with observations that help place the work into a larger context, but when you're starting out, stick to the facts.

It is helpful to break the writing of the review down according to Goethe's 3:

Evidence

In this section, you lay out the material you will analyze and evaluate. Be thorough, but selective. Give your reader everything he or she needs to understand your analysis, but make sure you analyze all the evidence you present. As the old saying goes, "Take all you want, but eat all you take."

- First, set the scene: what show—where—what company—when. What's the theater like? What was the audience like?
- Explain to us any weird genre issues or strange conventions we will need to understand before we get started.
- Do a short plot summary, followed by a brief discussion of the play's themes. This is useful so you can refer to it later and essential to your attempt to answer WTPN. Don't include information that is extraneous to your overall analysis—just tell us what we need to know to understand your overall point.
- Include a summarized production history of the play text, especially if it is an adaptation from an earlier work of art, including critical acclaim, awards, controversies, and so on. This helps the reader understand the context for the company's choice.

Analysis

- Was the action of the play clear? If not, why not?
- Was the direction coherent? Were the stage pictures meaningful? Did the show appear to have a unified sense of theme and purpose?
- Was the acting cohesive and fluid? Was it appropriate to the material? Was it skillful?
- How did the various design elements (costume, set, light, sound) influence the overall effect? Did they enhance or detract from the play's meaning?
- Was the adaptation of the script logical and coherent? Did any changes made to the script enhance or detract from the play's meaning?
- Were the various elements of the total production harmoniously integrated? Did it all make sense?
- What x-factors (events outside the control of the production, like weather, politics, traffic, riots, stampedes, or rains of fish) affected the audience's experience?
- Bring it into a larger context. What's up in the world? What's up with this theater? How are we supposed to understand such a performance? Bring in your critical theories here. Analyze audience reaction as far as you can.

Evaluation

Now discuss the worth of this work as a piece of art overall. What's it worth to the reader, the world, theater as a whole? Certainly, you can talk about if you "liked it." But your liking it or not liking it needs to be a total evaluation of ALL of the above points, including the play's relationship to the rest of the world and the audience's reaction.

Doing these steps out of order causes the reader to cast suspicion on your motives. If you say, "What a waste of my life" in the first paragraph, or "I didn't like this actor's choices" in the third paragraph, you're missing the point—first you have to come up with an explanation of WHY the actor chose that action. Maybe it seemed stiff and unrehearsed to you—but if it's a Brechtian piece, maybe it's supposed to! You can't make such a judgment until you get the whole picture. What is the production *trying* to do? If they're doing *Romeo and Juliet* on a basketball court with six orangutans, it's a safe bet they aren't looking for a traditional reaction.

As for the third question: was it worth doing? Obviously, there is an invitation here for your opinion and evaluation, but because you have grounded your analysis in a close examination of the information, what you are really trying to do here is articulate the value of the production's dramaturgy, which has a larger scope than "I loved it" or "I hated it." Just as you would not, for instance, compare the production values of the Palace's big-ticket *Legally Blonde* to those of *Chicken Little* by Miss Spalding's kids (in the latter, the production values aren't the point, while in the former, they're the main point), your evaluation of every aspect of the production needs to be made on the production's own merits and against a standard that was set for you by the production team, as well as by your own sense of what kind of theater is important. You might decide that despite the fact that Miss Spalding's kids consistently forgot their lines, waved to their moms, and cried when they got confused or hit by the acorns, *Chicken Little* was nevertheless worthwhile because the point of this show is far more pedagogical (to expose the kindergartners to the amazing world of the theater, to give them confidence about their own skills, and to teach the kids how to work as a team) than aesthetic (but don't mention that to the parents).

The final element of your review answers the question Why this play now? What's going on in the world that makes this play relevant? Does this production make me look at something in a new way? Does it improve my life? Did it teach me anything? Was I entertained? Were any artistic horizons crossed? Do I want to see more from this troupe?

Now that you have some sense of how a critic watches a play, you can bring these skills back into your own rehearsal hall and apply it to your work with your troupe, which is the focus of the chapters ahead.

Exercises

Go deep! Write a *production history* both for a contemporary play and for a significant modern production of a classic play.

Go wide! Select a production that you've seen in the last three months. Go online or into the newspaper archives at your library, and find as many reviews of the production as you can. Write a paragraph on each one, with an eye towards answering the following questions:

- Are there signs that the critic did preliminary research on the play and the author prior to attending the production? How about a production history?
- Has the critic considered Goethe's 3 or made a similar type of evaluation, and/or are his or her critical criteria appropriate to the material? Is the evaluation consistent and coherent throughout the review?
- Does the critic address WTPN by putting the production into a larger context? How knowledgeable is the critic about this theater, the theater of the region, of the world, and of history?
- How many "me messages" are in there? Any other "noise" that distracts you from the above two criteria in this review?

Go long! Write a five-thousand-word WTPN-driven *performance review* for the next show you see.

THREE

Practice

7

New Plays

> The question put to us is "How do you talk to a playwright?" and like any good dramaturg I'll start by critiquing the question. It's fraught with potholes. The question implies that there is a methodology that can be codified and then communicated to other people. I don't know if I believe that's true. I know that when I work as a dramaturg, it's a liquid process and it's at least 50 percent instinct. . . . you don't talk *to* a playwright. You talk *with* a playwright, or you don't have a conversation at all.
>
> —John Glore, "How to Talk to a Playwright"

Dramaturgy is a process of artistic discovery and creation that intersects many creative disciplines, and a dramaturg is a specialist in that process. Having discussed the history and philosophy of dramaturgy and created a frame for the development of dramatic analysis (the dramaturg's most central skill), we are able to discern that there is a method to that process, a mechanism that can be described, if not simply, then at least fairly clearly and logically. Now, finally, we can begin to see how the dramaturg can *apply* all of this knowledge into practice and to be an agent of Aristotelian phronesis, applying that practical wisdom to the creation of enlightening, harmonious, powerful, affecting, and significant theater.

Dramaturgs enter the profession in many ways. There is certainly no "set path" for advancement in the field, but it is likely that the first paying job a new dramaturg will get, and most of the subsequent ones, will have to do in some way with the development of new plays, so that seems as good a place as any to begin a discussion of professional practice.

In the United States, a new-plays movement has persisted since the 1960s that is deeply committed to fostering the works of emerging playwrights and in workshopping new work by established playwrights. Theaters foster new plays in many ways, including:

- Specifically soliciting new scripts for production
- Sponsoring new-play competitions
- Hosting in-house writer's workshops
- Providing staged readings for plays in development
- Providing resources to facilitate established playwrights to develop their pieces

Other companies, usually those with an explicit political agenda and an experimental aesthetic philosophy, will devise plays from an in-company process of creative collaboration, and others will create documentary dramas out of news and other nonfiction sources. There is also a great deal of interest in adapting established scripts into new forms. The dramaturg's task in these situations is to spearhead a process that cultivates the script toward a production of some kind—usually in phases. Since the late 1990s, dramaturgs have come to be considered more or less indispensable for this kind of work, and this field provides some of the best (and most regular) opportunities for dramaturgs to participate in the evolution of American drama. Many dramaturgs, particularly those who are playwrights themselves, find this kind of work to be rewarding and exciting, and many dramaturgs become specialists in new-play development. The four kinds of new-play Development are working with playwrights, devised theater, documentary theater, and adaptation.

Working with Playwrights: Forging an Alliance

Working with a new play is the ghost-lighting equivalent of navigating a ship into unexplored waters. There is no helpful guide for you and no map scribbled by those who have come before. Neither the dramaturg nor the playwright knows exactly what's out there, but there the script must go, and the dramaturg's job is to help the script get there in one piece. There are some institutional guidelines, however. If you are hired as a new play dramaturg, you will generally be expected to do three things:

- Prepare the script for a preliminary production (usually a staged reading)
- Facilitate the artistic relationship between the playwright and the producing agency (especially with the director)
- Help the playwright get and assimilate the most useful knowledge possible from the production

It's important to remember that there is no clear model for working with playwrights, but as with directors, the relationships that dramaturgs develop with particular playwrights can be quite rich and can last throughout professional lifetimes. As John Glore describes in the epigraph, each relationship is different, and it's half instinct. In the pages that follow, I attempt to detail what the other half can sometimes look like.

Years ago, there was a lot of suspicion towards dramaturgs from playwrights in the United States. Some playwrights thought of dramaturgs as people who did not write plays and yet held themselves up as advisors to those who could, or as dusty academics who didn't understand the difference between a "good" play and a "well-crafted" one, or as people too divorced from the proper sociocultural contexts to properly understand what the writer was trying to do, or as interlopers who would try to seize control of the play's creation. Other playwrights, however, welcomed dramaturgs as champions of their work and as valuable sounding boards and collaborators in development. These days, dramaturgs are known to have a lot of exposure to theater *practice*, and the best new-play dramaturgs are deeply engaged ones who are as committed to the playwright's mission as the playwright, who use their skills in dramatic analysis as the *beginning* of their process, not the end, and who bring to the table immense critical acumen and broad knowledge sharply focused by the production realities of the art. Also, many dramaturgs are also playwrights or directors themselves. Playwrights and directors both have come to recognize the value of having a multiply skilled ally around during the new-play development process.

Established playwrights usually have their own ideas about how they like to work with dramaturgs—if lucky enough to be paired early in your career with an established playwright, take your cues from him or her. You'll probably learn a lot, particularly if you are just starting out. For a new playwright, however, working with a dramaturg can be initially very intimidating. Inexperienced writers who don't understand the dramaturg's function well may fear that a dramaturg will try to guide the script in a way the playwright doesn't wish it to go or that if they don't get along, the dramaturg will give a bad report to the artistic director. This can manifest itself in trepidation or hostility. In the first meeting, you and the playwright should agree on some "ground rules" as clearly as you can—the more clarity exists in a relationship between a playwright and dramaturg, the more successful it will be. Again, there is no hard-and-fast rule, but the dramaturg should inform the playwright that the dramaturg is at the service of the play; it is the dramaturg's job to help the playwright prepare the script for production, to ask constructive questions, to give advice, and to facilitate exchanges with the director and the rest of the production team, not to take over the writing process. In fact, the dramaturg isn't going to do any writing on the script at all.

A great deal of very knowledgeable debate, particularly in the United Kingdom and Germany, is going on about how much influence a dramaturg should have in the writing process. Is the dramaturg the writer's pal, nurturing him or her gently along to production? Or is he an acknowledged authority, like a professor, there to give direction? There are ups and downs to both of these characterizations, of course. In my experience working on both sides of the table in the United States, what a playwright really needs from a dramaturg is neither a buddy nor a teacher but an *ally*. Playwriting can be a very isolating process, particularly if the playwright is covering new territory or trying something controversial. The playwright needs to know that the dramaturg will get right in there alongside to fight those battles. The playwright needs to be able to trust the dramaturg not only to be there to support the good changes but also to provide honest, engaged criticism for the improvement of the script. The playwright needs someone in the trenches who understands what he or she is trying to say and helps to say it in a way that will work on stage. The playwright needs an objective, critical eye, one that is smart and informed by years of training in theater history, theory, and practice. "Attaboys" and "attagirls" are all well and fine, but at the end of the day, what we're looking to create is a script that will stand up to the immense pressures of production, and a dramaturg who is an engaged but critical ally rather than an intimate buddy or an aloof professor will be better able to predict and prepare for the worst. Conversely, a dramaturg may have spent a lifetime developing a powerful theatrical vision of his or her own, but if he or she unduly imposes it upon the playwright, the play will, at best, not belong to the playwright anymore. The key here, as in most of the dramaturg's relationships, is achieving the proper balance.

When a theater decides to foster the development of a new script, it brings in the dramaturg for the same reason a shipping company would hire a navigator: to protect its investment. Putting up a new play is risky—it requires time, money, personnel hours, and physical space, and the costs of these resources add up. And while you may discover the next Sam Shepard whose play will cause dump trucks full of money to arrive on your loading dock, the chance of that happening is actually pretty slim, nor is it particularly looked for (a play doesn't have to be *True West* to be worth producing). The dramaturg's presence provides a contact point for the theater and a skilled critical eye to help the playwright make the best out of the work at hand.

Most dramaturgs these days have some experience in playwriting, maybe a lot. An aspiring dramaturg should definitely take at least some playwriting classes, because the more he or she understands what the playwright's mission is, the more effective that person will be as a new-play dramaturg. Conversely, working as a dramaturg is one of the best ways of improving skills as a playwright—helping someone else navigate the perils of script craft gives great insights about one's own. Many established playwrights, like Glore and Tony

Kushner, regularly act as dramaturgs because the two skills inform and amplify one another and help playwrights form lasting, supportive relationships with one another as well. The important thing is not to confuse the two positions; think of *dramaturg* and *playwright* as two different hats to wear. When acting as dramaturg on a new play, never pursue the thought "I could write this play a lot better than this playwright." You couldn't, because it wouldn't be *this* play. If you want to write a play, go and write a play—who's stopping you? But if you are acting as dramaturg on someone else's play, do that with the total commitment and dedication that *you* would want from a dramaturg working on *your* play.

One more note of caution. Some playwrights have complained that the dramaturgs they work with don't have the proper cultural backgrounds to understand the writer's work. When the playwright is attempting to capture a particular ethnic, historic, or community experience that the dramaturg simply has not had, this can be a problem. However, the culturally specific plays of writers like Luis Valdez, August Wilson, and David Henry Hwang have attracted a much-broader audience than Hispanic Americans, African Americans, and Asian Americans, respectively. Their well-deserved fame has a lot to do with their ability to comment on the *human* condition even as they specifically talk only about one aspect of it. No doubt there is a lot of meaning in the *Oresteia* that, not being Ancient Greeks, we are never going to fully understand, but there's an awful lot of great stuff there that speaks directly to us as if the intervening millennia were nothing more than a gossamer veil. The dramaturg is supposed to be a bridge—in this case, between the playwright and the potential audience. A dramaturg who has the same background as a playwright can be extremely useful, but a playwright can take tremendous advantage of a dramaturg from a different background by asking, "Is this getting through to you?" It is possible be *overqualified* to dramaturg a play; if you know much more than the playwright about the topic of a play, you may have a hard time developing the necessary objectivity to work as a dramaturg. By the way, here is one of the places that critical theory comes in most handy. Critical theory trains the mind to extend beyond the narrow lived experiences of the thinker. It enables us to *philosophize*, which is to consider the human condition from more positions than the one that fate decreed we must occupy. That's more or less the point of philosophy, and a dramaturg with that kind of ability can be a powerfully ally to almost any writer.

The Process

New-play dramaturgy begins when a dramaturg is brought in to work with a particular playwright. Sometimes, this playwright is the winner of a contest that the theater sponsored to solicit new plays, but he or she might also be someone who submitted a play to the theater for production, or the theater may have commissioned a more established playwright to write for the theater. Either way, an in-house dramaturg has probably already been exposed to the writer's work, either as a judge for the contest or as a preliminary reader of a draft of the script (perhaps the very one who suggested that the play be produced). Whatever the case may be, the organization is now prepared to commit its resources, and the dramaturg's task is to help the playwright prepare for the next step. Before beginning, if possible, read anything else this playwright has written to get a sense of where the writer is coming from.

In the trenches, working with the playwright has three steps, which match neatly with Goethe's 3:

- *Analysis. What is the playwright trying to do?* The first task of the dramaturg is to *read* the new play, and I mean *really* read it. Go back to this book's chapters four and five. Do a full-bore analysis of each of the play's beats, and an equally rigorous analysis of how the beats fit together to create a total plot. Is the play Aristotelian/climactic? Or does it employ some other structure or variant? Analyze character breakdowns: isolate motives and analyze decisions. Identify the various lines of conflict. Is the playwright thinking about individual problems, social ones, spiritual ones, or what? Is the play an allegory? Is it funny or serious? Finally, do thematic analysis. What is the playwright trying to say?

- *Diagnosis. Did he or she do it?* Is the action of the play clear? Is it easy or hard to follow the plotlines? Is it clear or unclear how the playwright's ideas are communicated by the character's actions? Are the characters presented coherently? Is their behavior consistent? Is the dialogue cohesive and fluid? Do the various elements of the production integrate harmoniously? Is it original, or has it been done before? How well do the play's themes come across? Is there reason to suspect that any of it has been plagiarized?[1] Then, ask questions about the practicality of the piece. Is it producible? Can it be cast? Can it be directed? Can actors act these roles? Can the sets, lights, and costumes be designed and built?[2] Is there anything in it that might be considered controversial?

- *Evaluation. Is it worth producing?* Start with Why This Play Now? (WTPN). Can you articulate why this play is worth doing right now? If not, what needs to change in order to make it worth doing? If yes, how can it be made sharper, clearer, or more moving in the time left? Remember, many of the greatest plays in American theater history had early productions that enabled the writer to make revisions.

Just like when writing a performance review, it is important to keep these questions as separate as possible. A good dramaturg has an open, questioning mind. If the play is untraditional, noncohesive, incoherent, ambiguous, or controversial, that hardly means that it is automatically "not good": that's exactly the kind of narrow-minded theater criticism that Gotthold Ephraim Lessing deplored so strongly all those centuries ago. Chaos, to paraphrase dramaturg Jayme Koszyn, may come to rescue us.[3] Today, we have but to consider Euripides, Shakespeare, Ibsen, August Wilson, Constance Congdon, Sarah Ruhl, Sarah Kane, and many others to see that great playwrights break rules. But, and it's a big but, *not at random*. Of course, each play is different, but the more self-aware the playwright is about the choices he or she is making, the better the play will work in front of an audience.

By asking the above questions of the script, you should be able to develop a pretty good idea of where you and the playwright can start your work. You need to *earn* your alliance, and you do this by perceiving the playwright's intentions as best as possible. A word of warning: if you can't find something to love in the play, you will likely be unable to forge the necessary alliance with the writer, and you should try to excuse yourself from the project. As Glore says, "If you don't have that commitment to the project, you have no business trying to exert an influence on it."[4]

Once the intense analysis is done and you feel that you have a strong connection with the script and a fairly deep sense of the writer's intentions, meet with the playwright. Particularly when just starting a relationship with a playwright, your main focus should be (like always) to ask questions, and like all the questions you ask as a dramaturg, these should be pointed, direct, and constructive, designed to help the playwright clarify *what* he or she is trying to say, and *why*, and *how* best to say it. Many dramaturgs find that it puts the writer at ease to begin the conversation by stating what they like most about the play, in the process summarizing the play's action and themes and asking if that was what the writer meant. Done gently, this summary can reinforce the playwright's senses both of maintaining control and of your commitment to realizing the script's potential, while helping the playwright focus on some possibilities for improvement. I am opposed to the idea that playwrights need to be treated like hothouse orchids, coddled and gently misted—playwrights are tough (or they should be), and my experience on both sides of the table has always been that once the playwright knows that the dramaturg is an ally and a supporter, the level of serious (but engaged) criticism the playwright can receive is actually pretty extensive. Let the playwright know it is okay to mix it up a little, even to argue. After all, the criticism a playwright gets from a dramaturg is *nothing* compared to what critics might say about the play in the media (positive *and* negative), and that's one of the storms that a dramaturg is helping the playwright to weather.

Working toward Production

Once you have established an alliance and gone over the script with the writer, from here on in it's largely a question of using your own instincts and judgment (honed by your analytical skills, historical knowledge, and philosophical acumen) for the remainder of the process. It helps a lot to keep your eyes on the prize, which is preparing the play for its next encounter with an audience. Here are some broad guidelines for this next step:

- DO question! And requestion!
- DO share your concerns about the road ahead; point out potential problems and crises.
- DO reinforce your commitment to the play.
- DO know when to shut up and listen to the writer.
- DO help the writer answer questions by drawing on your own skills as a researcher, philosopher, and lover of drama.
- DO admit when you are wrong or don't know something.
- DON'T tell the writer how to solve a problem.
- DON'T write any of the script yourself.

This last point is very important (see "Maintaining Boundaries" below). Remember that the dramaturg's most important goal in this process is helping the playwright to find his or her voice—that is, to be able to articulate what, why, and how. The tight wire that the dramaturg walks in this relationship is balancing the level of input. You don't take over the process, but on the other hand you do not serve the playwright well by utterly subverting your knowledge, instincts, and skills. After all, you got into this position, ostensibly, because you know a little something (both practical and theoretical) about rendering drama from page to stage, particularly in different aesthetic, cultural, social and political contexts. Many playwrights have this knowledge as well, but a dramaturg brings something to the table that the playwright cannot: objectivity (or we might say *philosophy*). That's why, as is the case with your relationship with the director (and everybody else), it's important to keep your own ego out of it and concentrate on the big picture of the production and its place in the ongoing conversations of our art. The sense of fulfillment and satisfaction will come when you see that you've helped your ally accomplish his or her goal and that you've ghost-lit him or her through the uncharted territory, for with that knowledge comes the realization of one more small victory that contributes to your greater mission as a dramaturg: improving the theater culture of your community, as Aristotle demanded.

Apart from working closely with the playwright, dramaturgs often find themselves called upon to act as intermediaries between the writer and the rest of the production team, particularly the director. Again, take this task on a case-by-case basis—most directors and playwrights are not too bad at dramaturgy themselves, so sometimes the *knowledge* can be redundant, but the *perspectives* rarely are (and remember, redundancy is productive). Nevertheless, relationships between directors and playwrights are often fraught with tension, and this is particularly true when new scripts are being produced. The playwright wants to see a "faithful" first production, while the director wants to "interpret" the script according to the dictates of his or her own artistic sensibility. The dramaturg (as the one with the least ego involvement) can often act as a representative of both parties, fostering the amicable (or at least functional) collaboration that is indispensable to theatrical production.[5]

Maintaining Boundaries

Because the skill sets of dramaturgy and playwriting overlap so often, the professions tend to attract the same kinds of people—passionate, smart, text-oriented people who understand both writing and the translation of writing into performance. If in the past the problem was dramaturgs and playwrights not getting along, the danger now seems to be that dramaturgs and playwrights will get along *too well*. This is particularly true as the avant-garde is again flexing its muscles in the United States, and cutting-edge collaborative companies generate performance scripts in wildly untraditional ways. But in the mid-1990s, a case of a dramaturg and playwright getting too close shook both disciplines, and it is important to examine this case now so as to become aware of the perils that attend.

The events surrounding the development of the blockbuster musical *Rent* were deeply painful to the dramaturgical and playwriting communities of the United States. I have no wish to reopen the case here, or to go into great detail about these unfortunate matters, or to derive any new conclusions. The court documents and the reactions of the various communities are easily accessible online and in periodicals. I only summarize them here.

In 1994, the New York Theatre Workshop mounted a studio production of *Rent* and after getting feedback from various parties, expressed a desire to produce the show Off-Broadway, provided that some significant improvements were made. The workshop hired Lynn Thomson as a dramaturg to work with the author, Jonathan Larson, paying her a fee for her services. At the time, *Rent*, a modernization of *La Boheme*, was considered a minor show at best. For many months, Thomson and Larson collaborated intensively on the project, and in October of 1995, a new script emerged that all observers agreed was substantially, even radically different from the previous version. NYTW was pleased, and production began in December of 1995. Lamentably, Larson passed away in January of 1996 and would not live to see the fruits of this labor. The show opened on February 13 and moved to Broadway on February 26, where it became one of the most successful runs in American theater history, netting a Pulitzer Prize and even spawning a hit movie. Suddenly, a lot of money was at stake.

Thomson asserted that she herself had actually written a certain percentage of the script and in 1998 sued to be recognized as a coauthor and for an appropriate share of the show's profits. The court case that ensued was highly publicized, and some of the nation's most celebrated dramaturgs and playwrights appeared as witnesses, including Kushner, Craig Lucas, Morgan Jenness, Mark Bly, and Anne Cattaneo. The judge found that Thomson had made what amounted to a "copyrightable contribution" to the script, but because the details of her working relationship with Larson were so unclear (and Larson was, tragically, unavailable to clarify matters), she should not be awarded legal coauthorship. The case was ultimately settled out of court, but the New York theater community and dramaturgy as a whole were left shaken and divided.

Elsewhere in this book, I have written (in agreement with others) that the metamorphic, indefinable, and even marginal position of the dramaturg in the American theatre is something to be celebrated and even cherished, because that's what gives dramaturgs dynamic fluidity and a philosopher's ability to let their egos fall by the wayside. But here are seen the perils of that fluidity. Thomson's contention was that she was only seeking fair remuneration for her labor and asserted that had he lived to see what the financial rewards would be, Larson would have made a provision for her that would have compensated her fairly; the defendants argued that Larson never thought of Thomson as a coauthor and that no contractual basis for such a relationship existed.

Again, I have no wish to make any assertion that one of the sides of this case was justified, and one was not. I only remark on it because the outcome of the case has had a significant impact on the professional status of dramaturgs. One result of this highly publicized case has been that dramaturgs are now usually made to sign contracts that stipulate the dramaturg's work as work-for-hire, which means that the dramaturg is relinquishing claims to royalties or other future remunerations.

The lesson of *Thomson v. Larson* for dramaturgs entering the profession is simply this: among the questions a dramaturg must ask is whether the contractual obligations are being exceeded when working with the playwright. The dramaturg's job is to assist the playwright, not to do the playwright's job for him or her. This can be a tough call, but the question of "Am I making a 'copyrightable contribution' to this play?" is one that must remain in the forefront of the dramaturg's mind, because he or she will likely not be able to claim coauthorship later. A dramaturg must maintain an engaged objectivity to work as a dramaturg. If in a situation where work is feeling more like coauthorship than dramaturgy, the dramaturg must either excuse him- or herself from the project or renegotiate status. Once on board as a joint author, a dramaturg's entire relationship to the production changes, and so should the remuneration. This is the dramaturg's responsibility to work out, but remember a change in status might not always be to one's financial benefit. Dramaturgs usually get paid up-front; playwrights rarely do.

As if that weren't complex enough . . .

Devised Theater

Since the late 1800s, some theater artists have experimented with finding ways of generating performance "scripts" in a collaborative, ensemble way. One of the influential progenitors of this movement was Antonin Artaud (1895–1948). A director, critic, theorist, and visionary, Artaud's "Theatre of Cruelty" was envisioned as one that would not be a spectacle to be consumed but rather a sort of communion ritual to be participated in. Although he founded his ideas on Marxist principles about the purpose of art, Artaud split with the politically left surrealists when he insisted upon putting theater into a strongly metaphysical context (outside the bailiwick of dialectical materialism). For Artaud, theater was not mimetic but actually a completely different form of reality that is poorly understood by our logical, individualistic society and much better understood by "primitive" and collectivist cultures. His theater would present itself as a kind of excursion to a primal state, one that would induce delirium and therapeutic exorcisms in the audience, who would participate in the creation of the piece. Such a theatrical experience could rely neither on texts nor on intellectual interpretation but instead would rely on inspiration and transcendent spontaneity.

Visionary or crackpot (or both), Artaud's dramaturgy became a dominant guiding force for the emerging European avant-garde and an American neo-avant-garde that would follow in its footsteps. These companies, which in America include but are certainly not limited to the Open Theatre, the Living Theatre, the Ontological-Hysteric, the Bread-and-Puppet, and the Wooster Group, have all developed methods for putting performances together that do not rely on an individual playwright to act as "author."

In their 2008 book, Cathy Turner and Synne K. Behrndt define a devised performance as one for which "the performance text is, to put it simply, 'written' not *before* but *as a consequence of* the process."[6] In other words, instead of direct-ing the rehearsal, the text emerges *from* (and is therefore directed by) rehearsal.

The results of such a process can be quite extraordinary, but the process and the dramaturg's role in it are hard to describe because each performance group has its own process. It is possible to make a few generalizations, however, and important to do so because the devising process is one to which dramaturgy is particularly and explicitly central.

In a conventional performance, the script is the structural and ideological frame upon which the performance is built, and the dramaturgy is the approach that guides the construction of the one upon the other. In a devised piece, the *dramaturgy* itself is the frame, and the script is a consequence of it. From a ghost-lighting perspective, it is as if the company is creating the terrain even as they explore it. Perception is equal to creation. It is utterly inconceivable to devise a piece of theater without some explicit dedication to some kind of dramaturgical approach; without it, the company would go off the deep end and never return (and this does happen). When it works well, everyone involved in the process is actively and consciously collaborating in the dramaturgy, so having an expert on dramaturgy who is intimately involved is essential. A canny dramaturg recognizes that someone needs to keep an eye on the big picture, which frees the director and actors up to work on the individual moments.

One word of caution: experimental companies are typically united by a common ideology or set of principles, whether political, metaphysical, or aesthetic, and are often grounded in the shared lived experiences of the members, whether cultural, geographic, or religious. If a dramaturg does not share the value systems that bring the troupe together (or does not think he or she will share those values in short order), the dramaturg will likely serve poorly in the kind of facilitation dramaturgs provide in this context. On the other hand, if there are not a certain level of distance and objectivity from the creative process, the dramaturg will not be able to function as the translator of the troupe's ideas into a larger context, understandable by a wider audience. Again, the dramaturg walks a tight rope.

So what exactly does a dramaturg *do* when he or she finds him or herself in an empty space full of brilliant, passionate, cutting-edge actors and a like-minded, visionary, experimental director, all really excited but with no idea what comes next? Again, there is no hard and fast rule, because the process generates itself out of its own action. A devising rehearsal is the true garden of forking paths; Turner and Behrndt note, "If we could draw a map of a typical devising process, it might lead to a labyrinthine journey of blind alleys, dead ends, associative leaps, mysterious paths and links between passages."[7] But as dramaturgs *live* in such gardens, they should be quite at home showing their allies and collaborators the landmarks and sharing some secrets. It's going to be chaotic and irrational, but by comparing the writings of several dramaturgs who have worked on such processes,[8] I have assembled a basic list of tasks (or, at least, points to keep in mind) for dramaturgs working in this exciting creative atmosphere.

- *Facilitate the process of exploration.* A dramaturg does this partially by providing visual, historical, and contemporary research, just as for any production. But there are no particular "right" ways to take the development of this research into a text. The process is full of dead ends, false leads, sudden stops, unexpected triumphs, crossovers, and backtracks. Mistakes turn out to be brilliant. Accidents turn out to be the perfect solutions. Companies often find themselves returning to their first ideas after weeks of exploration. Keep an open mind as well as a critical eye to encourage the process.

- *Look for emerging patterns.* Research methodology and critical theory are all about training one's mind to see connections between things that would otherwise seem very disparate. Use those tools refined by hard work in the library here in rehearsal. Find similarities. Note when the process seems to dwell on a particular theme, idea, image, or moment. Uncover the hidden tunnels; if necessary, dig them yourself. From such connections, a dramaturg will perceive (and thereby create) the eventual shape of the whole, and it will enable suggestions of strategies for the next step. Some dramaturgs put these observations up on a corkboard, with index cards arranging the actions in a way that gradually suggests a cohesive whole, and discusses the board with the company. Once a structure begins to emerge, it will be clearer what gaps need to be filled. The ultimate structure of the piece should emerge naturally from the piece itself and need not be Aristotelian/climactic, but keep in mind that it will eventually need to communicate clearly to an audience.

- *Record the journey.* This is a critical task of the dramaturg in the devising process, even more so than in a traditional production, because one never knows in a devising process when the company is going to have to backtrack to the last crossroads and go the other way. Without a map of the area already explored, the dramaturg will have to rely on people's memories of a chaotic and unstructured process and invent new terrain and explore it all over again to get there. The dramaturg is the company's mapmaker as well as navigator. The dramaturg is not the production's secretary and if taking too many notes, is not really listening and engaged. Perhaps recording the rehearsal on video is the right thing to do, or have an assistant document the process in greater depth.

- *Watch in the place of the future audience.* One problem that devisers sometimes encounter is that stuff that makes perfect sense in rehearsal might make less sense to the audience (for several minutes of Artaud's radio broadcast *"Pour en finir avec le jugement de Dieu,"* he and his actors stand in a stairwell screaming at the top of their lungs, for instance). While the others submerge themselves completely in exploring the garden, a dramaturg's job is to keep consulting the map he or she is drawing and trying to see where it might be headed. What is this going to look like when it's finished to someone who wasn't privy to the process?

- *Ask questions.* The dramaturg's main task is if anything more important in this context. The question is WTPN, and the job is to constantly ask it of everyone involved, including the dramaturg, in the process. Why are we doing this? What do we hope to achieve? What is this going to mean to an audience? What does it mean to us? Does this choice make sense in context with these other choices? Where have we been? Where are we headed? What's working? What's not? Are we faithful to our original ideas? Have we moved on to something better, or do we need to go back to our first principles?

A final note of caution is warranted. In this context, the dramaturg is often called upon to do the work of a playwright; to actually transform the emerging patterns, scenes, and ideas into a performance text, weaving the moments together. This means writing, developing characters, and creating dialogue and action. And that's great, especially when the dramaturg is also a playwright. But here as in other new-play development situations, the dramaturg needs to be as clear as possible about ownership and attribution. Will the dramaturg be credited as the author of the eventual piece? If so, certain ownership rights attach. If the troupe isn't willing to give up that kind of ownership, they need to share equally in the labor of writing. If they can't or won't, the dramaturg needs to decide what credit and remuneration are appropriate to receive for the work put in.

Documentary Theater

All plays succeed to the extent that the audience finds them relevant and topical. But the idea of creating performances based on current events (as opposed to "history") is not really a new one. In his documentary-play anthology *Voicings*, Attilo Favorini traces the "documentary impulse" from the ancient playwright Phyrnicus (whose 492 BCE play *The Capture of Miletus* chronicled events of the Persian War) through the medieval era and the French Revolution up to today.[9] "Documentary theater" took on a unique character in the twentieth century as both the right and left wings of the avant-garde experimented with consciously using the theater as a way to spread the news (even as it comments upon it). A characteristic of the avant-garde, from whatever political leaning, was its Lessing-like desire to liberate itself from reliance on established texts and their authoritative interpretation. Like Artaud, an Italian group known as the Futurists sought to create a theater based on improvisation and intuition, one that would be grounded in the *now*, using cutting-edge technology and disdaining extensive preparation or attention to history. The progenitor and chief dramaturg of the Futurists, F. T. Marinetti, wrote his 1904 poem *Destruction* to "the Demon of Speed" that dissolves and remakes everything with its fearful passage and wrote in his 1913 *Futurist Manifesto* that his theater should involve commentary on current events and create "a more or less amusing newspaper."[10] Like Bertolt Brecht, Marinetti was interested in variety theater and cabarets, where he could communicate with ordinary people instead of the cultural elite that attended "highbrow" theater.

Prominent Russian director Vsevolod Meyerhold, meanwhile, was conducting some major groundbreaking experiments of his own in Moscow. In 1919, the Communist Party in Russia issued a decree advocating the public reading of the news accompanied by performances of various kinds (in the proper revolutionary context, of course). In response, Meyerhold created a Living Newspaper–style theater. In 1923, a theater troupe called the Blue Blouse, heavily influenced by Meyerhold's innovation, was formed by Russian journalists precisely to perform Living Newspapers ordinary workers around the Soviet Union.

Blue Blouse's work was improvisational and to some degree experimental in the Meyerhold fashion but within certain limits delineated by the Central Committee of the Communist Party. The actor-journalists would condense real newspaper stories into loose performance outlines in which they performed as easily recognizable stock characters (workers, bosses, and so on). The actors wore blue smocks like the factory workers, who composed their audience (hence the name). Blue Blouse was tremendously popular and even toured internationally but could not survive Stalin's brutal crackdown on the dissemination of information (and the government's promotion of Socialist Realism) and was disbanded in 1927. Before it did, however, it spawned Blue Blouse imitators all over the world (Hallie Flanagan saw them in Moscow, and the concept became vital to her own dramaturgy with Seki Sano, another Blue Blouse imitator who joined Flanagan in the United States after fleeing arrest in Japan). These performances required the evolution of a new international dramaturgy of documentary theater.[11]

One of these early dramaturgs was Jacob Levy Moreno, who wrote *Theatre of Spontaneity* in 1924, and trained his actors not merely to dramatize the news but to be investigative reporters themselves, seeking out the stories as material for their performances rather than reporting news that had been vetted by the authorities. He described this in 1946:

> An event, soon after it has happened, loses its news value. It has therefore a natural affinity to the form of the spontaneous drama, which requires for its unrehearsed, immediate form an equally spontaneous and immediate context, for instance the ever new and ever-changing social and cultural events that are flashed from moment to moment to the editorial office of a newspaper. In this sense, the living newspaper was not only dramatic, but rather sociodramatic.[12]

For Moreno, as John W. Casson observes, documentary theater was a means for stimulating spontaneous and ultimately therapeutic (socially and psychologically) acts in both the performers and the audience.

Moreno's troupe performed in New York in 1931. By then, many Living Newspapers were already active in the United States, some of them captained by artists who had been exposed to Brecht or Blue Blouse and who were trying to start a worker's theater in America. The pinnacle of the genre would be in the work of the Federal Theatre Project, but Casson reports that Moreno didn't much care for it and denounced it for its "lack of spontaneity and for trivializing and distorting his original concept. . . He may not have realized that, despite the similarity of the ideas, the source of the American Living Newspapers was (through Flanagan, Rice, and others) Blue Blouse."[13] Moreno was growing more concerned with the utility of his "spontaneous theatre" as a form of therapy, while Flanagan was more concerned about the possibility for enlightened political action, writing in 1969 in *Arena* that "the dramatization of the news stories had liveliness and vitality, the two short plays were skillful intensifications of social problems."[14] First Lady Eleanor Roosevelt described the movement as far more meaningful "than any amount of speeches which . . . I or even the President might make."[15] Using presentational, Brechtian staging techniques including music and dance, projections, and a disembodied "Voice of the Living Newspaper," American Living Newspaper theater would form a dramaturgical guide for activist (usually left-wing) documentary theater makers John Allen, Aloke Roy, and Augusto Boal.

Possibly the most influential of these was Boal, born in Brazil in 1931, who founded a radical form of political theater that was popular with dissident left-wing activists and artists in São Paulo in the 1960s. Associated with an equally radical social-education movement, Boal was considered a threat by the Brazilian government. In 1971, he was arrested, tortured, and exiled. In 1973, he wrote his influential dramaturgy *Theatre of the Oppressed*. This book starts with a detailed repudiation of Aristotle's *Poetics* as elitist and antirevolutionary and advocated a Hegelian performance that is more engaged, interactive, and confrontational. Dramaturgy of the Oppressed emphasizes breaking down the barriers between performer and audience and encourages audiences to stop the action and explore with the actors possible alternative choices that the characters might make to achieve a better outcome. One of the best-known techniques innovated by Boal is the "Invisible Theatre," in which performances take place in crowded public places without any prior warning. Initially devised as a way of staying out of jail while performing, invisible performances coax audiences to respond more freely and naturally than they would in the formal environment of the theater. In a 2005 interview on *Democracy Now!* Boal opined. "Everyone can do theater. Even actors. And theater can be done anywhere, even inside theater."[16]

From a dramaturgical perspective, documentary theater overlaps with "drama therapy" (the psychotherapeutic use of various kinds of role-playing) as well as "devised theater" somewhat but diverge from either in their explicitly political and educational mission. Today, documentary theater is growing in popularity, particularly as artists feel a growing need to respond to political crises. Recent theater plays tend to share a lot of elements with their predecessors: they are presentational rather than mimetic, are Brechtian rather than Aristotelian, and use projections, voice-overs, and other technologies. They are typically leftist politically, but there's no particular reason they have to be. They are sometimes authored by individual writers but are also assembled collectively by troupes.

Some of most interesting and popular creators of documentary theater of the past twenty-five years are:

- *Anna Deveare Smith*. Her play *Fires in the Mirror: Crown Heights, Brooklyn and Other Identities* (1993) chronicles the 1991 Crown Heights, Brooklyn, New York, race riots. For this play, Smith assembled and edited dozens of interviews she conducted with black and Jewish individuals connected with the riots, from nameless shadowy criminals to the Reverend Al Sharpton. The result is an astonishingly complete look at a moment of great violence and tragedy. In her 1991 stage show, Smith performed each interview as a short monologue. She repeated her documentary theater success in 1992 with *Twilight Los Angeles*, in 2000 with *House Arrest*, and in 2008 with *Let Me Down Easy*.
- *Porte Parole*. This Montreal-based, bilingual theater company, spearheaded by Annabel Soutar, created the award-winning 2005 *Seeds*. This documentary play chronicles the six-year legal battle between the global Monsanto Corporation and one unlikely Saskatchewan farmer.

- *Culture Clash*. This San Francisco–based Chicano/Latino company adapts personal interviews into cutting-edge satirical and revolutionary comedy. Their *Chavez Ravine*, which tells the story of the destruction of a poor Los Angeles community to make way for Dodgers Stadium, appeared at the Mark Taper Forum in 2003 to critical acclaim.
- *Tectonic Theater Project*. A collective troupe of multi-disciplinary dramaturgs fronted by Israeli playwright Moisés Kaufman, Tectonic is best known for *The Laramie Project*. After the brutal, homophobic murder of student Matthew Shepard in Laramie, Wyoming, in 1998, the company descended on the small town and conducted hundreds of interviews, which they compiled with news items, their own journals, and other materials. The result is a moving and celebrated text that has been performed around the world, from high-school and community theaters to Broadway, as a beacon of tolerance and understanding.

The process of transforming fragmentary materials into complete piece of documentary theater is really more of a dramaturgical task than it is one of playwriting. The troupe (or a single individual) must first research and collect documents of real-life facts and events. These can include:

- Newspaper items
- Editorials
- Interviews
- Diaries
- Trial transcripts
- Public-hearing transcripts
- Minutes from corporate meetings
- Declassified government documents (or classified ones, if you can get them and don't mind risking arrest)
- Radio and TV broadcasts
- E-mails, text messages, and other forms of electronic communication
- Speeches
- Laws, edicts, decrees, and papal bulls
- Anything else composed of real nonfictional material

Once gathered, the material requires refining in order to be presented as a theatrical event with a dramatic arc to it. Again, this is a dramaturgical task (even if a playwright is the one doing it) because it requires a clearly articulate methodology and a fidelity to the original material, and this in turn requires the brand of critical engagement and perpetual questioning that define what dramaturgy is. The beginning, middle, and end of documentary-theater is

WTPN. The end result is a piece of art, however, so bringing those dialogue skills (or bringing in a playwright, if you prefer) to bear in the service of the dramaturgical enterprise is necessary as historical events become enlisted as plot points, and real people get flattened into characters. Naturally, this process demands that artistic choices be made, and it is in those choices that the dramaturg articulates what exactly the WTPN of this piece of drama actually is. The end result is a passionate, politicized, performative retelling of these real-life events that offers a new perspective.

Adaptation

This chapter concludes with a very short section on a very complex and important aspect of the dramaturg's work: the adapting of canonical texts into new production contexts. There is a high demand for such texts—indeed, some of the great adaptations are ranked alongside their ancestors in terms of literary quality. Many texts that considered authentic stand-alones are adaptations of classical works—Eugene O'Neill's *Mourning Becomes Elektra*, for example.

Like generating devised theater and documentary theater, adaptation requires many of the skills of the playwright, but it is at its heart a dramaturgical activity. From a certain point of view, it could be considered the pinnacle of the dramaturg's art: the ultimate consummation of Why This Play Now in the complete reconstruction of a performance text. Of all the more complicated tasks a dramaturg undertakes, adaptation is unquestionably my personal favorite, as it gives me the chance to bring my skills as a researcher, a historian, a theorist, a critic, a teacher, and a playwright together.

Dramaturgs turn their hands to adaptation for a variety of secondary reasons, but the main reason derives from a need to retell a well-known, solidly established dramatic story in order to reveal some truth about it that has been obscured by its age, fame, production history, criticism, changes in production values or theatrical conventions, or any or all of these. Adaptation can do many things: it can unlock an immediacy and relevance to the play that has been lost (Chuck Mee's *Big Love* and Edward Kemp's *Nathan the Wise* are examples); it can reveal a radical truth subversive to the play itself that the author did not intend (as happens in Aimé Césaire's *Tempest* and Wole Soyinka's *Bacchae of Euripides*); or it can use an ancient story as a platform for a new dialectic of ideas (as in Mabou Mines's *Gospel at Colonus* and Ruhl's *Eurydice*).

I will not go into the process here in further detail, for two reasons. Firstly, as a cumulative peak of the dramaturg's art, adaptation requires nothing more than judicious and artistic application of all of the philosophies, analyses, and practical skills described in the preceding chapters. Secondly, I find that I am unable to add much of substance to what writing on adaptation already exists, most notably Susan Jonas's wonderful essay "Aiming the Canon at Now: Strate-gies for Adaptation" in *Dramaturgy in American Theatre: A Source Book*. Also, anyone interested in adaptation should secure a copy of Daniel Fischlin and Mark Fortier's *Adaptation of Shakespeare* (2000), which highlights the many options open to adapting well-known traditional texts to particular modern contexts. More resources on this subject can be found in appendix B.

Exercises

Go deep! Partner up with someone else, and each of you write a ten-minute play on any topic. When you are done with a complete draft of the play, give it to your partner, and take his or hers in turn. Begin a critical analysis of your partner's play, thinking of yourself as the playwright's ally in production. Use all your analytical skills, following Goethe's 3, to review the work. Does the play work by itself? Is it aesthetically cohesive and structurally sound? Can you answer WTPN? Now, spend a half hour with your partner discussing the play. Bring up these issues, and help the writer figure out what needs to be fixed and how. Then, switch, and have your partner dramaturg *your* play. When the process is complete, each of you write a two-to-three-page response about the process. How did your partner take your criticisms? How did it feel being the playwright? What techniques for creating alliances worked, and what didn't? Finally, share your papers with your partner, and discuss your insights about the relationship between playwrights and dramaturgs.

Go wide! Create a ten-minute Living Newspaper. Begin by reading today's newspaper and finding a story in the local or national news that you think is worth exploring. Use your own developing dramaturgy: what kind of issues are important to you? What do you think theater is for? Those questions will help you pick a stage-worthy topic. Research this story as deeply as you can. Collect news reports, interviews, court proceedings, and whatever documents you can find. Assemble them into a dramatic narrative, and fill in the gaps with your own speculation. Try to find a protagonist and an antagonist, and follow their struggles as the main arc of your piece. If you like, use the "Voice of the Living Newspaper" as a narrator.

Go long! Find a play written prior to 1800 or from a culture very different than your own. After doing a full analysis of the play and a production history, write an essay of no fewer than eight pages that argues for adapting the play into a more modern or more local context. First, lay out the evidence—the play, its impact in its time or place, and your overall analysis. Next, explain why there's a need for this play now, in your theatrical community. What insights does it grant about here and now? What challenges does it present to our way of thinking about its topic? What gaps of time and space will have to be bridged for it to work? Finally, map out the contours of your adaptation. How, specifically, will you bridge those gaps? What will have to happen to the play to make it charged and relevant for your envisioned audience? What problems does an adaptation like this generate, and how will you master them? Ground your work in an appropriate theoretical model. The more you use clear evidence and solid analysis, the stronger your adaptation argument will be.

8

The Company

A dramaturg is a man of letters who rashly interferes in the business of theatre.
—Edwin Zeydel

Edwin Zeydel's quotation is tongue-in-cheek, but it is a reminder that there is sometimes a gulf between a theatrical event that is artistically or socially relevant, on the one hand, and what makes money for a theater on the other. But a good dramaturg's "rash interference" can actually bridge this gap by providing a critical (but supportive) eye within the production process. The best troupes use dramaturgs the same way that a ship uses a navigator, as a resident expert in plotting a course from A to B, avoiding hazards known and unknown, and for finding the way again after getting lost. When working with the administration, cast, and crew of a production, here are some ways that dramaturgs are practically employed keeping their theatrical ships on course.

Working with the Artistic Director

Theaters in America employ many models of organizational hierarchies that provide chains-of-command for various types of decision making. Some Broadway houses and other commercial entities have different management structures than the approximately seventy-five theaters that are members of the League of Resident Theatres (LORT, the administrative organization to which most non-Broadway or "regional" American theaters belong). But generally speaking, LORT theaters follow a model that divides the company's responsibilities into departments, as shown in figure 2.

An *artistic director* (AD) is an individual typically hired by the theater's board of directors who is responsible for the artistic vision of a theater. The AD usually works hand-in-hand with a *managing director* who is responsible for

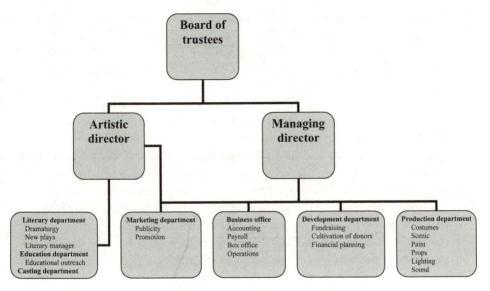

Fig. 2. Theater organization chart

the day-to-day business and audience relations. With the managing director, the AD plans the season, hires many of the artists, supervises the press materials, and supervises artistic decisions made by others. The artistic director is distinct from the director of an individual production, who is responsible for the artistic execution of a single production within a season. The director is the primary artistic voice of an individual production but is usually hired by (and reports to) the artistic director. In this model, dramaturgs are placed in the *literary department*, which reports to the artistic director. Most other departments are accountable, more or less, to both the artistic director and the managing director.

Some dramaturgs remain in residence year-round at a particular theater company, working not only in rehearsal but also closely with the artistic director. In the United States, the director of the literary department is often called *literary manager*, and this position involves the selection of scripts and a season, the cultivation of authors and audiences and education and outreach (although some theaters have a separate education department with its own director), and support of individual productions. The specific responsibilities made by a dramaturg in such a position depend on the nature of the company itself. The in-house dramaturg has to ask not just "Why this play now?" but "Why this play now HERE?" Different theaters have different identities and different contexts, and the dramaturg must take these issues into account. Usually, the in-house dramaturg or the literary manager reports directly to the artistic director as well. In concrete terms, the responsibilities of a literary manager or resident dramaturg require detailed knowledge of the general provenance of the theater's income (in terms of both patrons and audience) and the theater's mission.

Mission Statements

A mission statement is a prerequisite for the legal creation of any not-for-profit organization. The board of trustees is mainly responsible for keeping the organization financially afloat and following this mission. In this way, the board represents the interests of the community that funds the theater with its taxes, and the board hires the artistic director, the managing director, and other senior staff specifically to realize the mission. Even if the artistic product of a theater is very good, if the theater does not maintain its mission, it runs the risk of alienating its audience and donors, thereby losing its funding. Theater missions are generally broken down into broad categories:

- *Artist driven.* The theater's mission is to advance the work of a single artist or artistic vision (possibly that of the theater's founder, or of a major figure like Shakespeare or Shaw).
- *Management driven.* The theater's mission is determined by the artists who brought the company into being (such as the Steppenwolf Theatre in Chicago).
- *Community driven.* The theater's mission is a direct response to a need from the community (most children's theaters have this kind of mission).

A dramaturg ought to have a detailed understanding of the theater's mission and how it was executed in past seasons. This information is not difficult to find; it is usually printed in the programs, kept in archives, or posted on the theater's Web site. The dramaturg helps to contextualize the work in productions and with audiences within that larger view. Understanding the theater's mission doesn't mean that the dramaturg needs to abandon his or her own artistic vision; it would hardly be useful to become an aesthetic philosopher only to be a cipher for someone else's ideas. Remember, the dramaturg is the one who questions, and the theater's mission is, like everything else, subject to that questioning. But the dramaturg needs to work within the company, always striving to improve the mission and to refine and clarify its goals and practices.

Representation in Rehearsal

The dramaturg may be called upon to act as a representative of the theater's mission in the rehearsal hall. This representation is necessary because theaters make promises to their patrons and audiences, and it is part of the AD's job to make sure those promises are fulfilled. Imagine, for instance, that the theater's budget comes from a big grant that stipulates that the productions will have certain qualities; that the theater will do a certain number of plays by African American authors, for instance, or will do plays about scientific advancement, or will educate audiences about AIDS.[1] Working conscientiously in this manner allows dramaturgs also to develop close relationships with the theater's regular audience. A director, often visiting for the first time, can check in with the dramaturg as a sort of mobile history of the house to gauge how some choice or other will be received. The dramaturg can also provide a rich basis for collaboration by suggesting innovative choices that will engage this particular audience. Dramaturgs also have a responsibility to defend the intellectual and artistic integrity of the scripts they encounter, and sometimes, of playwrights themselves if they are present.

Negotiating these relationships is sometimes pretty tricky. The dramaturg can damage the production process if he or she is too willing to stifle the creativity of the production team in the service of the theater's mission but can also run the risk of alienating the audience or the patrons (or being unfaithful to a text or playwright) if he or she is too lax in representing these concerns.[2] Generally speaking, the dramaturg should be committed to promoting debate rather than repressing it and to acting as a mediator between the various concerns, with an eye on the big picture of how the work of the company affects and is affected by aesthetic, philosophical, and social conditions. The dramaturg has an ethical responsibility to be faithful to these high ideals.

Season Selection

A chief task of the literary manager is in helping the AD choose the season, which is again a process of negotiating between the needs of the house, the personnel, and the art of drama itself. Literary managers have a responsibility to provide the AD with ideas for production. Therefore, literary managers read a lot of scripts, including those that the artistic director is considering, new submissions to the theater, those that members of the company particularly want to do, and those that seem particularly topical or ripe for production. A good literary manager also has an ear to the ground and keeps up with theatrical trends, watches the behavior of other theaters, and reads the newspaper a lot to stay current with the spirit of the times, all so he or she can present material to the AD for the season-selection process.

These choices also depend on the nature of the theatrical company. Theaters choose programming according to the demographics of their patronage. A commercial house is primarily interested in making money for its producers and so has a responsibility to choose plays that will bring in big audiences. A national or "people's theater" company is funded by the government and so is responsible to the people of the nation (at least, insofar as those people are genuinely represented by the government officials who oversee the theater); a theater like this chooses plays that raise national consciousness about particular issues or engages in cultural diplomacy with other countries. A small community theater is focused on its local audience and its membership. An academic or university theater, funded by student tuitions, makes choices that are largely pedagogical (that is, concerned with the education and edification of students). Each approach has its own benefits and hindrances, and it is part of the dramaturg's job to maximize the potential enrichment of the company's particular audience.

Creating a Dossier

Different theaters have different submissions protocols, but once the dramaturg has found a play he or she would like to see in next season's lineup, the next step should be the production of a *play dossier*. These can take many forms, but a good dramaturg will create dossiers composed of the following:

- A *production history.* This includes a critical-response summary, copies of reviews, significant revivals, and production stills or other images if available (this is not applicable, of course, for a new play) (see chapter 7).
- An *authorial biography.* A quick summary of the facts of an author's life and a description of the impact that author has had on the theater (use the biographies in chapter 2 as a model) are included.
- A formal *letter to the artistic director.* This letter is a formal document proposing a script for production (see the next paragraph for details).

The more detailed the letter to the AD is, the more useful it will be to him or her in the play-selection process. Not every AD requires this level of formality, but keep this skill in practice anyway: a well-crafted letter to the AD conveys professionalism and insight and becomes the seed of later work. A good letter to the AD should include the following:

- A *plot summary*, based on one's own analysis of the play's action (see chapter 4) with a discussion of the play's major themes
- A preliminary *theoretical outline*, that is, a critically engaged concept of how to approach the script
- A cast breakdown
- An articulation of any significant design or production challenges, including to do with casting
- A discussion of the larger *sociopolitical context* of the play
- An articulation of WTPN that is specific to this theater

Below is a sample letter to the artistic director that came out of a class exercise, as a model for this kind of project.

OCTOBER 15, 2006
TO: ELIZABETH BRADLEY, ARTISTIC DIRECTOR
CARNEGIE MELLON SCHOOL OF DRAMA
210 PURNELL CENTER FOR THE ARTS
5000 FORBES AVENUE
PITTSBURGH, PA 15213

DEAR PROFESSOR BRADLEY,

I would like to formally request that you consider Terrence McNally's play *Corpus Christi* for inclusion in our 2007–2008 season. *Corpus Christi* is a retelling of the gospel life of Christ story set in modern day Corpus Christi, Texas. The catch with this retelling is that the Jesus character (Joshua) and his 12 apostles are portrayed as gay men. The story follows Joshua from his birth in a seedy hotel room, through his very close relationship with Judas and the gathering of his apostles, to his brutal murder at the hands of his childhood bullies.

I think this show would be perfect for a performance at Carnegie Mellon University because this play has a very bold message. It uses scripture passages filled with Christ's words of love and acceptance for all people and juxtaposes them with the Church's arguments against homosexuality. However, it does this in a very subtle way. When it was first performed by the Manhattan Theatre Club in 1997, the play caused more than a few waves, including high-profile public protests from the Catholic League for Religious and Civil Rights, and threats of violence against the theater, its staff, and the playwright. The Manhattan Theatre Club elected to cease production, but relented when several well-known playwrights (including Tony Kushner) threatened a boycott. 2000 protesters appeared on opening night. However, after so much hype was created by so many parties, some without having read the play, many critics came away disappointed with the show, noting that it was not the bold smack in the face of Christianity it was made out to be. In all reality, it has a very loving message. The characters have "no tricks up our sleeves. No malice in our hearts." The play doesn't, in the end, attack Christianity or show Joshua's love of his disciples in a crass or gratuitous manner. There is even a wedding of two of Joshua's followers onstage, performed by Joshua himself.

Difficulties in staging this at Carnegie Mellon are not technical at all; the show is performed on an almost empty stage with two benches for the actors to sit on and very sparse scenic props. Perhaps the only issue with this show would be the cast of 13 male actors. The Drama School does have more male actors than female actors, but I know it is difficult to cast only male actors in a show.

The show has caused protest from fundamentalist religious groups at many revivals, and we could likely expect a protest here, in the largely Catholic city of Pittsburgh. I consider this a reason to do this play now, for our audience, because frankly this play terrifies me. As a devout Catholic, simply reading this play was very difficult. Although it rubs against the grain of everything I've been taught, I cannot in good conscience find grounds to argue against it. It brings to the surface the personal conflicts I have with what I've been taught and the people I know. I think this play is important because theater often isn't terrifying anymore. We need more plays that shake up our beliefs and encourage discussion of controversial issues that most people prefer to ignore and sweep under the rug of affected tolerance. This play is especially important for our audience, the students of Carnegie Mellon. They are at a time in their lives when many of their beliefs are being tested and defined, and they are at an age where they must learn acceptance of people who are different from them. Also, I do not think I am being judgmental when I say that the issue of homosexuality is one that is especially prominent in our school community. This play could be a message from our students that would help encourage understanding and acceptance in lieu of fear and rejection. I think that this show would be most effective with audience discussion with the actors after the show, facilitated by the dramaturg, to begin an open dialogue among the students that will help the message of the play to continue beyond our theater doors.

Thank you, and good luck in the ongoing process of season selection.

Sincerely,
Rose Sengenberger
Dramaturg

Working with the Director

John Glore admonishes, "There is no room for arrogance among dramaturgs. God knows there's enough arrogance and ego in the theater as it is, so dramaturgs have to be the least arrogant and most self-abasing. Maybe that's concomitant with having one of the most over-arching views of the process."[3] At no time is it more important to remember that than at the moment when the dramaturg's focus shifts from a whole season to working as a production dramaturg on an individual show.

Productions are headed by the *production director* (usually just called the *director*). The relationship between director and dramaturg is possibly the most important one developed as a dramaturg. Directors are the people with whom dramaturgs will have the most extensive contact, the members of the troupe whose work is most similar to the dramaturg's own, and the ones who will rely on them most strongly. In a career as a dramaturg, it is essential to get some directing training to have a good idea what the process is like for the most important collaborator.

The director is responsible for the successful execution of the production. His or her primary job is to provide a vision for the production. The basic task a dramaturg does for a director is to help develop WTPN. In the best-case scenarios, the director and the dramaturg collaborate at every stage of the process, adapting the production's vision to emerging circumstances and research to ultimately create a powerful and relevant piece of theater. The director's task doesn't end there, of course—it's the director's job to provide leadership to a complex organization, to bring the various disparate elements of the production (including the dramaturgy) into a single cohesive whole, to deal with actors who sprain their ankles or get the wrong haircut, and to keep everybody from storming out at any given moment because of what *he* said about *her* at the last production meeting. In other words, many factors that have nothing to do with WTPN affect the production's success or failure, and the dramaturg is not responsible for these issues (although they should be recorded). Once in rehearsal, a dramaturg's job is not to direct the show nor to give notes to the director in the context of "If *I* were directing this show, here's what I'd do . . ." That's not the show the dramaturg is doing. In any event, the dramaturg has other fish to fry; and some of those are very big fish indeed.

Often, the first contact a dramaturg has with a director is shortly after the director has been hired. In preparation of this meeting, some dramaturgs compile a *director's packet*, which includes the following:

- A letter of introduction, which includes a description of what dramaturgy means at this particular house (what a dramaturg is expected to do in prerehearsal and in rehearsal, what kinds of outreach will be done, and whatever special skills the dramaturg brings to assist the director in developing and implementing his or her vision for the production)
- A well-theorized preliminary dramaturgical approach to the script, focused on answering WTPN with a sense of why the AD chose the play for the season (and including any suggestions for cutting)
- The play dossier created previously for the AD

- New contemporary and historical research, which includes:
  - Any notes, interviews, or commentary from the playwright
  - Scholarly articles and essays about the play and its context
  - Information about recent productions elsewhere, if possible
  - Information about the sociopolitical context in which the play was written and in which it is going to be performed
  - Anything else you think the director will need to get a jump on developing the vision
- Visual research, which includes:
  - Images relating to the sociopolitical context of the play's writing
  - Images relating to references within the play (historical figures, important places, pieces of art, whatever is appropriate)
  - Maps
  - Timelines

Be creative in producing these elements. If the director is any good, he or she will have started working on the dramaturgy of the production and will be developing ideas already. It is okay to be redundant, but this first meeting is also the dramaturg's opportunity to demonstrate that he or she can bring materials to the table that can significantly enrich the production for the director, the cast and crew, and the audience. Dramaturgs work best when they offer the director a collaborative menu of skills and when they demonstrate their acumen as aesthetic philosophers who are there to support, refine, and enhance the director's choices, not to control them.

As the weeks pass, the dramaturg should speak regularly with the director to share the results of new research and develop ideas for further exploration. As these collaborations continue, the dramaturg adds them to the director's packet, reframing them with commentary and notes as necessary or taking away materials that are no longer relevant (put these aside somewhere safe—for later).

A dramaturg can become a director's most intimate professional confidant, a sounding board for ideas, even an aesthetic conscience. Since the late-eighteenth-century team-up of Friedrich Schiller and Johann Wolfgang von Goethe at the Weimarer Hoftheatre, dramaturgs have been fostering relationships with directors that can turn into lifelong collaborations. Since increasingly many production directors started their own careers as dramaturgs (and vice versa), directorial relationships with dramaturgs are becoming much more "normal" and easier to negotiate. American theater is in the process of becoming smarter and more relevant, and directors have learned the value of having someone artistic, smart, well-read, and passionate as the go-to guy or gal, particularly when the going gets rough.

You may have noticed that the dossier created for the AD becomes the seed of the director's packet. This packet becomes the seed of what a dramaturg presents to the actors and the designers as well, and *that* work becomes the seed of the production casebook. There's a method to this madness, and it all starts (and ends) with WTPN.

Working with Designers

While a dramaturg is working with the director in developing WTPN, the director is also engaged in working with a design team. Dramaturgy is demonstrably central to theater design, as it is to all other aspects of theatrical production. In training programs, students of theater design learn how to dissect scripts and then resurrect them as productions, using research and other creative tools to bring the text to life; but some designers do not always put emphasis on this aspect of their work. Since the Renaissance, designers have acted as "conceptual engines" for the theater, responsible for generating many significant innovations. Some designers have radically altered the way the general public thinks about and consumes the theater, like Czech scenographer Joseph Svoboda (1920–2002), who developed the magic-lantern projection technique that allowed for new fluidity of visual ideas on stage; Russian designer George Tsypin (1954–), noted for colossal grand-scale architectural spectacles; and American costumer/puppeteer turned auteur Julie Taymor (1952–). So when working with designers, dramaturgs have a tremendous opportunity to exchange knowledge, viewpoints, and theoretical approaches to germinating scripts into living theater pieces. Like dramaturgs, designers rejoice in the redundancy of research because it is in that overlap that important thematic patterns appear. A dramaturg works best when he or she helps designers solidify those patterns, and a dramaturg adds depth and focus to the designer's research in order to help construct a conceptual framework for production.

In order to be effective, a dramaturg should have some familiarity with the basic principles and lexicon of design and some understanding of how designers go about realizing the unified aspirations of the production team. This knowledge increases ability to communicate with the designer and also makes a dramaturg a better collaborator.

In professional practice, a "design launch," where all the designers meet in a single large group to discuss their ideas and make plans, is ideal but fairly rare. If one exists, the dramaturg must be there to share the background information and contextualizing theories already assembled. If not, the dramaturg should make an effort to be available to the designers during preproduction for discussions about the production and the research developed in concert. The dramaturg's presence in these discussions is essential when the designers want to talk about WTPN or have questions about where to take the research. In the hectic modern world, the design team very rarely works together in the same building or even the same city, and the director will likely be only intermittently available, while the dramaturg is often in-house. If the dramaturg and the director have established a good, trusting, collaborative relationship, the dramaturg can act as a touchstone for ideas and explorations in the absence of the director. The dramaturg should privately discuss with the director how to proceed in this area, before the designers are brought in, and should discuss all interactions with the design team with the director. Remember, it is the director's job to integrate the totality of the production elements. Misinterpreting (intentionally or not) the director's vision or authority will jeopardize the production.

In production, dramaturgs can be even more valuable to designers, as unexpected questions come up. As the process goes on, the research direction moves from themes and concepts to more tangible solutions. The larger questions get translated into solid objects. What kind of gun does Hedda Gabler use in Ibsen's *Hedda Gabler*? What kind of stove appropriately sits in a Chekhovian parlor? What does an assegai look like? These are important questions and ones for which a dramaturg's input can be profoundly impactful on the overall production.[4]

Working with Actors

If dramaturgy is the blood of a production, as Mark Bly notes, then acting is its eyes, its ears, its breath, and its beating heart. Actors are what make theater alive. The acting of a production is arguably its most important quality, because if the acting is weak, the audience will not even notice how great the directing, design, or dramaturgy is. Playwright Dennis Reardon once told me, "Good acting can save bad playwriting, bad directing, bad design, and bad dramaturgy, but *nothing* can save bad acting."

How does dramaturgy inform the actor's project? This is a tricky question. Acting relies on instinct and split-second decisions as much as on extensive training, deep discipline, and unshakeable self-control. Acting training in many parts of the world teaches the actor to "look inward" for answers to questions of performance as much as to search the historical record. In addition, the production calendars of most United States companies are cruelly tight, and actors often feel as if they have barely enough time to learn their cues and blocking, much less engage in time-consuming analysis and contextualization. As a result of these factors, some actors (usually at the beginnings of their careers) balk at the rigorous, theorized work of the dramaturg and may not at once appreciate the potential benefits of such collaboration.

The more experienced an actor grows, the better he or she learns how central the dramaturg's work is to the process and the more often he or she will take advantage of it, but it is unrealistic to expect actors to emerge as professionals ready to work with dramaturgs. Like all of the relationships a dramaturg has, this one must be carefully cultivated; the dramaturg must be ready to articulate to the actor why his or her work will be enriched by the dramaturg's art. This includes but is not limited to:

- Helping articulate the director's vision and WTPN in a way that is useful to the actor's process of making choices
- Providing essential support materials and contextualization to help the actor understand the purposes of the playwright
- Forming a vital bridge between the actor and the audience with outreach
- Helping the actor maximize his own research, emphasizing the important and eliminating the nonessential

The dramaturg interacts with actors on a given production in various stages, which usually follow the pattern described below.

Auditions. After the launch, if there is one, this next big milestone in the production calendar occurs some weeks later. These might be done in a day but often stretch out over several sessions. The dramaturg should be present for every minute of the auditions, sitting close to the director at all times to be ready to consult. Because the dramaturg has been part of the process as long as (or longer than) the director, the dramaturg is the perfect person to act as a sounding board for ideas as the director tries to puzzle out the best combination of actors. Critical changes in the director's vision can occur at this stage, as critical as a sudden decision to double-cast or even to eliminate a character. The dramaturg has to be available and prepared to discuss how such changes might impact the production's overall meaning and to illuminate potential pitfalls or opportunities. Things happen fast in auditions—be ready.

Actor's packets. When the auditions are complete, the dramaturg gets to work on the actor's packet. This is a modified version of the director's packet, with the following elements included:

- A short statement from the dramaturg regarding WTPN
- The play's production history
- Articles and essays about the play (perhaps including one written by the dramaturg) and notes from the playwright
- A glossary of unfamiliar terms, phrases, and ideas (including visuals is often a good idea)
- A guide to pronunciation for strange words

- Contemporary research that puts the WTPN in context
- An explanation of any cuts
- Visual research, including maps and timelines
- Anything else that will help the actors do their jobs

As important as it is to provide good information for the actors, it is equally important to eliminate weak or unclear information and to use short, accessible articles and playwright's notes. This is not because actors are incapable of understanding the material—far from it! Actors need to be supremely flexible and disciplined, intellectually speaking, and they also need to have a strong grasp of their work within a larger context. But given the extremely short rehearsal schedules that prevail in American theaters, the actors simply do not have the resources to pursue those wonderful philosophical tangents that keep dramaturgs obsessed. Winnow data down to the most relevant, the most critical, the most compelling, and set the rest aside (don't throw it away—it'll be needed later!). The actors have to work very fast—an actor's packet that is longer than thirty or so pages is going to look daunting and superfluous to most actors, and that risks the possibility that they will ignore the packet completely. Remember that the actors (if they are any good) will also be doing their own research, like the designers, and the dramaturg can always add more to the packet or do further specific research with individual actors.

Making a good actor's packet requires a lot of forethought, particularly in the area of the glossary. The dramaturg needs to read the play very carefully, with an extremely sharp critical eye geared towards answering this question: "What does the actor need to know to convey the proper meaning of this line?" Consider this speech of Biondello from *The Taming of the Shrew*:

> Why, Petruchio is coming in a new hat and an old jerkin, a pair of old breeches thrice turn'd, a pair of boots that have been candle-cases, one buckled, another laced, an old rusty sword ta'en out of the town-armoury, with a broken hilt, and chapeless; with two broken points: his horse hipp'd, with an old mothy saddle and stirrups of no kindred; besides, possess'd with the glanders and like to mose in the chine; troubled with the lampas, infected with the fashions, full of windgalls, sped with spavins, 'wray'd with the yellows, past cure of the fives, stark spoil'd with the staggers, begnawn with the bots, sway'd in the back and shoulder-shotten; near-legg'd before and with a half-cheek'd bit and a head-stall of sheep's leather which, being restrain'd to keep him from stumbling, hath been often burst and now repair'd with knots; one girth six times pieced and a woman's crupper of velure, which hath two letters for her name fairly set down in studs, and here and there pieced with pack-thread. (3.2)

Imagine being an actor confronting this speech for the first time. The purpose of the speech is to prepare the audience for Petruchio's arrival and his outrageous behavior at the upcoming wedding. But there's something else going on here—the horse that Petruchio is riding is afflicted with just about every ailment in the Renaissance veterinary manual. Shakespeare wrote these words for a reason—there's tremendous comic potential there, if the actor can pull it off, but it starts with knowing what windgalls, spavins, and the staggers actually *are*.[5]

As another example, for a production of *Guys and Dolls*, a dramaturg might produce a glossary that includes definitions of all the 1930s slang (with images of things like cauliflower ears), explanations of all the 1950s in-jokes, a description of how to place bets on horses, and a description of how to shoot craps (possibly with a line-by-line explanation of what is happening in the scene where Harry the Horse is cheating Nathan). Always be asking questions: what else does an actor need to know? The best way to figure that out is to get to know actors and as much about their process as possible.

First rehearsal. Once the dramaturg has developed the actor's packet and gone over it with the director, the dramaturg arranges with the director to make a ten-minute presentation at the first rehearsal. During this presentation, the dramaturg introduces him- or herself to the actors and explains his or her role in the production and what he or she and the director have determined by way of WTPN. The dramaturg hands out copies of the actor's packet for each actor, the stage manager, and the director and explains that he or she will keep a master copy and bring it to rehearsal. The dramaturg walks the actors through the packet, explaining what each section is for and inviting their questions, and closes the presentation by asserting that the actor's packet is a living document and that the dramaturg particularly encourages the actors to bring in their own material to add to the file. Finally, the dramaturg makes him- or herself available to the cast for research consultation outside of rehearsal.

The actor's packet comes with the dramaturg to each rehearsal, and anyone, including designers and others, should feel welcome to consult it and add to it. If done right, the actor's packet can become a central clearinghouse of information for the whole show. The dramaturg is its custodian and ultimately makes the choices about what stays in, but the more openly the dramaturg employs it, the more useful it will be to the production.

Sidebar: Rehearsal Etiquette and Protocols

Rehearsal is a delicate time and in the United States usually proceeds under strict rules governed by the various unions and by the inevitable tick of the clock towards opening night. The dramaturg should be sure to discuss his or her role in rehearsal beforehand with each new director. In general, observe the following protocols:

- *Punctuality.* Call time is the beginning of the rehearsal, not arrival time. Be early! This is often a good time to exchange a few words with the director. Be set up and ready to work when the rehearsal starts.

- *Courtesy.* Turn off the cell phone, and mute the laptop. The dramaturg should never, ever draw focus away from the director, unless the director specifically requests that the dramaturg speak to the actors. Some commonsense rules for dramaturgs: Do not make noise. Do not make a mess. Do not lounge. Do not socialize. In professional settings, the dramaturg is often the only person in the hall who has a legitimate reason to be using a laptop (apart from the stage manager). Don't abuse this privilege! Do not surf the Web, instant message, or check e-mail during rehearsal. You'd be amazed how distracting these activities can be even to someone across the room. Stay close to the director in case he or she wants to consult with you. Never leave during rehearsal; the director will often want to talk to you during breaks.

- *Watch.* If a dramaturg is bored, he or she is not doing the job properly. The dramaturg is not sitting in rehearsal waiting to be given a task. He or she is watching the rehearsal process, also taking notes to share with the director at a later time: these notes are details on rehearsal process, in relation to how the production is answering WTPN. The other purpose of these notes is to record the process for later consultation. The dramaturg holds up his or her end of the contract to be the director's confidant and sounding board by being present, focused, and engaged. Don't worry; they'll need you soon enough.

- *Engage in appropriate activities.* It is appropriate for the dramaturg to pitch in as a full, responsible, friendly, helpful member of the professional team. That said, the only "boss" in the rehearsal room is the director. Only the director may give the dramaturg assignments in rehearsal. It is appropriate for the director to:

  - consult with the dramaturg privately in rehearsal or on break
  - ask the dramaturg to respond openly to a question, idea, or action on stage
  - ask the dramaturg to work one-on-one with an actor on issues related to research and interpretation
  - ask the dramaturg to explain or enhance some element of the packet
  - ask the dramaturg to share new materials he or she has brought to the rehearsal
  - ask the dramaturg to give *dramaturgical* notes to actors or designers[6]

- present detailed research questions to the dramaturg, to which he or she will respond *at the next break*, or if it is a more difficult question *at the next rehearsal*

It is *not appropriate* for the dramaturg to:

- fill in for a crew member, assistant director, or assistant stage manager
- give acting, directing, or design notes of any kind
- be made responsible for props, costumes, or security
- cease watching the rehearsal to complete a detailed research assignment

- *Some don'ts*:

  - Don't walk between the director and the actors during rehearsal or notes.
  - Don't give any member of the team other than the director notes unless specifically asked by the director to do so (*especially* if the person asks you for notes!).[7]
  - Don't touch props, scenery, weapons, or costumes.
  - Don't take up rehearsal time to give notes to the director. Set aside private time for that.
  - Don't abdicate research responsibilities to *anyone else on the team*.
  - Don't appear at rehearsal under the influence of anything stronger than the Saint Crispin's Day Speech from *Henry V*.[8]

Table Work

The first three or four days of rehearsal are ones in which the dramaturg plays a critical role. Here, the actors are reading through the script together for the first time. The dramaturg should be right in the thick of it, prepared to define any strange terms, to provide a larger context, to explain how an individual moment fits into the work of the larger plot, to provide guidance if new cuts are proposed, and to *question*, at every moment, whether the team as a whole completely gets what's happening in the scene. Here, the close reading skills developed in part 2 of this book are critical. Although the rehearsal protocols should take into account the centrality of the dramaturg's role in this phase, take nothing for granted, ask many questions of the cast, and if the dramaturg is asked a question he or she cannot answer, provide it at the earliest opportunity (usually the next rehearsal), but do not stop the table work to do research. One final word of advice—mind the old saying, "Only a knave borrows books, and only a fool lends them," especially when it comes to library books.

The dramaturg will work with actors and designers throughout the process, just as he or she will continue the collaboration with the director. For the first week or two, the dramaturg should be in rehearsal every night. However, during the period when the director is blocking the play, the dramaturg's presence in rehearsal becomes less necessary, and he or she can scale back to two or three nights a week, checking in with the director at least once a day for notes until the final week or so of performance, when he or she will reenter the rehearsal hall with a vengeance to help the director make sure that the final product is in accord with the adapted vision.

During the rehearsal process, keep a *production journal.* Take the notes from each night, and record them in this journal, along with information about interesting things that happened in rehearsal. These days, a top-notch stage manager will send rehearsal reports by e-mail every night—these can be very helpful in compiling the dramaturg's own journal. See appendix A for more information.

In the meantime, the dramaturg will be entering the next intense phase of the job: working with the audience.

Exercises

Go deep! Take one of the plays for which you created a production history from the last chapter, and create a complete *dossier* for it. Include everything you think an AD will need to know about the play.

Go wide! Take that dossier you just created, and write a letter to the artistic director for it, arguing in favor of its production. But here's the catch, it must be addressed to a real artistic director at a real theater. Before you write the letter, research the theater—find out its mission and who its donors are (easy enough to do, just look in their programs!), and scrutinize the season productions before *and* after the current artistic director was in place. What trends do you see? What has this AD done differently? What has the AD said in the press about the theater and about drama in general? Pitch your letter *directly* to that person. If you really want to find out how good you are, send it after you're done. Who knows? You might get a job.

Go long! Turn the dossier into an actor's packet of between twenty and thirty pages. Since you don't have a director to collaborate with on this exercise, imagine one who agrees with everything you say. Use your research skills to collect information, then use your critical judgment to winnow it down to a streamlined, efficient document that would be ready to go on the first day of rehearsal.

9

Audiences

> I don't think there's enough effort to get under the skin of audiences, to try to understand who they are and why they come. To know what their motivations are . . . it's about taking the risk of seeing risk-taking work as less risky, if you know what I mean?
> —Mark Ball, "Curators on Audiences"

In the intense and high-powered machine that is theater production in America, the dramaturg is something of a liminal figure, neither this exactly nor that exactly. Some students of dramaturgy initially find this liminality frustrating, but it is indeed what makes dramaturgy work because the dramaturg is at home in the worlds of criticism and scholarship as well as administration, preproduction, and rehearsal. The dramaturg is as comfortable working with writers, actors, and designers as with directors and artistic directors. The dramaturg understands what's going on in rehearsal in a way the artistic director cannot and knows what goes on in the boardroom in a way the cast and crew cannot. The dramaturg knows the company's history and helps plan its future. As a result, the dramaturg is uniquely able to build bridges of understanding among all of these groups, who must collaborate in order to produce exciting and relevant theater. Just as the dramaturg keeps his or her eye on the "big picture" in terms of history, philosophy, and aesthetic movements, so does the dramaturg become privy to the "big picture" of the theater company as well. This perspective is what gives the dramaturg the ability to follow through on one of Gotthold Ephraim Lessing's most important goals for modern dramaturgy: the education and development of an audience.

The Front Line

Theater production in America has become extremely specialized and streamlined, but everyone in the theater must agree that audience is the most important component of what we do. After all, without the audience, what exactly are we doing? As the Player in Tom Stoppard's *Rosencrantz and Guildenstern Are Dead* famously ranted, "The single assumption that makes our existence bearable [is] that somebody is watching!" Actors bow at the end of each performance not to accept praise but to *thank*, on behalf of the whole company, the audience for coming. Thinking about audiences in general terms is the responsibility of every member of the troupe, but the dramaturg is particularly concerned with the specific people who are coming to see the plays and must ask questions of them as of everything else. Who exactly are they? Why are they coming? What do they expect? What do they want out of the experience? How will they react to something new and different?

The lesson here is partially about artistic visions colliding, but it is also about how the needs of the artists dovetail (or fail to dovetail) with the needs of the people who pay for the art (audiences and patrons). All artists, except those who can bankroll themselves, need to deal with this issue at some level, but for dramaturgs it is a critical and ever-present issue because it directly informs the philosophical underpinnings of the work. Patrons never (or almost never) give money without some idea in mind of how they want it to be spent, and like it or not, those priorities affect the choices a theater makes. Ideally, the patron doesn't make any overt demands of the artists, but this happy situation is usual only when the patron knows that his or her values and the company's were compatible *before* any money changes hands.

Lessing's tone towards his audience in *Hamburg Dramaturgy* shows a certain level of frustration—as someone who has studied theater for most of his life with a philosopher's critical engagement, he sees the theater achieving great things and transcending a stultifying conformity to alien rules. Lessing sees the theater as a tool for social and individual liberation, and he's miffed that few others seem to get it or even to want it. But all theaters must follow a model that includes getting productions paid for. Is this automatically at odds with producing challenging and cutting-edge theater? Certainly not. Audiences will pay for good theater, and there's no reason whatsoever why a big-ticket Broadway lung-buster can't also be serious, innovative, and challenging; recent examples include popular productions of intense musicals like *Threepenny Opera*, *Rocky Horror Show*, *Spring Awakening*, and *Urinetown!* But there is also a steady, committed audience across the country that is equally dedicated to other genres of drama and willing to pay for it. We might observe that as American theater becomes increasingly thoughtful, topical, and innovative, it is looked to by the general public not only as a place for great entertainment but also as a bastion of serious and progressive art. Brilliant and passionate dramaturgs are required for both.

In practice, the dramaturg (as the ghost-lighter for the troupe) is out there on the front lines, in contact with the audience long before anyone else. Dramaturgs who are in-house develop deep and sometimes quite intimate relationships with their audiences, but even freelancers get into the trenches. Below are several ways that dramaturgs interact with audiences.

Outreach is the process by which the theater extends itself into the community to bring audiences in. It has many components, including but not limited to:

- Publicity and marketing
- Educational programs, workshops, and lectures
- Program notes
- Lobby displays
- Preshows and postshow talkbacks
- Blogs

The dramaturg can play a role in all of these events, but some are more central than others to the dramaturg's job.

Publicity

Most of the larger theaters have their own marketing departments, in charge of getting the theater exposure and studying the audience demographics to get "butts in seats." This is not the dramaturg's job (although in smaller houses, the dramaturg is often called upon to do some of this kind of work), but a close working relationship with marketing has two upsides—it facilitates the dramaturg's connection with the audience, and it keeps the publicity faithful to the artistic vision of the production. After all, the first contact that most audiences have with the production will be in the form of a press release, season brochure, or advertisement. Getting butts in seats is marketing's job; the dramaturg's job is making sure those butts belong to people who are well prepared to be the production's ideal audience.

Developing a marketing strategy around a production can sometimes be a little tricky, because once again the dramaturg must address both the fiscal needs of the theater and the artistic needs of the production. The two need not be in conflict, however, particularly in light of the fact that good dramaturgy will actually *increase* an audience's receptiveness to challenging drama. An audience can come to trust a theater to make good artistic choices, and in that environment of trust, the tolerance for something radically different will increase. That milestone reached, the next season gives new opportunities for new experiments and so on. It's worth reiterating that audiences in the United States seem ready for more challenging, more serious drama, and dramaturgs have a responsibility to respond to (and, indeed, to foster) that desire. There is a decreasing need to pander, and the ideal audience will be insulted by pandering, anyway.

When it comes to brochures and press releases, the dramaturg can be extremely helpful by providing thoughtful and engaged copy (written material for distribution) to whoever is writing the release. Like everything else dramaturgs write, marketing copy should be driven by WTPN, which is essentially the same question we are asking in rehearsal, "Why would anyone come and see this?" except now we are making a case for "YOU should come and see this." The best part is that the dramaturg has *already written this*, in the dossier. It is a relatively simple matter to transfer this argument to the artistic director into a statement of the production's intentions to its expected audience. One note: a little pizzazz doesn't hurt. False modesty (or, conversely, scholarly objectivity) about the dramaturg's house is not appropriate here. Why would anyone come see the show if the dramaturg doesn't sound excited about it?

Education

Theater companies across the country are engaged in aggressive programs to reach out to schools and other groups in the community. Many theaters are required, as a condition of their grants, to provide some form of education; others do it as part of their regular missions. A lot of ghost-lighting is really teaching in one form or another, so it should come as no surprise that theater companies tap dramaturgs to devise and implement various types of educational programs. Some theaters have educational directors, who are separate from dramaturgs, but dramaturgs always need to be prepared to speak to a variety of audiences in the context of education.

Theater, as the adage goes, is life. Every play ever written touches on some aspect of the human condition, and people respond to that. The dramaturg must include in his or her list of questions new ones like, "What kind of people would want to see this play apart from the subscribers? What new audiences can we bring in?" As practitioners, we all know that theater is extremely habit-forming, even addictive. Someone who has never thought of him- or herself in relation to the theater might come in because a particular play appealed to some special interest, and that patron might become a lifelong theater lover. It happens every day. Our livelihoods in many ways depend on this phenomenon.

As they ghost-light, dramaturgs should constantly be scanning the horizon for groups that might appreciate the production and on finding them should extend an invitation to participate. One of the best ways of extending this invitation is to develop educational programs around particular shows. Ideally, these are mobile; a dramaturg can write lectures with slides or PowerPoint presentations and deliver them to the groups. But many theaters also host regular classes and workshops in the theater building. Both are great; going to the audience conveys a sense of respect and interest, and bringing the audience to the theater conveys a sense of welcome and familiarity.

As to *who* exactly should be included, candidates will present themselves as a dramaturg pursues regular activities that keep him or her in touch with the spirit of the times. These sources will reveal a few likely suspects:

- *The newspaper. What's going on in the community? Region? Nation? Don't forget, this should be part of the reason why the dramaturg presented the play to the AD in the first place. If an antiwar protest made the company think Lysistrata would be a topical play to do, who organized the protest? Who attended? What are they doing now? Did a recent dust-up over immigration impel the company to do Zoot Suit? Who was involved in that event? Contact them. Doing Boys on the Side or Creeps? Where is the local group home or disability-services office? Is the local art gallery doing a big Seurat retrospective? Sounds like a great opportunity for cross-promotion with Sunday in the Park with George. Write elected officials in the state legislature and Congress. One never knows how the production might intersect with someone's political agenda.*

- *University course catalogs. It's likely that someone is teaching a course near your theater that relates strongly to your show. Plays regularly encompass issues of science, psychology, sociology, history, art, language, literature, politics—there's literally no limit. Call up the professor, explain what a dramaturg is about, and offer to give a presentation to a class. Most professors will jump at this chance.*

- *High school and elementary school lists. If the play is appropriate for such audiences, get in touch with principals or teachers and offer to come in and make a presentation. Develop regular relationships with local teachers. These will pay off big time.*

- *Adult education programs. Continuing education is becoming very popular in the United States. These are ideal targets for a dramaturg's work.*

- *Be creative!*

Talk with the box-office manager about securing group rates for these groups brought in, perhaps with a couple of comps for professors, teachers, principals, organization leaders, or parent chaperones. If possible, arrange for the groups to attend the show on a night when the dramaturg will do a talkback (see the section "Preshows and Postshow Talkbacks," below). They'll enjoy seeing their dramaturg again, and it will make for a livelier interaction.

Creating an educational presentation requires creativity and finesse. The dramaturg, using materials he or she has already developed, like the dossier and the various packets, and starting with WTPN, can craft a twenty-to-thirty-minute presentation designed to be a "peek behind the scenes" of the production. Prepare this talk ahead of time, and *rehearse it*. This might include:

- A discussion of why this play was initially proposed and selected
- Historical background about the play and its productions
- Biographical information about the author(s)
- Visual research
- The sociopolitical context for the production
- Exciting things that are happening in rehearsal
- Why the play is of particular interest to this group

Include these elements in a *study guide* for distribution to these groups and also made available to the general audience at the show who might be looking for a supplement to the program notes. Bring slides, overheads, or PowerPoints, but find out ahead of time what technology is available. Bring brochures and other information about the theater.

When giving the presentation, the dramaturg needs to remember that he or she is both an ambassador of the company and probably the first contact most of the audience will have with the production. Dress, speak, and act professionally. Be prepared, open, and friendly. Let them know how important the audience is to the production. Again, without compromising philosophical integrity, a little razzmatazz won't hurt. Make it interesting. Make it *compelling*. But remember, for a dramaturg, it's less about getting butts in seats than it is about creating an audience that is ideally prepared to get the most enriched experience possible out of attending the production.

Many theaters host workshops (in acting, design, directing, playwriting, and what-have-you) and one-time "master classes." Depending on circumstances, look for opportunities to participate in those, which will help the workshops connect to the theater's programming. Better yet, the dramaturg can develop his or her own workshops; perhaps host an adult-education class that meets regularly to discuss dramaturgy issues. The only limit here is the imagination.

Program Notes

Many dramaturgs consider their program notes one of their chief artistic products. It is one of the few discrete elements of the production that a dramaturg can point to and say, "I did that." It is a critical piece of the artistic pie, because once the audience has arrived, checked their coats, found their seats, and schmoozed a little, they will check the program. At this moment, they are set up to love the show or hate it. The program will also be heavily exploited by the critics later that night when they are writing their reviews. Finally, the program will provide one of the only lasting traces of the production, the main source of information for future historians. Companies underestimate the impact of the program at their extreme and lasting peril.

Doing program notes right requires patience and tremendous forethought. As with the actor's packet, a dramaturg does not want to overburden the reader; instead, he or she wants to use the five or ten minutes the reader will give the program to create the perfect viewer of the piece. A very good overview of the purpose of program notes was written by music professor J. Michael Allsen for a course at the University of Wisconsin–Whitewater.[1] Allsen asserts that the main purpose of notes is to give the audience a sense of the piece's history and what to expect from this performance. I would add, for plays particularly, that the program notes are not meant to *explain* the production, only to *enrich* the audience's experience of it. Director Jed Allen Harris once told me, "If the production *needs* to be explained in the program, the director hasn't done his job very well."

At base, notes should include the following:

- Biographical information about the author(s)/adaptors/ translators/ lyricists/and the like.
- Summary of production history of show
- *Brief* WTPN: Significance of show, summary of dramaturgical theory, hopes, challenges, and so on.
- Historical context, glossary of strange terms, maps, timelines, images, anything else the audience needs to know to be the perfect viewer for the production.
- Resources for pursuing more information

Obviously, there will be variations in intensity—a program for *Guys and Dolls* probably needs something of a glossary (a fun one), but it won't need nearly as much supporting materials as a program for *Arcadia*.

Program notes are not meant to match the scholarly rigor of an academic paper, so they should be written in an easy, accessible style without jargon or obscure references. There is no need to cite sources, as for a scholarly article. However, as Allsen warns, plagiarism is just as serious a peril here as anywhere, and with more and more dramaturgs posting their notes to the Internet (see the section "Blogs" below), the temptation is great to just cut-and-paste. Apart from plagiarism being a dark and horrible crime, one that can terminate a career, it is also a fundamental violation of the process. If the production can use the same notes as someone else's, then the dramaturg obviously hasn't done his or her job. A dramaturg's notes need to be a direct outgrowth of *his or her* own process of questioning the play, the theater, the audience, the director, and the production team. If a dramaturg is stealing someone else's notes, what other responsibilities is he or she abdicating? Maybe this person is in the wrong line of work.

Program notes are usually due well in advance of opening night because of the time necessary to print them (and usually the director will wish to review them and give notes). There is a danger, then, that the content of the notes will be out of context with the process. Some of the great innovations and discoveries in a production occur in the final weeks of rehearsal, and that's too late for them to be included in the notes. So a dramaturg must be as prescient as he or she can be, anticipating the possibility of change between the time the programs go to press and opening night. In short, don't overreach or come to premature conclusions. That said, there is no reason why one can't be creative, vital, compelling, and even funny in the notes. Remember, the *Hamburg Dramaturgy* started out as program notes. For all you know, the majority of the eventual readers of the program haven't even been born yet.

Some of the up-and-coming dramaturgs are starting to present program notes in ways other than as traditional text in a traditional program. At a recent production of *Accidental Death of an Anarchist*, a play written by celebrated radical Italian playwright Dario Fo about the absurdity and violence necessary in a police state, the audience was handed a program that looked like a piece of government propaganda. At a production of Bertolt Brecht's tragic antiwar comedy, *Man Is Man*, the programs appeared to be military recruitment pamphlets. At a production of Czech playwright and humanist Václav Havel's *The Memorandum*, the programs looked like declassified political documents. I attended a production of *Cabaret* in which the actors met the patrons outside the theater and yelled information about Nazi Germany at them. I attended a production of *Urinetown!* where dramaturg Lavina Jadhwani had taken snippets of information on water use that would normally go in the program and instead taped them to the insides of the lavatory stalls, so that a patron at intermission was suddenly confronted with the fact that the single flush of his toilet would use the same amount of water as a poor family in South Africa might use in a day. I have heard ideas for projecting program notes onto the walls of the theater or for presenting them in graphic form (like a comic strip) and for creating interactive online and multimedia experiences. And as someone who was trained in a very traditional way to do rigorous, disciplined, scholarly work, I have only one thing to say to these kinds of newfangled, boundary-breaking ideas: Go for it.

Lobby Displays

In some theaters, dramaturgs have the responsibility of curating lobby displays. Such displays can take virtually any form, but many theaters have display cases or other hardware especially designed for this kind of presentation. It is an opportunity for the designers to showcase their work by displaying renderings and models, and audiences love to see these kinds of things because they convey a certain level of insight into the process usually reserved for insiders. This is another opportunity for the dramaturg to cultivate the ideal mindset in the audience. The display is a great place for exploring the production more deeply, for instance, by presenting information that doesn't fit into the program notes or including visual research that enriches the audience experience (like charts, timelines, maps, photographs, and the like). Remember, the lobby display is something the audience will probably confront three times: before the show, at intermission, and after the show. Consider how their attitudes and insights will change with each confrontation. Making a provocative lobby display requires forethought and creativity but can really pay off for the dramaturgy of the show. One example that stands out in my mind was the display at a 2007 production of a documentary-theater piece entitled *In Their Own Words*, which was set in 1900 and dealt with issues of Europeans immigrating to the United States. The dramaturg, Brianna Allen, had erected a tall board that posted in two columns quotes from immigration (and anti-immigration) activists from 1900 and from 2007; the reader was staggered by how similar the rhetoric was. Nothing could have brought home WTPN better.

Preshows and Postshow Talkbacks

Talkbacks are events that connect the audience directly to the artists and when moderated by a dramaturg, can be extremely rich opportunities for increasing your theater's audience and helping them towards a deeper appreciation of your company's work. Preshows and postshow talkbacks have in common that they are held in the theater, but they differ in several ways. Preshows are events that occur in the theater itself, often right on stage. Preshows are much like the educational outreach presentations but will be directed to particular "friends of the theater"; these could be adult-education classes, donors, potential donors, special guests, or anyone else to whom the theater wants to give the red-carpet treatment. Again, the key here is professionalism. Gear the presentation to the audience, and if they are experienced theatergoers, a dramaturg can up the ante a little in terms of provocative content. Don't hesitate to be creative, but remember the audience.

Postshow talkbacks are a different matter. These special events are held immediately after a performance that are open to any ticket holder who attended the show that night. It is a very good idea to invite any groups you have met with previously to attend on talkback nights—as noted above, they'll feel comfortable with you, and that will help get the conversation going. Talkbacks are typically led by the dramaturg, but members of the cast, the playwright (if available), the director, and some of the design team are typically present. Generally, it is not difficult to get the production's personnel to show up to these events because they are great fun and provide a rare opportunity for the artists to connect directly with the audience. That said, a dramaturg doesn't want to be left out in the cold all alone on this one. My advice is to take it upon yourself, as dramaturg, to remind people when the talkback is by doing any of the following:

- Ask the stage manager to put the talkback date in his or her report and to include reminders.
- Put up an eye-catching sign on the callboard.
- Comment casually on how the talkback is one of the few times the company gets direct feedback from their target audience.
- Remind the team that special-interest groups, classes, and people you've personally cultivated are coming, and they want to see the team!

To get the audience to show up:

- Make sure the date of the talkback is included in the press materials, brochures, and on the online schedule.
- Put up a sign in the lobby with the date of the talkback.
- Put a slip or sticker in that night's program.
- Ask the house manager to announce the talkback during the preshow announcement on that night (when he or she explains where the fire exits are and requests everyone turn off cell phones).

The night of the talkback, follow this procedure:

- At the end of the last act, be ready just offstage (or if using a PA, in the booth). Do NOT get in anybody's way. Do NOT interfere with a curtain call or an encore!
- As soon as the house lights come up, step onto the stage (or get on the PA), and announce "Ladies and gentlemen, if I could have your attention, there will be a TALKBACK with the cast and crew of the show here in the theater in FIVE MINUTES. Once again, TALKBACK with the cast and crew in FIVE MINUTES, thank you!"

- Let the main audience filter out, and from the stage, encourage the remaining patrons to sit in the center section close to the stage.
- While onstage, do not touch the set or props, and do not sit on chairs that are part of the set. If chairs are needed, have one of the run crew help bring some out, and place them as far downstage as possible.

After five minutes, some of the team should have wandered out on stage. Don't wait for the rest—jump right in.

- Welcome the audience and thank them for staying.
- Thank the stage manager, the board operator, the production manager, and the run crew by name—these people are staying late to accommodate you, and they rarely get any applause.
- Introduce yourself, and explain what a talkback is. Here is a sample sentence: "We like to have these direct question-and-answer sessions to give our cast and crew a chance to get direct feedback from the most important people in the theater—the audience—whom we otherwise rarely hear from. It's a chance for us to get to know you and to learn how effective we have been, and how we can serve you better in the future."
- Ask others to introduce themselves and note what they did on the show. If people filter in late, you can have them introduce themselves when there is a break between questions.
- You might want to set up the conversation with some "fun facts," any interesting or engaging information you discovered or facts about the show, particularly while you are waiting for folks to wander on stage. "You may not know that we found original antiques to be part of this set," for instance. This loosens up the audience and sets the right mood.
- Beforehand, prepare at least ten questions, and list them in order of importance. These can be directed to the audience or the cast. You will start things off by asking your first and possibly your second question. Usually by then, the audience will be ready to pitch in. Keep your questions in reserve in case the talk bogs down or if you really want to get the audience's feedback on a particular point. Remember, your questions will set the tone of the whole discussion. Use serious, engaged questions rather than easy, softball ones. Encourage people to ask questions about things that surprised or moved them particularly, or ask those questions yourself, for example, "As the dramaturg, I want to know particularly what surprised you or moved you in this performance."
- Call on people yourself, as if you were teaching a class, but call them "sir" and "ma'am" or "the gentleman in the dapper gray jacket" or "the

lady with the lovely corsage." Repeat all audience questions in a loud, projecting voice: this makes sure everyone can hear the question and also solidifies your control over the event, and being on top of everything makes you seem charming and engaged.

- Your job is moderator. Make sure the audience gets their questions answered.
- Direct the questions to particular members of your team. For instance, you might say, "The lady's question was, 'What did the actors have to do to prepare for this performance?' Robert, I know you did some unusual things in your process, perhaps you'd like to answer that?" You can, of course, answer dramaturgical questions yourself. You can pepper the discussion (lightly) with your own observations or quick anecdotes about the process, but keep it moving.
- If someone on stage is going off on a tangent, cut him or her off (politely). If anyone gets unruly, rude, or abusive, cut that person off (you can do this in a constructive way, such as "Okay, I think we've heard that you didn't like the choice in act 2. Jim, how would you respond to that?"). On the other hand, if someone has a genuine criticism, delve. Air it out. Be brave.
- If the company has questions for the audience, that's great! Make sure they get heard but not at the expense of the audience.
- Bring people in. If in the classes or in your outreach, certain issues came up, bring those issues to the fore. "When I was talking to the City Women's Coalition last week, a question was raised about the way women are depicted in the show. Who would like to talk about that?"
- Talkbacks can last from fifteen minutes to an hour, depending on the kind of house you are in (commercial houses often have very short sessions, while children's theaters, academic theaters, and small experimental houses will want to devote more time). When figuring out the time for these, err on the side of "Always leave 'em wanting more." Make sure you know the run times for the shows and how big a window you have before the union will crack down on your crew or when the show has to be reset. Keep a close eye on the time; when you get down to five minutes, say, "I think we have time for only three more questions."
- Get a friend, colleague, or assistant to attend the talkback and take notes for you, and include them in your casebook. Include the number of people who showed up.

Things to remember:

- It's great to get positive feedback, and it's important to know what you are doing *right*, but if the audience only wants to talk about how great the performance was, then the play's deeper issues have likely not come across. Go back to your training about themes—remember that they are *dialectical*. If everyone loved the performance (unlikely!), gently steer the conversation towards the exploration of the show's themes. This is your intellectual payoff, after all—your chance to see whether your own dramaturgical theories have borne fruit.
- Nothing's worse than being on the front line when someone decides to take out a personal grudge by trashing someone in front of an audience. It's not professional, and it makes the whole company look bad. Steer the conversation towards constructive areas, and stay away from personal attacks.
- The dramaturg's job is not to rigidly direct the course of the discussion—that should flow naturally. But it is important to have someone at the helm to focus the discussion, cut off useless debate, encourage useful questions, and discourage extraneous comments.

When done right, talkbacks can be powerfully enriching and even fun!

Blogs

A few years ago, no one had heard this term *blogging*, that is, keeping an online journal or "Web log." In a short time, blogging has gone from a new concept to an omnipresent fact of life. Dramaturgs are all over the blogosphere and use blogs widely for any of the following functions:

- To keep a philosophically astute diary of the theater culture of their region
- To post (sometimes anonymous) criticisms or commentaries about productions or dramaturgical news
- To provide a forum for discussions about particular issues
- To keep running production journals
- To post actor's packets and casebooks online (cuts down on paper and allows actors, designers, and directors to contribute directly)
- To keep in touch with an international network of like-minded artists and thinkers.
- To give detailed information to the public about their work

Blogs are a terrific tool for dramaturgs. To see what some of the cyberturgs are up to, follow these links:

- *Literary Managers and Dramaturgs of the Americas (LMDA). www.lmda. org. LMDA is the main organization of dramaturgs in the Western Hemisphere. This Web site has terrific resources and opportunities to contribute directly to the ongoing discourse about the discipline.*

- *Julie Ohl's blogs. http://www.blogger.com/profile/12534884728503234396. Boston Dramaturg Julie Ohl sets the gold standard for online production dramaturgy. Check out her cyber casebooks for Zeitgeist Theatre's productions of The Kentucky Cycle (http://www.kentuckycycle.blogspot.com/) and Sacred Heart (http://dramaturgy-sacred-hearts.blogspot.com/).*

- *Rat Sass. www.ratconference.com/blog/. The irreverent culture critics of the "Rat Conference" wrap a unique blend of research, passion, and international theater acumen into a dramaturgy blog that's dripping with bad attitude and great information.*

- *Dark Knight Dramaturgy. http://darkknightdramaturgy.wordpress.com/. Taking Batman as a model dramaturg (both superhero and detective), Chicago-area dramaturg and playwright Dan Rubin's mission is "seeking truth and battling mediocrity in a theater near you." The Dark Knight provides commentary on productions, pedagogy, and people in his theater community.*

- *PDC Dramaturgy. http://www.pdc1.org/index.html. A sort of online clearinghouse for news, articles, theoretical essays, and commentary from a Philadelphia-based community of writers and thinkers.*

- *Dramaturgy Northwest. http://www2.ups.edu/professionalorgs/dramaturgy. This is a blog from a northwestern collective stays very current.*

Of course, blogs have a tendency to come and go, so it can be difficult to stay abreast, but on the whole, these are a terrific way to keep in touch with the community of dramaturgs and to accomplish outreach at the same time.

Exercises

Go deep! Make some kind of contribution to at least five online dramaturgy blogs or Web sites, or better yet, start your own (they're free)! Make sure you provide links to other online dramaturgy networks.

Go wide! Do the following with the actor's packet that you completed in the last chapter:
- Write a press release of 250 to 500 words for a hypothetical production of your show, putting WTPN into the context of "Why YOU should see this!" Put a little pizzazz into it.

- Then, create a list of at least ten organizations in your immediate community that you think would be interested in seeing this show and who you think would appreciate an educational presentation.
- Write a study guide for your show, and use it as the basis of creating a twenty-to-thirty-minute presentation designed for these groups.

Go long! Collect the season brochures and one production program from five different theaters. Evaluate them in terms of the principles in this chapter. What strategies are they using to bring people in? How are they presenting themselves? What themes or hooks are they employing? Are they excited about their own work? Can you see evidence that whoever has written these is considering WTPN and making a case for it? How does that affect your reaction? Do you want to go to these shows or not? Write a summary of your findings, rating the companies from best (most compelling and interesting) to worst (least compelling and interesting).

APPENDIXES
NOTES
INDEX

Appendix A

The Casebook

The *casebook*, also called a *protocol*, is the last stage of the process of working on an individual production, project, or theatrical experiment. It is a document that contains everything that happened in the process and a lot of information on things that didn't happen. It is a map of the garden of forking paths that made during a dramaturg's time with the production. It is the record of the event and includes a summation of the projects' goals, hopes and dreams, successes and failures, and overall worth.

The dramaturg is a bridge: between the script and the production, between the author's time and now, between the administration and the artistic team, between the playwright and the director, between the production and the audience, and between the scholar and the artist. The casebook enables the dramaturg to be the most important bridge of all (from our humble perspective): between one dramaturg and another.

Performance is ephemeral. It exists in a fixed time and at a fixed place, and when a performance is complete, poof, it's gone. It leaves only fragmented traces, from which future researchers attempt to piece together a whole. Dramaturgs look to past productions all the time, seeking guidance in how previous companies navigated the terrain and what perils and triumphs they encountered.

Craft your casebook to be exactly the document you would like to have if you were working on a future production of this play. In it, record as much as possible about your concept, process, research, what was used (and what wasn't used), and the events that shaped your production. Be sure to include information about the role you played as dramaturg. Your objectivity and critical eye are essential components of this document.

Please, please, please do not include commentary along the lines of "if I had been directing this show" or "if only the playwright had done what I said." Those aren't the shows you are working on. This venting is unprofessional and demonstrates that something was guiding your work as a dramaturg other than dramaturgy: your ego. Working in this way only contributes to the idea that dramaturgy is a "second prize" instead of a discrete art form with its own principles and goals. When you are directing, direct, when you are writing, write, and when you are the dramaturg, be the dramaturg.

The casebook should include the following items:

- A cover sheet with the basic production information (what, who, where, when)
- A table of contents
- Letter to the artistic director
- Letter to the director
- Production history with critical commentary
- Historical and contemporary research
- Visual research
- Production stills, designer renderings, other visual records of the show, if permitted
- Program notes (or a copy of the program itself)
- Notes on the lobby display, including photos, if possible
- Notes on any outreach, preshows, or specific audience development
- Notes on postshow talkbacks
- The dramaturg's production journal, a day-to-day account of the whole process, which includes his or her summary of the production and the performances
- Any reviews, criticism, or media feedback
- The entire script, showing cuts, revisions, retranslations, translations, adaptations, new material, and the like

Your theater should maintain an archive of past productions, and this is where you can establish (or contribute to) a casebook library. If you do have a library of casebooks, it is a professional courtesy to allow other dramaturgs and scholars to consult it (although no one is allowed to steal the ideas they contain—directors and companies have been sued for re-creating design and even blocking, so be warned). More and more dramaturgs are putting their casebooks online to give other researchers easy access, but if you do this, make sure you are not violating any copyrights (not only for material you uncovered doing research but for material owned by the designers and the theater company). Get permissions in writing if you need to, and include them in the casebook.

The Dramaturg's Library

Books are the main tools of the dramaturg's trade, and dramaturgs must develop a solid library of resources on the practice of dramaturgy, research in theatre history and interpretive theory. As a dramaturg becomes specialized in particular styles and practices, his or her library will reflect that. For starters, I have included this (necessarily incomplete) list of strong resources in various categories. No doubt you will discover (or have already discovered) other books you will consider indispensable, but these lists can be useful to jump-start research in particular areas.

On Dramaturgy (Including Script Analysis, Adaptation, and Translation)

Ball, David. *Backwards and Forwards: A Technical Manual for Reading Plays.* Carbondale: Southern Illinois University Press, 1983.

Bly, Mark. *The Production Notebooks: Theatre in Process.* Vols. 1 and 2. 1995. New York: Theatre Communications Group, 2001.

Gounaridou, Kiki, ed. "Theatre Translation." Special issue, *Metamorphoses* 9, no. 1 (Spring 2001).

Hartley, Andrew James. *The Shakespearean Dramaturg: A Theoretical and Practical Guide.* New York: Palgrave MacMillan, 2005.

Heyman, Ronald. *How to Read a Play.* New York: Grove 1977.

Johnston, David, ed. *Stages of Translation: Translators on Translating for the Stage.* London: Oberon, 1996.

Jonas, Susan, Geoffrey S. Poehl, and Michael Lupu, eds. *Dramaturgy in American Theatre: A Source Book.* New York: Wadsworth, 1996.

Londré, Felicia Hardison. *Words at Play: Creative Writing and Dramaturgy.* Carbondale: Southern Illinois University Press, 2005.

Luckhurst, Mary. *Dramaturgy: A Revolution in Theatre.* Cambridge: Cambridge University Press, 2006.

Proehl, Geoff. *Toward a Dramaturgical Sensibility: Landscape and Journey.* Fairleigh Dickinson University Press, 2008.

Rush, David. *A Student Guide to Play Analysis.* Carbondale: Southern Illinois University Press, 2005.

Turner, Cathy, and Synne K. Behrndt. *Dramaturgy and Performance.* London: Palgrave MacMillan, 2008.

Weschler, Robert. *Performing without a Stage: The Art of Literary Translation.* North Haven, CT: Catbird, 1998.

Zatlin, Phyllis. *Theatrical Translation and Film Adaptation: A Practitioner's View.* Clevedon, UK: Multilingual Matters, 2005.

Some Important Dramaturgies

Artaud, Antonin. *The Theater and Its Double.* New York: Grove, 1994. This definitive text on experimental theater written in 1938 by the visionary artist elevates theater to a site of metaphysical and social therapy and shatters conventional boundaries about what as possible on stage.

Boal, Augusto. *Theatre of the Oppressed.* New York: Theatre Communications Group, 1993. This is the radical Brazilian activist's manifesto that challenges deeply held assumptions about the role of theater as art, as education, and as a political tool.

Brecht, Bertolt. *Brecht on Theatre: The Development of an Aesthetic.* Trans. John Willett. New York: Hill and Wang, 1992. A collection of critical essays that mark the development of Brecht's thinking about theater, this text is extremely helpful in clarifying Brecht's dramaturgy and marking its influence.

Brook, Peter. *The Empty Space: A Book about the Theatre.* New York: Touchstone, 1996. The prominent director's radical review of the state of the profession in the 1960s has been profoundly influential on the development of avant-garde and traditional directing alike ever since.

Flanagan, Hallie. *Arena.* New York: Blom, 1940. Flanagan's memoir details the inception, philosophies, development, and destruction of the Federal Theatre Project.

Grotowski, Jerzy. *Towards a Poor Theatre.* New York: Theatre Arts, 2002. A sort of mega-casebook on experimental theatre in Poland by one of the great theater minds of the last century.

Lessing, Gotthold Ephraim. *The Hamburg Dramaturgy.* Trans. Helen Zimmern. 1890. New York: Dover, 1962. Lessing's landmark output as dramaturg for the Hamburg Nationaltheatre in the eighteenth century establishes the foundation of Hegelian dramaturgy.

Stanislavski, Konstantin. *An Actor Prepares.* New York: Theatre Arts, 1989. This primary sourcebook for Stanislavski's method of actor training is now a standard text for actors all over the world.

———. *My Life in Art.* New York: Theatre Arts, 1996. This is the memoirs of the legendary director who lead the Moscow Art Theatre to international prominence in the early twentieth century.

Theater History

Applause. *Theatre World.* New York: Applause, 1944–present. These editions are a pictorial record of Broadway, Off-Broadway, and Off-Off Broadway.

Aronson, Arnold. *American Avant-Garde Theatre*. London: Routledge, 2000.

Baker, Henry Barton. *History of the London Stage and Its Famous Players 1576–1903*. Whitefish, MT: Kessenger, 2006.

Banham, Martin. *The Cambridge Guide to Theatre*. Cambridge: Cambridge University Press 1995.

———, ed. *A History of Theatre in Africa*. Cambridge: Cambridge University Press, 2004.

Beadle, Richard, ed. *The Cambridge Companion to Medieval English Theatre*. Cambridge: Cambridge University Press, 1994.

Bean, Annemarie. *A Sourcebook of African-American Performance: Plays, People, Movements*. London: Routledge, 1999.

Ben-Zvi, Linda. *Theatre in Israel*. Ann Arbor: University of Michigan Press, 1996.

Brown, John Russell, ed. *The Oxford Illustrated History of the Theatre*. Oxford: Oxford University Press, 2001.

Cavaye, Ronald, Paul Griffith, and Akihiko Senda. *A Guide to the Japanese Stage: From Traditional to Cutting Edge*. Tokyo: Kodansha, 2005.

Cody, Gabrielle H., and Evert Sprinchorn, eds. *The Columbia Encyclopedia of Modern Drama*. New York: Columbia University Press, 2007.

Cortes, Eladio, and Mirta Barrea-Marlys, eds. *Encyclopedia of Latin American Theatre*. Westport, CT: Greenwood, 2003.

Critics' Theatre Reviews and *New York Theatre Critics' Reviews*. New York: Critics Theatre Reviews, 1940–96.

Fischer-Lichte, Erika. *History of European Drama and Theatre*. London: Routledge, 2004.

Fisher, James, and Felicia Hardison Londré. *Historical Dictionary of American Theatre: Modernism*. Lanham, MD: Scarecrow, 2007.

Grange, William. *Historical Dictionary of German Theatre*. Lanham, MD: Scarecrow, 2006.

Greenblatt, Stephen. *Will in the World: How Shakespeare Became Shakespeare*. New York: Norton, 2004.

Hauser, Arnold. *The Social History of Art*. London: Routledge, 1962.

Hill, Errol G., and James V. Hatch. *A History of African American Theatre*. Cambridge: Cambridge University Press, 2006.

Kastan, David Scott. *A Companion to Shakespeare*. Oxford: Blackwell, 1999.

Krasner, David. *American Drama 1945–2000: An Introduction*. Oxford: Wiley-Blackwell, 2006.

Lal, Ananda. *The Oxford Companion to Indian Theatre*. Oxford: Oxford University Press, 2004.

Lee, Esther Kim. *A History of Asian American Theatre*. Cambridge: Cambridge University Press 2006.

Leiter, Samuel. *Encyclopedia of Asian Theatre*. Westport, CT: Greenwood, 2006.

Magill, Frank N., ed. *Critical Survey of Drama*. New York: Salem, 1985.

Meyer-Dinkgrafe, Daniel. *Who's Who in Contemporary World Theatre*. London: Routledge, 2002.

New York Times. *New York Times Theater Reviews*. New York: New York Times, 1870–present.

Ortolani, Benito. *The Japanese Theatre*. Princeton, NJ: Princeton University Press, 1990.

Peterson, Bernard L. *Early Black American Playwrights and Dramatic Writers*. Westport, CT: Greenwood, 1990.

Richmond, Farley, Darius Swann, and Phillip B. Zarilli, eds. *Indian Theatre: Traditions of Performance*. Delhi: Motilal Banarsidass, 1993.

Riley, Jo. *Chinese Theatre and the Actor in Performance*. Cambridge: Cambridge University Press, 1997.

Roach, Joseph R. *The Player's Passion: Studies in the Science of Acting*. Ann Arbor: University of Michigan Press, 1993.

Schechner, Richard, and Lisa Wolford. *The Grotowksi Sourcebook*. New York: Routledge, 2001.

Senelick, Laurence. *Historical Dictionary of Russian Theatre*. Lanham, MD: Scarecrow, 2007.

Theatre Communications Group. *Theatre Profiles: The Illustrated Guides to America's Nonprofit Professional Theaters*. New York: Theatre Communications Group, 1973–present. This source is a record of TCG's membership theaters (see Applause, Theatre World).

Thomson, Peter, and Glendyr Sacks. *The Cambridge Companion to Brecht*. Cambridge: Cambridge University Press, 2006.

Trussler, Simon. *The Cambridge Illustrated History of British Theatre*. Cambridge: Cambridge University Press, 2000.

Tydeman, William, ed. *The Medieval European Stage*. Cambridge: Cambridge University Press, 2001.

Wells, Stanley, and Lena Cowen Orlin, eds. *Shakespeare: An Oxford Guide*. Oxford: Oxford University Press, 2003.

Wilmeth, Don B. *The Cambridge Guide to American Theatre*. Cambridge: Cambridge University Press 2007.

———. *Variety Entertainment and Outdoor Amusements, A Reference Guide*. Westport, CT: Greenwood, 1982.

Witham, Barry B. *The Federal Theatre Project: A Case Study*. Cambridge: Cambridge University Press, 2003.

Critical Theory

Adams, Hazard. *Critical Theory since Plato*. New York: Harcourt, 1992.

Adams, Hazard, and Leroy Searle, eds. *Critical Theory since 1965*. Tallahassee: Florida State University Press, 1992.

Benjamin, Walter. *Illuminations*. New York: Schocken, 1969.

Bial, Henry. *The Performance Studies Reader*. London: Routledge 2003.

Blau, Herbert. *The Eye of Prey*. Bloomington: University of Indiana Press, 1987.

Carlson, Marvin. *The Haunted Stage: The Theatre as Memory Machine*. Ann Arbor: University of Michigan Press, 2001.

———. *Theatre Semiotics: Signs of Life*. Bloomington: Indiana University Press, 1990.

———. *Theories of the Theatre: A Historical and Critical Survey from the Greeks to the Present*. Ithaca, NY: Cornell University Press, 1993.

Case, Sue-Ellen, and Janelle Reinelt, eds. *The Performance of Power: Theatrical Discourse and Politics*. Iowa City: University of Iowa Press, 1991.

Curtin, Kaier. *We Can Always Call Them Bulgarians: The Emergence of Lesbians and Gay Men on the American Stage*. Boston: Alyson, 1987.

Deleuze, Gilles, and Felix Guattari. *Anti-Oedipus*. Minneapolis: University of Minnesota Press, 1985.

Dollimore, James. *Radical Tragedy: Religion, Ideology, and Power in the Drama of Shakespeare and His Contemporaries*. Chicago: University of Chicago Press, 1984.

Dukore, Bernard, ed. *Dramatic Theory and Criticism: Greeks to Grotowski*. New York: Holt, 1973.

Elam, Kier. *The Semiotics of Theatre and Drama*. London: Routledge, 1980.

Fischer-Lichte, Erika. *The Semiotics of Theatre*. Bloomington: Indiana University Press, 1992.

Fortier, Mark. *Theory/Theatre: An Introduction*. New York: Routledge, 2002.

Fuchs, Elinor. *The Death of Character: Perspectives on Theatre after Modernism*. Bloomington: Indiana University Press, 1997.

Freud, Sigmund. *Interpretation of Dreams*. Hertfordshire, UK: Wordsworth, 1997.

Johnston, Brian. *The Ibsen Cycle: The Design of the Plays from Pillars of Society to When We Dead Awaken*. University Park: Penn State University Press, 1992.

Moreno, Jacob L. *Psychodrama*. 3 vols. New York: Beacon House, 1946.

Pavis, Patrice. *Languages of the Stage: Essays in the Semiology of Theatre*. New York: PAJ, 1982.

Pavis, Patrice, Christine Shantz, and Marvin Carlson. *Dictionary of the Theatre: Terms, Concepts, and Analysis*. Toronto: University of Toronto Press, 1998.

Reinelt, Janelle G., and Joseph R. Roach, eds. *Critical Theory and Performance: Revised and Enlarged Edition*. Ann Arbor: University of Michigan Press, 2007.

Rifkin, Julie, and Michael Ryan, eds. *Literary Theory: An Anthology*. Malden, MA: Blackwell, 2001.

Roach, Joseph R. *Cities of the Dead: Circum-Atlantic Performance*. New York: Columbia University Press, 1996.

Rustin, Margaret and Michael Rustin, *Mirror to Nature: Drama Psychoanalysis and Society*. London: Karnak, 2002.

Schanke, Robert, and Kimberly Bell Marra, eds. *Passing Performances: Queer Readings of Leading Players in American Theatre History*. Ann Arbor: University of Michigan Press, 1998.

———, eds. *Staging Desire: Queer Readings of American Theater History*. Ann Arbor: University of Michigan Press, 2002.

Senelick, Laurence, ed. *Gender in Performance: The Presentation of Difference in the Performing Arts*. Danvers, MA: University Press of New England, 1992.

———. *Russian Dramatic Theory from Pushkin to the Symbolists*. Austin: University of Texas Press, 1981.

Straub, Kristina. *Sexual Suspects: Eighteenth-Century Players and Sexual Ideology*. Princeton, NJ: Princeton University Press, 2006.

Societies of Interest to Dramaturgs

The *American Society for Theatre Research* (ASTR) (http://www.astr.org/) is a U.S.-based organization created in 1956 to foster "scholarship on worldwide theatre and performance, both historical and contemporary." In practice, ASTR is a central clearinghouse for scholars of the theater in the Americas. ASTR is *the* organization for American theater historians and theorists, and gives out a variety of theater-research grants and awards each year. ASTR hosts an international conference every November, and publishes the top-ranked journal *Theatre Survey*. ASTR also keeps a detailed database of doctoral programs in theater studies. Dramaturgs form a vocal and visible subset of this community. ASTR also hosts an e-mail-based discussion list-serv, which is very active and provides a forum for extended discussions about history, research, and course planning: for more information, e-mail ASTR at ASTR-L@listserv.uiuc.edu. You need not be a member of ASTR to join the list-serv.

The *Association for Theatre in Higher Education* (ATHE) (http://www.athe.org) is a large, established society composed primarily of faculty and graduate students involved in theater at colleges and universities from around the world, although the association is majority American. ATHE sponsors two list-servs, offer resources for promotion and tenure guidelines, maintain an academic job bank, and publish *Theatre Journal* and *Theatre Topics* (the latter is particularly concerned with dramaturgy). The organization hosts a national conference in late July, which may be anywhere in the United States, and a leadership-development program that helps train professors for administrative posts. The conference features a dramaturgy focus group, usually administrated by members of LMDA.

The *International Association of Critics of Theatre* (IACT) (www.aict-iatc.org) is an established not-for-profit nongovernmental organization, established under UNESCO, and based in Paris that brings theater critics from all over the world to foster the discipline of theater criticism. The association is concerned with methodologies, ethics, professional rights and interests, and cultural exchange among critics. IACT hosts a world congress every two years and symposia and seminars that meet more often. It particularly works to foster young critics and maintains an exchange network of theater periodicals that includes and also maintains lists of links to online resources (journals, institutes, individuals, associations, awards, and festivals) for critics and dramaturgs from all over the world.

The *International Federation for Theatre Research* (IFTR) (http://www.firt-iftr. org/) is a global community of researchers. The annual conference takes place in July, may convene anywhere in the world, on any theme, and attracts scholars from across the planet. They also host the IFTR World Congress, which meets once every four years, and smaller themed conferences. IFTR is composed of working groups that develop research themes and provide leadership and continuity. Working groups focus on topics like research methodologies, performance practice, stage forms, cultural studies, and theater technologies. On the Web site are links to associated theater-research societies from around the world. IFTR gives members support in obtaining grants, establishing databases, communicating with governments, and creating their own theater-research societies. They publish the top-ranked journal *Theatre Research International*.

The *Kennedy Center/American College Theatre Festival* (KC/ACTF) (http://www.kcactf.org) is a branch of the John F. Kennedy Center for the Performing Arts that dedicates itself to advocacy in the field of national performing arts education. The festival provides leadership in creating education policy and programs, commissions work specifically focused on students, offers professional development for teachers, fosters outreach programs, and maintains several performing-arts databases. The festival functions as a year-round program divided into eight regions. In each region, participating schools enter productions that are considered for awards in playwriting, design, and dramaturgy (in cooperation with LMDA). The dramaturgy-award postmark deadline is in early December. The festival also invites "guerrilla dramaturgs" to collaborate on the fly with developing plays for the festival. With the Eugene O'Neill Institute, the festival also sponsors the National Critics Institute (NCI), which pairs student critics with professionals at the festival. Student critics write reviews of the festival's works and may be selected to attend the national playwriting conference at the O'Neill Theatre Center.

Literary Managers and Dramaturgs of the Americas (LMDA) (www.lmda. org/blog) is the central organization for dramaturgs operating in the Western Hemisphere. This group includes America's most prominent dramaturgs and provides a worldwide forum for communication with other members of the discipline. LMDA hosts an annual conference that meets in late June somewhere in North America. With the Kennedy Center/American College Theatre Festival (KC/ACTF), LMDA sponsors a national dramaturgy award available to undergraduates. LMDA also sponsors regional miniconferences, fundraisers (including the Lessing's Birthday Bake Sale), and social events. On the Web site, LMDA provides resources including a bank of jobs and internships, a guide to dramaturgy programs in universities and colleges, sourcebooks, bibliographies, a script exchange, play lists, member biographies, and information on legal issues like copyright and employment guidelines. LMDA also publishes the *LMDA Review*, a journal dedicated to dramaturgy issues, and provides many other resources and contact points.

Performance Studies International (PSi) (www.psi-web.org/index.html) is a smaller international professional association of scholars and practitioners. Their annual conferences are held around the world. PSi also supports working groups in such topics as performance and human rights, biopolitics, community performance, music, site-specific, documenting performance, and philosophy. PSi sponsors the Dwight Conquergood award for performance-based work (including scholarship and dramaturgy) in underrepresented communities.

Theatre Communications Group (TCG) (www.tcg.org) is a broad consortium of over 450 theaters and 17,000 individuals dedicated to the promotion of nonprofit professional theater in the United States. They publish *American Theatre Magazine* and *Artsearch*, a theater/performing arts employment resource. They also manage grants for theater professionals, host many yearly events and a national conference, and provide other resources for arts research as well as legal and political advocacy for theater artists.

The *Theatre Library Association* (TLA) (http://tla.library.unt.edu/) is an association of librarians and archivists particularly affiliated with performance studies of every kind. The organization provides excellent resources for researchers, including lists of libraries, archives, exhibitions, both public and private collections, and forums for discussing best practices. TLA preserves and publishes rare and out-of-print documents and a thrice-annual newsletter called *Broadside*, which includes articles and book reviews. TLA's annual conference is held jointly with ASTR's, and it sponsors two prestigious book awards.

Journals, Periodicals, and Online Databases

Journals and Periodicals

American Theatre Magazine, Theatre Communications Group, is a professional trade magazine and is a tremendous resource, particularly for noting important developments in the American regional theater. It includes articles, season previews, summaries of the fiscal condition of various theaters, and previously unpublished scripts of new plays.

Assaph, Tel Aviv University Press, edited by professors from the Department of Theatre Studies, at Tel Aviv University, Israel, is a distinguished international journal that attracts some of the biggest names in scholarship and theater practice. Published yearly since 1984, issues are generally themed to a particular research topic, with a regular section on Jewish and Israeli theater.

Comparative Drama, Western Michigan University Press, published quarterly since 1967, is an established journal that is interdisciplinary with particular strengths in medieval and modern drama.

TheatreForum, University of California–San Diego Press, has been published twice yearly since 1993. This slick periodical has an international scope focused on innovative theater artists around the world. Each issue includes unpublished scripts, articles written by dramaturgs, scholars, and practitioners, and many photographs.

Theatre Journal, Johns Hopkins University Press, also chartered by ATHE, is a well-established, top-shelf journal that publishes articles, book reviews, and performance reviews both from emerging writers and from the most highly regarded theater scholars and practitioners in the world. Published annually since 1948, the journal contains social and historical essays as well as more theoretical and methodological treatises.

Theatre Survey, Cambridge University Press, chartered by American Society for Theatre Research (ASTR), is one of the most serious scholarly journals available, published twice yearly since 1959. The journal covers theater history, practice, theory, and reviews from all periods, featuring articles from the most accomplished scholars and dramaturgs in the world.

Theatre Topics, Johns Hopkins University Press, chartered by Association for Theatre in Higher Education (ATHE), is specifically aimed at practitioners. Published annually since 1990, its performance orientation and scholarly rigor make it an ideal resource for dramaturgs and theater educators.

Online Searchable Journal Databases

These databases charge a subscription fee for their services but are available for free to students or at university libraries.

FirstSearch (http://www.firstsearch.oclc.org/) is an exhaustive searching tool of the full text of journal articles, articles, and books available through all of the largest informative databases.

IngentaConnect (http://www.ingentaconnect.com/) is similar to JSTOR, with more science and business resources.

JSTOR (http://www.jstor.org/) contains full-text articles from a variety of disciplines. This is the first stop for articles by scholars in the arts and humanities.

Proquest Direct (http://www.proquest.com/en-US/) is a search function that finds newspaper articles, historical and current, from many international and national newspapers.

The Times Digital Archive (http://archive.timesonline.co.uk/tol/archive) is a searchable database for the *Times of London*, which has published theater reviews since 1785 and is a source of information on much experimental theater in the 1960s and 1970s.

Accessing Original Texts Online

This is a list of Web sites that contain particularly extensive collections of original texts and that are free for researchers (but not necessarily for performance). These sources will help in finding original texts to build a network of sources.

Accessible Archives (http://www.accessible.com/accessible/) is a full-text searchable database that contains periodicals from the eighteenth and nineteenth centuries. Used in conjunction with Paratext's "19th Century Masterfile" (http://poolesplus. odyssi.com/19centWelcome.htm), the site grants access to a staggering amount of documents from the period.

All about Jewish Theatre (http://www.jewish-theatre.com/) is Moti Sandak's award-winning clearinghouse and world network for all things conceivably related to Jewish drama.

Artslynx International Arts Resources (http://www.artslynx.org), associated with the Literary Managers and Dramaturgs of the Americas (LMDA), is a major bibliography and "link dump" containing an exhaustive and well-organized theater archive. Particularly useful in terms of nineteenth-century theater in England and the United States and in its multi-art form eclecticism.

Christian Classics Ethereal Library (http://www.ccel.org/), hosted at Calvin College, contains a tremendous amount of Christian literature, extending from the birth of Jesus to the *Chronicles of Narnia*. Especially of concern are the Fall of Rome and excerpts of the Early Church Fathers. The site features audiobooks and cross-referencing of arcane passages with the Bible.

Eighteenth Century Resources (http://andromeda.rutgers.edu/~jlynch/18th/index.html), hosted by Jack Lynch and Rutgers University, tracks the movement of Americans into the English literary landscape. It is unique in terms of its variety and organization, but use the subject links rather than the search mechanism provided to navigate effectively.

HarpWeek (http://www.harpweek.com/) provides the complete archive of *Harper's Weekly*, an excellent source of information and theater criticism, from its first publication in 1850.

Ibsen Voyages with Brian Johnston (http://www.ibsenvoyages.com) is a repository of the dramaturgical work of Brian Johnston, including Hegelian analyses of Ibsen, extensive historical notes, criticism, and information on important productions.

Internet Archive (http://www.archive.org) archives eighty-five billion Web pages. Just about anything one can find online, one can find here.

Internet Broadway Database (http://ibdb.com) is an increasingly useful resource for information on Broadway shows, including many useful links and production data not found elsewhere.

The Internet Classics Archive (http://classics.mit.edu/index.html), hosted at the Massachusetts Institute of Technology, contains complete full, searchable text works of Aeschylus, Aristophanes, Aristotle, Julius Caesar, Cicero, Euripides, Sophocles, Virgil, and many more, extending from the early eighth century BCE to later writings by authors such as Omar Khayyam and Sa'di. The archive is networked with online booksellers to facilitate the purchase of different translations and various commentaries.

Internet Medieval Sourcebook (http://www.fordham.edu/halsall/sbook.html), hosted at Fordham University, contains letters, diaries, court records, theological treatises, pacts, papal bulls, and a useful section on Islam and its medieval relationship to Christendom. There are also bibliographies that provide useful commentary.

Luminarium (http://www.luminarium.org/lumina.htm) focuses in Renaissance and seventeenth-century literature that is difficult to find elsewhere online, including many plays and dramaturgical essays. The external links (located just below the painting centerpiece on the Web site) are remarkably useful.

Perseus Project (http://www.perseus.tufts.edu), hosted at Tufts University, contains resources and original texts extending from Ancient Greece to the English Renaissance. The project is convenient because it uses Java tools to display facsimiles of original text. Perseus also has a number of reference works available. All of these texts are searchable in an efficient manner: by subject, author, and individual wording. An indispensable resource.

Project Gutenberg (http://www.gutenberg.org) maintains an archive of at least eighteen thousands books with deep collections in German, French, and Italian.

TheatreHistory.com (http://www.theatrehistory.com/) is an extensive collection of resources ranging from topical summaries and encyclopedia-style articles to images. It contains an online bookstore, a script archive, and an interesting "Today in Theatre History" feature. A useful early stop in research.

Twentieth Century North American Drama (http://www.alexanderstreet2.com/), compiled by the Alexander Street Press and the University of Chicago, contains texts from North American drama along with great production information, including twenty-one hundred plays by black authors from 1850 to the present.

Recommended Play Anthologies

Play anthologies are useful resources for dramaturgs not merely because they collect significant dramas together in one volume but because the supporting materials (introductions to the plays, thematic models, and other research) can be extremely valuable sources of information, helping to frame ideas about production. Below are some collections published in the last twenty years that will hopefully whet the appetite for finding more on your own. A good dramaturg has many anthologies near at hand, ready for when someone asks for a play recommendation.

Barker, Simon. *Routledge Anthology of Renaissance Drama*. London: Routledge, 2002. This is a useful text that contains a broad cross-section of English early modern drama.

Corrigan, Robert W. *Classical Tragedy: Greek and Roman*. New York: Applause, 1990. This anthology contains solid translations as well as essays by contemporary dramaturgs and directors dealing with both thematic and production issues.

Cox, Jeffrey N., and Michael Garner, eds. *The Broadview Anthology of Romantic Drama*. Peterborough, ON: Broadview, 2003. Broadview publishes a series of reliable anthologies. This one is notable for its wide scope, multiple genres, and inclusion of women writers.

Elam, Harry, and Robert Alexander. *Colored Contradictions: An Anthology of Contemporary African-American Plays*. New York: Plume 1996. This book collects a broad sampling of styles from twelve modern authors and provides some strong meditations on black cultural expression.

Evans, G. Blakemore, and J. M. Tobin. *The Riverside Shakespeare*. 2nd ed. Boston: Heinle, 1996. This is the standard repository of the complete works of William Shakespeare, with critical essays, illustrations, and excellent notes on the texts themselves. This edition includes poems, as well as *Edward III* and other works now thought to have been by Shakespeare.

Fischlin, Daniel, and Mark Fortier. *Adaptation of Shakespeare*. London: Routledge, 2000. This book assembles adaptations of Shakespeare from the seventeenth century to the present and from all over the world. A must-have for anyone interested in adaptations.

Halman, Talat S., and Jayne L. Warner. *Ibrahim the Mad and Other Plays: An Anthology of Modern Turkish Drama.* Syracuse, NY: Syracuse University Press, 2008. This recent publication exposes readers to the variety and vitality of Turkish playwriting, which has a long and brilliant history.

Jeyifo, Biodun. *Modern African Drama.* New York: Norton, 2002. A widely representative collection that includes writers from every corner of the continent, this book also contains some eye-opening criticism on issues and materials rarely encountered by Western readers.

Johnston, Brian, and Rick Davis. *Ibsen's Selected Plays.* New York: Norton, 2003. Johnston and Davis's translations of the Norwegian master are among the best available, with some sharp contextual materials as well.

Kelly, Katherine. *Modern Drama by Women 1880s–1930s.* London: Routledge, 1996. Kelly's book collects and translates dramas from the period that are customarily excluded from the canon of emergent realist and antirealist works.

King, Woodie, Jr. *The National Black Drama Anthology: Eleven Plays from America's Leading African-American Theaters.* New York: Applause, 2000. This is a good resource for some underrepresented authors of the black theater.

Kinney, Arthur. *Renaissance Drama: An Anthology of Plays and Entertainments.* Oxford, UK: Wiley-Blackwell, 2000. This text includes a rich sampling of plays and other performance traditions to give a strong sense of the "theatrical culture" of the period.

Lonergan, Patrick. *The Methuen Drama Anthology of Irish Plays.* London: Methuen, 2009. This book contains five landmark dramas of the latter half of the twentieth century.

Sandoval-Sanchez, Alberto, and Nancy Saporta Sternbach. *Puro Teatro, a Latina Anthology.* Tuscon: University of Arizona, 1999. This is a captivating assembly of both well-known and almost unheard-of authors from extremely diverse Latina backgrounds and production contexts.

Senelick, Laurence. *Anton Chekhov's Selected Plays.* New York: Norton, 2004. Another of the Norton Critical Edition series, Senelick's translations of Chekhov are much-lauded as vibrant and modern. This edition includes commentary from some of the great twentieth-century directors of Chekhov as well.

Stanton, Stephen S. *Camille and Other Plays.* New York: Hill and Wang, 1990. This is a good source for translations of the great French "well-made" plays of the nineteenth century.

Walker, Greg. *Medieval Drama: An Anthology.* Oxford, UK: Wiley-Blackwell, 2000. This is an excellent edition of drama from many periods and places in Europe of the period.

Whybrow, Graham. *The Methuen Book of Modern Drama: Plays of the '80s and '90s.* London: Methuen, 2003. A collection of the most cutting-edge writers produced at the Royal Court in the previous decades: Caryl Churchill, Terry Johnston, Sarah Kane, Martin McDonough, and Mark Ravenhill.

Worthen, W. B. *The Wadsworth Anthology of Drama*. New York: Wadsworth, 2006. Worthen's text, which groups exemplary plays from many periods and cultures, is a standard for theater history classes. The introductions are learned and useful, and supporting materials on theory and production contexts are also provided.

Notes

1. What the #$%@ Is a Dramaturg?

1. A note on spelling and pronunciation: the convention within the field in the United States is generally to use *dramaturg* pronounced with a hard *g* as opposed to *dramaturge* with a soft *g* sound. This is standard practice, but it goes a bit further than mere convention. The hard-*g dramaturg* is affiliated with a kind of dramaturgy developed and adopted by German theater practitioners in the eighteenth century. This model of dramaturgy is held up as a powerful means of including specialist dramaturgs in theater practice. In any event, *dramaturgy* is usually pronounced with a soft *g*, as are *metallurgy* and *thaumaturgy*.

2. Mark Bly, "Bristling with Multiple Possibilities," *Theatre Symposium* 3 (1995): 12–17, rept. in Susan Jonas, Geoffrey S. Proehl, and Michael Lupu, eds., *Dramaturgy in the American Theatre: A Source Book* (New York: Harcourt Brace, 1997), 54.

3. The author overheard Joe Hanreddy make this comment at Carnegie Mellon University on April 4, 2008.

4. Jorge Luis Borges, "The Garden of Forking Paths," trans. Donald A. Yates, in *Labyrinths: Selected Stories and Other Writings*, ed. James E. Irby and Donald A. Yates (New York: New Directions, 1964), 20–24.

5. Bly, "Bristling," 53–54.

6. Ibid., 48–49.

7. For more on this subject, see Frank Rich, *Ghost Light: A Memoir* (New York: Random, 2001).

8. Sarah Gubbins, interview by Lucia Mauro, 2001, "Stage Persona: Sarah Gubbins," *Performink Online*, http://performink.com/archives/stagepersonae/2001/gubbinssarah.html.

2. Historicizing Dramaturgy

1. Henry James Breasted, trans., *Ancient Records of Egypt, Pt. I* (Chicago: University of Chicago Press, 1906), 298.

2. Plato, *The Great Dialogues of Plato*, trans. W. H. D. Rouse (Penguin: New York, 1984), 25–26.

3. Ibid., 27.

4. Plato, *The Dialogues of Plato, v. III*, 3rd ed., trans. R. Jowet (New York: Oxford University Press, 1892); qtd. in Bernard F. Dukore, ed., *Dramatic Theory and Criticism: Greeks to Grotwoski* (New York: Holt, 1974).

5. Aristotle, *Aristotle's Theory of Poetry and Fine Art*, 3rd ed., trans. S. H. Butcher (London: Macmillan, 1902), 71.

6. Ibid., 33–34.

7. Horace, *Horace on the Art of Poetry*, trans. Edward Henry Blakeney (London: Scholartis, 1928), qtd. in Dukore, *Dramatic Theory and Criticism*, 73.

8. Adya Rangacharya, trans., *The Natyasastra: English Translation with Critical Notes* (New Delhi: Munshiram Manoharial, 1996), 1–7. This is an excellent book.

9. Bharatamuni, *Natyasastra*, qtd. in G. H. Tarlekar, *Studies in the Natyasastra* (Delhi: Motilal Barnidassus, 2003), 66.

10. Aelius Donatus, *On Comedy and Tragedy*, trans. Charles Gattnig (1974), qtd. in Dukore, *Dramatic Theory and Criticism*, 99.

11. Hrosvitha, introduction, *Book of Drama*, trans. and qtd. in Nikolaus Scheid, "Hroswitha," in *The Catholic Encyclopedia*, vol. 7 (New York: Appleton, 1910). Nikolaus Scheid, "Hroswitha," *New Advent*, ed. Kevin Knight, 2009, http://www.newadvent.org/cathen/07504b.htm.

12. An extremely useful source on this is Donnalee Dox, *The Idea of the Theater in Latin Christian Thought* (Ann Arbor: University of Michigan Press, 2004).

13. Zeami Motokiyo, *The Flowering Spirit: Classic Teachings on the Art of* Nō, trans. William Scott Wilson (Tokyo: Kodansha International, 2006), 52.

14. Ibid., 55.

15. Ibid., 62.

16. J. Thomas Rimer and Yamazaki Masakazu, trans., *On the Art of the Noh Drama: The Major Treatises of Zeami* (Princeton, NJ: Princeton University Press, 1984).

17. William Shakespeare, *Henry V*, in *The Riverside Shakespeare*, ed. G. Blakemore Evans, 2nd ed. (Boston: Houghton Mifflin, 1996).

18. Lope Félix de Vega y Carpio, *El arte nuevo de hacer comedias* (*The New Art of Writing Plays*), 1609, trans. William T. Brewster, in Brander Matthews, ed., *Papers on Playmaking* (New York: Hill and Wang, 1957), qtd. in Dukore, *Dramatic Theory and Criticism*, 203.

19. Ibid., 198.

20. Pierre-Augustin Caron de Beaumarchais, *Essai Sur Le Genre Dramatique* (*Essay on Serious Drama*), 1767, trans. Thomas B. Markus, qtd. in Dukore, *Dramatic Theory and Criticism*, 300.

21. Gotthold Ephraim Lessing, "#101–104," *The Hamburg Dramaturgy*, trans. Helen Zimmern (1890; New York: Dover 1962), 263.

22. Ibid., 264.

3. Power Plays

1. Brian Johnston, "Revolution and the Romantic Theatre: III. Theatre's New Radical Supertext," *Ibsen Voyages*, www.ibsenvoyages.com/e-texts/revolution/III.html.

2. As a caveat, this is not to suggest that Shakespeare was not a profoundly philosophical writer. Indeed, his works were powerfully influential for the Romantics. However, a subtle dramaturgy is required to render his plays "dialectical" in the Hegelian sense. One such dramaturgy was offered by Bertolt Brecht, who argued that Shakespeare was a dialectical idealist, but because of the social pressures and censorship levied upon him,

he was forced to be covert about it. This dramaturgical approach gave Brecht permission (he felt) to alter the endings of plays like *Coriolanus* to bring them more in line with Brechtian ideals. After seeing a production of this play by the Berliner Ensemble, Peter Brook objected strongly to this dramaturgy in his landmark book *The Empty Space*.

3. Terry Prachett, *Jingo* (New York: HarperPrism, 1997), 426.

4. Bertolt Brecht, qtd. in *Brecht on Theatre: The Development of an Aesthetic*, trans. and ed. John Willett (London: Methuen, 1964), 23.

5. To be sure, even this simple statement is complicated by arguments including whether or not men can even *be* feminists, no matter how in accord they may be with the movement.

6. Elizabeth C. Stroppel, "Reconciling the Past and the Present: Feminist Perspectives on the Method in the Classroom and on the Stage," in *Method Acting Reconsidered: Theory, Practice, Future*, ed. David Krasner (New York: Macmillan, 2000), 111–26; 122.

7. Mark Fortier, *Theory/Theatre: An Introduction* (New York: Routledge, 2002), 138–39.

8. Dan Latimer, *Contemporary Critical Theory* (Orlando, FL: Harcourt, 1989), 124.

4. The Twelve-Step Program for Script Analysts

1. Denis Diderot, *The Paradox of Acting*, trans. W. H. Pollock (1758; New York: Hill and Wang, 1957), 13.

2. T. S. Eliot, "Dry Salvages."

3. Shakespeare, *Macbeth*, 2.1.33–34.

4. Shakespeare, *Henry V*, 5.1.44–45.

5. Ronald Heyman, *How to Read a Play* (New York: Grove Weidenfeld, 1977), 14–15.

6. Sam Smiley, *Playwriting: The Structure of Action* (Upper Saddle River, NJ: Prentice Hall, 1971), 41.

7. David Ball, *Backwards and Forwards: A Technical Manual for Reading Plays* (Carbondale: Southern Illinois University Press, 1983), 15–17.

8. Paul Henning, "The Ballad of Jed Clampett," 1962.

9. Brian Johnston, *The Ibsen Cycle: The Design of the Plays from Pillars of Society to When We Dead Awaken* (University Park: Penn State University Press, 1992), 249.

10. Andrew Sofer, *The Stage Life of Props* (Ann Arbor: University of Michigan Press, 2003), 290.

11. Hayden White, "Bodies and Their Plots," in *Choreographing History*, ed. Susan Leigh Foster (Bloomington: Indiana University Press, 1995), 229.

5. Form Follows Function

1. Mikhail Bakhtin, *Rabelais and His World*, trans. Helene Isowolsky (Bloomington: Indiana University Press, 1984), 92.

2. Sarah Ruhl, qtd. in John Lahr, "Surreal Life," *New Yorker*, 17 March 2008.

3. Critics have argued about how well Brecht actually achieved these goals and accused him of slipping into tragedy and even melodrama when it suited his theatrical purposes, but he spent his life refining his ideas through practical experiments and left an influential legacy.

4. Qtd. in James Knowlson, *Damned to Fame: The Life of Samuel Beckett* (London: Bloomsbury, 1996), 409.

5. Martin Esslin, *Theatre of the Absurd*, 3rd ed. (1961; New York: Vintage 2004), 45-61.

7. New Plays

1. It is astonishing about plagiarism, but this does happen, and when it does, not only playwrights but also theater companies can get sued for it. It's not really the dramaturg's responsibility to ferret out misconduct, but if there is some, the dramaturg can save everyone a big headache by exposing it early on. If the play is a parody, it is protected by copyright law, but the difference between homage or supertextual references and plagiarism is sometimes hard to define. Often, playwrights do this quite innocently (the imagination rarely gives footnotes), and a quiet word to the playwright is all that is needed to rectify the problem. If large or significant portions of the work are lifted, the dramaturg may need to bring this to the attention of the artistic director. How the dramaturg proceeds is largely a matter of his or her own ethical sensibility, but the consequences of producing a plagiarized piece can be very dire.

2. I was once on a team that was presented with an idea for a show that called for a set composed of one thousand living human babies who would all soil their diapers simultaneously on cue. Visionary? Quite possibly? Producible? No.

3. Jayme Koszyn, "The Dramaturg and the Irrational," in Jonas, Proehl, and Lupu, *Dramaturgy in the American Theatre*, 276.

4. John Glore, "How to ?Talk to a Playwright," in Jonas, Proehl, and Lupu, *Dramaturgy in the American Theatre*, 182.

5. For further reading, I recommend Morgan Jenness and Paul Selig, "Morgan Jenness Tells the Truth to Paul Selig: An Interview," in Jonas, Proehl, and Lupu, *Dramaturgy in the American Theatre*, 401–11, and Tony Kushner and Susan Jonas, "Tony Kushner's Angels," in Jonas, Proehl, and Lupu, *Dramaturgy in the American Theatre*, 472–82.

6. Cathy Turner and Synne K. Berhndt, *Dramaturgy and Performance* (New York: Palgrave Macmillan, 2008), 170.

7. Ibid., 171.

8. Ibid., 168–84; also David Graber, "Antonin Artaud and the Authority of Text, Spectacle, and Performance," in James M. Harding, ed., *Contours of the Theatrical Avant-garde, Performance and Textuality* (Ann Arbor: University of Michigan Press, 2000), 43–57; Christopher Innes, "Text/Pre-Text/Pretext: The Language of Avant-garde Experimentation," in Harding, *Contours*, 58–78; Allen Kuharski, "Joseph Chaikin and the Presence of the Dramaturg," in Jonas, Proehl, and Lupu, *Dramaturgy in the American Theatre*, 144–58; Gregory Gunter, "Exploration through Imagery," in Jonas, Proehl, and Lupu, *Dramaturgy in the American Theatre*, 176–79; Norman Frisch, Marianne Weems, and Elizabeth Bennett, "Dramaturgy on the Road to Immortality," in Jonas, Proehl, and Lupu, *Dramaturgy in the American Theatre*, 483–516; and "A Library of Cultural Detritus: An Interview with Elisabeth Lecompte," *Theatreschrift* 5:6 (1994): 192–209.

9. Attilo Favorini, *Voicings: Ten Plays from the Documentary Theatre* (New York: Ecco, 1995).

10. F. T. Marinetti, qtd. in Richard Drain, *Twentieth-Century Theatre, A Sourcebook* (London: Routledge 1995), 173.

11. A good history of the movement is provided by John W. Casson, "Living Newspaper: Theatre and Therapy," *TDR: The Drama Review* 44.2 (2000): 107–22.

12. Jacob Levy Moreno, qtd. in ibid., 111.

13. Ibid., 113.

14. Hallie Flanagan, *Arena: The Story of the Federal Theatre* (New York: Blom, 1940), 167.

15. Eleanor Roosevelt, qtd. in Cosson, "Living Newspaper," 112.

16. Augusto Boal, "Famed Brazilian Artist Augusto Boal on the 'Theater of the Oppressed,'" interview by Amy Goodman and Juan Gonzalez, *Democracy Now!* June 3, 2005, http://www.democracynow.org/2005/6/3/famed_brazilian_artist_augusto_boal_on (accessed June 8, 2008).

8. The Company

1. All of these were stipulations in effect at organizations where I have worked, and since these stipulations influenced the theaters' existences, I made them part of the dramaturgy.

2. Consider the extreme case of Dr. Rainer Schlösser, the *Reischsdramaturg* for Hitler's propaganda ministry, whose domination of German theaters prior to World War II helped to indoctrinate Nazism and shift the population to a "total war" consciousness that supported the horrendous atrocities of the period.

3. John Glore, qtd. in Jonas, Proehl, and Lupu, *Dramaturgy in the American Theatre*, 182.

4. I once worked on a Carnegie Mellon University School of Drama production of August Wilson's *Piano Lesson*, which is set in the home of an African American family in the 1930s. The designer wanted to use liquid soap in the onstage sink and asked me if such a product would have been available. In my research, I discovered that liquid soap did exist but at the time would have been prohibitively expensive owing to the scarcity of animal fat between the wars. The soap this family would have used was a harsh chemical detergent powder that would have made dishwashing an agonizing, painful, and prolonged labor. This discovery became central to the production's action, as it emphasized the family's degradation and suffering.

5. Confronted with this speech in a production at Seattle's TheatreWorks West where I was the dramaturg, the director was ready to cut it rather than risk a stall at a critical moment in the play (right before the wedding of Kate and Petruchio). But the very talented actress playing Biondello and I took a quick trip to the library, and with little effort (because the research on Shakespeare is very extensive), we discovered the nature of each of these strange sixteenth-century veterinary colloquialisms, and the actress developed descriptive gestures and vocal intonations to illustrate each one, with the end result that she brought the house down every night. Because she knew the words' meanings, the actress was able to convey those meanings quite fluidly to an audience who had never even heard them before, and her speech became one of the most talked-about moments in the production reviews.

6. *Dramaturgical* notes are ones that concern the script, research, WTPN, aesthetic philosophy, sociopolitical and cultural contexts, adaptation, pronunciation, and interpretation. It is *never* appropriate for dramaturgs to make suggestions on a particular actor's choices, to give a line reading, to suggest blocking or other directorial functions, or to comment on any element of the design except insofar as it affects the *dramaturgy*. Be conservative on this: an actor may indeed be completely missing the point of the line, or the script might call for a red carpet when what has appeared on stage is quite obviously blue, but addressing these issues is the director's job. Bring up any dramaturgical problems (especially ones like these) privately with the director outside of rehearsal.

7. If a member of the troupe has a dramaturgical question, the appropriate protocol is for him or her to address it to the director, who may ask the dramaturg to pursue

it either on his or her own or with the member; the dramaturg should then report back to the director on how it went and what was discussed. Otherwise, watch out: the danger here is that an actor or designer might solicit privately given advice from the dramaturg to challenge a directorial choice they don't like. You do not want to go there. Keep it all up-front.

8. That is, about three cups of coffee.

9. Audiences

1. See J. Michael Allsen, "Writing Concert Program Notes: A Guide for UWW Students," University of Wisconsin–Whitewater, January 2004, rev. August 2008 http:// facstaff.uww.edu/allsenj/MSO/NOTES/WritingNotes.htm.

Index

Michael Mark Chemers is the founding director of the Bachelor of Fine Arts in Production Dramaturgy Program at Carnegie Mellon University's School of Drama. He holds an MFA in playwriting from Indiana University (1997) and a PhD in theater history and theory from the University of Washington at Seattle (2001). He is the author of *Staging Stigma: A Critical Examination of the American Freak Show* (2008) and has authored or collaborated on many adaptations of classical texts, including *Lysistrata* with J. A. Ball (2008). His playwriting, which is performed across the United States, has been honored with eleven national awards. Chemers, who has over two decades of experience in production dramaturgy in the United States and abroad, worked most recently with the Rhodopi International Theatre Collective in Smolyan, Bulgaria. He lives in Pittsburgh, Pennsylvania, with his wife, Farhana, and son, Zain.

THEATER IN THE AMERICAS

The goal of the series is to publish a wide range of scholarship on theater and performance, defining theater in its broadest terms and including subjects that encompass all of the Americas.

The series focuses on the performance and production of theater and theater artists and practitioners but welcomes studies of dramatic literature as well. Meant to be inclusive, the series invites studies of traditional, experimental, and ethnic forms of theater; celebrations, festivals, and rituals that perform culture; and acts of civil disobedience that are performative in nature. We publish studies of theater and performance activities of all cultural groups within the Americas, including biographies of individuals, histories of theater companies, studies of cultural traditions, and collections of plays.